*"I am prepared to show that he was
a triple-powered superman."*
John B. Cowden

THEY CALLED HIM
SUPERMAN

THE LIFE OF T.W. BRENTS

By Kyle D. Frank,
John B. Cowden,
and
T.W. Brents

Volume One

Charleston, AR:
COBB PUBLISHING
2017

Published in the United States of America by:

Cobb Publishing
704 E. Main St.
Charleston, AR 72933
CobbPublishing@gmail.com
(479) 747-8372

ISBN: 978-1-947622-03-6

Table of Contents

The Life of T.W. Brents

The Early Days 2
Brents, the Physician 6
The State of Medicine in the 1800s 9
Burritt College 13
His Religion 17
His Work 27
Denominational Matters 51
His Debates 56
His Books 65
His Declining Years 71

The Alien's Department

The Story Behind the Alien's Department 84
Election and Reprobation 85
Hereditary Total Depravity. 90
Establishment of the Church 123
The Identity of the Church 138
The New Birth. 147
Repentance 162
The Confession 175
What is Baptism? 184
The Holy Spirit 193
The Gifts of the Holy Spirit. 216
The Operation of the Holy Spirit in Conversion, ... 229
The Reception of the Holy Spirit. 254

Bibliography 269

Forward

I would like to recognize Mr. John Cowden for the work that he did on his small book "**The Life of Dr. Brents**." It has been extremely helpful to me in the preparation of this work. I have borrowed a lot of ideas and in some places, the actual text is used. Being unable to say it better than he says, I defer to him. We have his work as well as the records left behind in the pages of the *Gospel Advocate*. These records are all that we have of the remarkable man, Dr. Thomas Wesley Brents. His sources were Mr. C.E.W. Dorris, who was married to Mr. Brents' daughter. Also, Mr. Cowden's father was a close friend with Dr. Brents. These sources are the best that we have after all of these years.

Mr. Cowden mused in his book over whether there was anyone else who cared for Dr. Brents as much as he did. I can unequivocally say "yes, someone does care."

Kyle D. Frank

The Life of T.W. Brents

THE EARLY DAYS

The subject of our story was born in the pioneer wilderness of what was to become the southern part of Marshall County in Middle Tennessee. A thorough search of the property record does not give us any concrete idea of the original Brents homestead though we are certain that it was in this area where he entered the world on February 10, 1823. Two suggestions were put forward later, as being either McClelland's Pillows or McCrory's in the valley of Richmond Creek. Keeping in common with the general knowledge that we have about shelters of this time and area we can be sure that it was a dirt-floored cabin which would be more like our "pole barn" rather than what we seem to think all the pioneers had now, which was a log cabin. For some reason, perhaps most likely the greater ease of construction, the pole-barn type made faster, easier construction; though the word "ease" should never be used in the same sentence as the word "pioneer." There was nothing of "ease" associated with anything which they endeavored to do. Everyone was a farmer in those days, as that was the only occupation. In their area, there were towering trees over the weeds, and briars that covered the ground. There were also dense canes that had to be dealt with to clear any ground for houses or the fields. These early settlers were forced to create out of virtual wilderness. Also, native Americans were still in the land, as well as wild animals and reptiles. These all combined to create great hardship for those who were trying to eke out a living from such harshness.

Dr. Brents' parents were originally from Kentucky. His father, Thomas Brents Sr. and mother Jane McWhorter Brents were among the mass of pioneers that were constantly on the move, looking for a better life where the pastures were greener. They came to Tennessee in 1800. Dr. Brents states that his father was a man of great intelligence, far beyond that of the neighbors and associates. They must have had something special to produce a son who accomplished so very much in such a harsh condition. These held very little of the necessities and advantages which would be available to later generations. Both the father and the son were mighty men with large families. Dr. Brents tells nothing of his early family life. This respectful silence expresses their poor and lowly state. He also is silent about his early life, so we have nothing other than the writings of others who lived around the same time and in the same area.

The first record that we find of T.W. Brents is when he was age eighteen, in 1841. At this point, like other pioneers, he was married. He married Angilina Scott. It was with her help that he learned to read and write. She got him started on the road of education that he would so doggedly follow for the rest of his life. He states that his real education began when he received his first English Grammar. This was no ordinary grammar but one of Victorian English. He was known for speaking and writing in perfect Victorian English. His books show him to be a master of this form of communication and this undoubtedly was a matter of personal pride to him as well. Besides this textbook, he was soon devouring any other books as quickly as he could locate and borrow them. Thus, with a candle and with a wall wick lamp he pursued his self-education by both day and by night. It was this method of self-education that allowed him to complete courses in English, Latin, Greek, and mathematics, which were the major fields of study in the average college of that day. Some of us had trouble with these courses under competent teachers, but Dr. Brents had such a mind and will that mastered all subjects that he undertook. It was, though, unfortunate that he would show little interest in anything other than his studies. He had very few recreations. The author of the earlier biography tells of being a small boy when he ran across Dr. Brents in the woods which lay between their farms. He remembers Dr. Brents holding a hunting horn, surrounded by a pack of hunting dogs. This was apparently one of his few recreational activities. The woods where this chance meeting took place was in the Richmond Creek Valley, one of the richest and most productive in the area. This valley is rimmed by Chestnut Ridge but the woods are gone. They have been replaced by the broad and fertile fields of this rich area.

In his early manhood, Dr. Brents had an occupation which helped make him into a fine specimen of manhood for the remainder of his life: he became a blacksmith. This is considered one the most difficult occupations among the earlier generations. To do this right, you not only needed the physical endurance which would enable you to swing the blacksmith's hammer for hours on end; the more difficult skill is being able to mentally picture what you are planning to create. No amount of hammering will create something if you are unable to picture what the finished product is going to look like. So, along with great strength and endurance, you need the mental power of design. Only by having both skills can you succeed. So, Dr. Brents had not just physical muscles, but also the mental "muscles" to accomplish what he began to do. Everybody worked and cleared land but there was only one blacksmith, which was hardest of all. Every single thing made of metal had to come from the hand of a blacksmith.

Being a blacksmith also contributed to his favorite occupation: studying. When he wasn't occupied in design work, he was able to sit and study his lessons. This blacksmith work, with its physical trials, created a mighty specimen of a man. Dr. Brents was known as a giant of a man his entire life. But, his muscles were mental as well as physical.

Returning to something mentioned before: Dr. Brents studied from a Victorian English Grammar. This grammar had models of speech worked out by an English scholar named Samuel Johnson, as well as other great writers and speakers, which supplemented and idealized Brents' writing and speaking in becoming an English scholar himself. Everything that he said and wrote for the public bore the Victorian form and art that has been the wonder and marvel of his readers. His vocabulary seems to have been unlimited, always with the exact and precise word for the thought. His style, however, is personal and recognizable in everything that he wrote and spoke. Simplicity and clearness seemed to have been his ideal. You may not agree with what he is saying, but you cannot claim to misunderstand it, even though it was written nearly 150 years ago.

In his day, English was not the universal language that it has become today. In those days, the common languages of science and scholarship—Latin and Greek—were long considered as dead. To do anything in the medical or ecclesiastical fields, you needed to know and to work well with those languages. Only Rome and Greece could help him in two of the three occupations that he would be involved with. Dr. Brents was self-educated and that meant obtaining textbooks and grammars and teaching these heretofore unknown languages to himself. Latin was absolutely essential in the medical profession to which Dr. Brents would soon turn. He needed to know Latin even before he began the process of anything in the medical field. It is here that he would go "underground" to learn these languages. I mean "underground" in that there is no record of his having done this: but it is obvious that he did in fact learn them or else he could not function in these realms. He says absolutely nothing about these times of his life.

Now, turning back to blacksmithing again, it must have been during this period that he learned Latin and Greek. He uses a rather unusual description of this time. He speaks of being "under flambo's flickering flame" which was his

5

name for reading by using a grease light. A grease light was a simple affair. It was made by putting old grease into a coffee-cup sized container and then placing a piece of wick into the grease and lighting the wick. It created a very smoky light. But, it was your go-to when all other forms of lighting, such as kerosene, or, whale oil were exhausted. If you didn't have any oil or kerosene, you were left in the dark.

This is the only mention that he makes of his effort to obtain an education. So, blacksmithing and studying in the idle intervals fill up the blanks in his life and equip him for his careers, in which he is now ready to begin. His first career was medicine.

BRENTS, THE PHYSICIAN

To begin with, we need to remember that Dr. Brents was entirely self-taught in whatever endeavor he undertook. Having studied every textbook that he could find, he ultimately learned how to write and speak in both Latin and Greek. Having reached the end of his self-generated education, he would have to apply to the first of his schools, the Eclectic Medical College: "An offer was made by the Society to establish the proposed school in the then young and aspiring village of Worthington, Ohio. A strong effort was being made to constitute that town the Capital City of Ohio, but its near neighbor Columbus won out. In Worthington, there had been established in 1808 a literary and scientific school known as the *Worthington Academy*. This was successfully conducted until 1819, when a new charter was granted it, with title *Worthington College*. One of Dr. Beach's appeals (for the Society) for a college site having reached Worthington College, the trustees, at the instance of Colonel James Kilbourne, offered the protection of the charter and the use of the college building for the proposed "Medical School in the West"

The train of emigration was rapidly moving westward in 1830; prospects for expansion were bright, and the offer was thankfully accepted. Doctor Steele came on to examine the place and approved of it. The *Reformed Medical College of Ohio*, better known as the *Medical Department of Worthington College*, was instituted, and Doctor Steele was made President. The latter proved wanting and was asked to vacate, when a stalwart young Kentuckian, Dr. Thomas Vaughan Morrow, full of vigor, resource, and ability, and fresh from the New York Institution, was installed at the head of the venture.

Under his presidency the school grew rapidly and proved immensely successful for a few years, when it was killed by the defection of some of its men and the machinations of its enemies of the regular school. That which has wrecked so many medical colleges, of whatever creed—jealousy—and particularly a "resurrection war," proved the fatal strokes to this new and unprotected school. The institution was closed and subsequently moved to Cincinnati, where it was to struggle for a year or two and then have a renewal of life such as is seldom experienced by a new and once crushed institution.

Nothing daunted by the failure of the college at Worthington, Professor Morrow decided to carry on the work of medical reform in a more auspicious locality. Cincinnati was determined upon for the center of operations, and accordingly, in the winter of 1842-3, limited accommodations were secured in the old Hay Scales House, corner of Sixth and Vine Streets, and a series of lectures was given to a small class.

In this venture Doctor Morrow was assisted by a Worthington graduate (of 1832), Professor Alexander H. Baldridge, and by a Professor Carr. In 1843 came Doctor Lorenzo E. Jones to assist in the work. He brought both zeal and business qualifications that made him a valuable acquisition. Lastly, Doctor James Kilbourne, Jr., son of Colonel Kilbourne, the staunch friend of Doctor Morrow and medical reform, was added to the faculty, in 1843. He had scarcely completed his first course of lectures, however, before consumption claimed him, and what promised a useful and brilliant career was brought to an abrupt close.

The school thus reorganized, was known as the "RE-FORMED MEDICAL SCHOOL OF CINCINNATI" and was the nucleus around which gathered the forces that ultimately established the Eclectic Medical Institute. The next removal was from the Hay Scales House to a house on Third Street. In 1845 "the large and spacious lecture room" known as the Fourth Street Hall, with adjoining rooms, was secured and accommodations were thus provided for two hundred to three hundred students. The *Western Medical Reformer* (1845, Vol. V, p. 15) announced that "in the course of the ensuing spring and summer the Institute will most probably have ample college buildings of its own."[1]

This is the school in which Dr. Brents first learned the art of medicine. This was the first of three schools that he attended.

The second school he attended was the University of Nashville Medical Department. As far as I have been able to ascertain, the school started in 1850 and closed in 1911.

The third and final school that Dr. Brents attended was the Reform Medical College of Georgia at Macon (Also known as Macon Medical College). The only reference to this college is: *Organized as a medical academy in 1829 and has been in constant operation ever since with the ex-*

---

[1] The following article was prepared, by request, for publication in the "Skull," the first annual publication of the student-body of the Eclectic Medical College, 1911

ception of the war.[2] He studied extra hard and graduated after three instead of four years, in 1855. After his graduation, he was requested by the institution to become a member of the faculty. He held a professorship of anatomy and surgery. Eventually he was appointed to head the Institution. He held this position until shortly before the Civil War. He resigned his post and returned home at that time. The early biographer of Dr. Brents felt that the reason for his departure was that Brents thought that the current state of medicine was false and he never tolerated that in his personal life. However, the reason Brents gave was personal health reasons. Medical schools of the period prior to the Civil War were far different than what we would think them to be. To begin with, the average course length would be two six month terms of lectures. Often, the second term was a repeat of the first term. Another way that an *aspiring* physician had for becoming a *practicing* physician was to in effect serve an apprenticeship with a practicing doctor who would take the student on. He would then serve for a predetermined period of time. This was also how young lawyers were set forward into their field.

Dr. Brents was the head of anatomy and surgery, which was much more sophisticated level than merely lecturing or even being an apprentice for a practicing physician.

THE STATE OF MEDICINE IN THE 1800S.

The medical field had advanced to a sufficient grade that it was truly helping those in its care. The uses of various

---

[2] Medical and Surgical Directory of the United States. Page 101

medications had progressed and pain relief was very advanced.

Morphine was discovered in 1803. It was named after Morpheus, the Greek God of Dreams. At first it was given orally, but when hypodermic needles were invented (1853), morphine was injected. It worked faster. It became popular for treating injured soldiers during the 1860s Civil War. Morphine was also used during childbirth, to suppress coughing, even to relieve diarrhea and dysentery. Side effects can include drowsiness, nausea, vomiting and constipation. In hospitals today, morphine is often the medication prescribed for severe pain.

Opiate is the broad term that covers any drug made from opium (the poppy plant). These drugs are also called narcotics. Morphine falls into this group. Extracts from poppy plants have been used for medicinal purposes since 4,000 B.C.

Hemp, or medicinal cannabis (also called marijuana) has been used for centuries. An Irish doctor, an herb specialist at a medical college in Calcutta 1830, is credited with training his Western colleagues in its benefits for relief of muscle spasm and pain. It was also used to treat migraines and insomnia, and as a primary pain reliever until the invention of aspirin. It became controversial in 1937 when the U.S. banned it.

Next, Aspirin ingredients originally came from extracts of willow bark. Indian tribes knew its value, and chewed on pieces of bark for pain relief. Even Hippocrates in 400 BC recommended it to his patients. Scientists began to study willow bark in the 1850s to see if they could isolate the analgesic ingredient.

Derived from the coca plant in South America, cocaine has been around for several years. Indigenous people chewed on the leaves to give them 'strength and energy.' Medicine men used it to wrap broken bones, reduce swelling, and treat festering wounds. The plant didn't grow in

Europe and spoiled easily during travel, so it wasn't until 1855 in Germany that the main ingredients were isolated. By 1885, cocaine was sold in corner stores in America in various forms – cigarettes, powder, even injection by needle (heroin was also widely available). In medicine, cocaine was commonly used as a local anesthetic. Sigmund Freud prescribed it for his patients to induce euphoria for those depressed. It wasn't until many years later they discovered its addictive nature.

Laudanum, or tincture of opium, was a very common painkiller because it was cheap and available to working class people. It came as a liquid, the main ingredients being morphine mixed with alcohol. There were different versions, with different ratios of opium (morphine). It was widely prescribed for many uses such as colds, pain relief, insomnia and heart ailments. Many writers and poets of the time were known to use it—Charles Dickens, Lewis Carroll and Elizabeth Barrett Browning.

Alcohol is a depressant on the central nervous system and a mood modifier. It was used not as an analgesic in itself, but because it made the person groggy and intoxicated, so he or she wouldn't notice the pain as much. As a local anesthetic (numbing agent) they used it for toothaches (ex. packing the hole in the gums left by a tooth extraction with gauze soaked in cognac). Doctors today do not recommend alcohol as a painkiller.

Home remedies included warm or cold compresses, poultices wrapped on the aching part of the body, herbal remedies (such as chamomile tea for stomach aches), liniments for muscle aches, electrical stimulation with batteries (Benjamin Franklin experimented with this in the 1750s although the ancient Greeks discovered that using electrical eels in foot baths relieved pain), and untold others.

Speaking of the problem of contagious diseases, not much was known about the transmission of infectious pathogens. Diseases such as small pox and tuberculosis were not commonly understood. Quite often, the healthy would stay in the same room as the infected because they did not realize that being in close proximity the one to the other could allow transmission. As an example of how little was understood regarding infectious pathogens, during the upcoming Civil War, the losses due to infectious pathogens were at almost the same level as at the losses due to combat-related injuries. The losses were around 650,000 overall—the combat losses being equal to infectious pathogens at 325,000 each. THAT was how little they understood infectious pathogens!

As for some of the things that medicine did not know at this point in time:

1. We know that they had no antibiotics, as they were discovered during World War 2.

2. They had no clue about avoiding contamination by germs and the vital importance of cleanliness in all areas of medicine, as during the soon upcoming Civil War doctors amputating arms and legs then wiped the saw-blades on their filthy aprons.

3. They had no other way of anesthetizing patients except by chloroform.

4. They also did not understand the concept of opioid addiction. It was merely referred to as "Old Soldier's Disease." All these things were outside the realm of common knowledge at the time. How much was known to the average doctor of the time is unknown, but we sure do see the huge difference now.

As has been earlier mentioned, Dr. Brents resigned from his position of the Reform Medical School of Georgia suddenly in the period prior to the Civil War. There is no light given about this particular occurrence, but three things are known: 1. He possibly resigned due to health issues. 2. He saw the Civil War coming and wanted to get away from that. 3. He possibly resigned to move to Spencer, Tenn. so his children could attend Burritt College.

My personal feelings are with number three because he placed a great deal of value with education. He had five children from his union with Angilina Scott. This union ended in 1857 with her death. He was a widower and solely responsible for providing for those five young lives. What better could he hold of value than the young lives of his poor motherless waifs?

BURRITT COLLEGE

The story of Burritt College is the story of Van Buren County, Tennessee, for whatever prestige the area has received has been the result of Burritt's presence. The town of Spencer owes its existence to Burritt College, for many parents who enrolled their children in the school moved to Spencer to eliminate many of the costs of education. Spencer was isolated from the main arteries of transportation of the area. The nearest towns were McMinnville, eighteen miles west, and Sparta, fifteen miles north. Roads leading to and from Spencer were extremely rough, and a journey to either of these towns usually required several hours, particularly on the return trip down the mountain. The Nashville, Chattanooga, and St. Louis railroad, the only other means of transportation serving the area, was not begun until 1848 and was not completed until 1853. The nearest branch of this line was located at Doyle Station, nine miles north of Spencer, in White County. Upon completion of the main structure, the school opened on February 26, 1849, with seventy-three students and three teachers. The total amount of money available to the college that year from all sources, primarily tuition and donations, amounted to $1,500. Expanding upon the start made by Jones and Carnes, made Burritt the well-respected institution it was, for he shaped its policies and set its standards. Isaac N. Jones and William D. "Pop" Carnes are the men who began

Burritt College. That the trustees were pleased with Carnes' administration is seen by the fact that Carnes, with the exceptions of William Newton Billingsley and Henry Eugene Scott, served as president of Burritt longer than any other man.

Shortly after Carnes arrived at Burritt, Dr. T. W. Brents, physician and a member of the Church of Christ, moved to Spencer and suggested the ideas of expanding the facilities of the college in an effort to restore the school's prestige and prosperity. It was Dr. Brents' belief that the school was unstable because it was not meeting the academic needs of the students, due to the conservative policies of the administration. Dr. Brents proposed the initiation of a fund drive to help build a new campus, purchase additional land, and buy new equipment for the school. Impressed with Dr. Brents' enthusiasm and suggestion, the trustees with Carnes' approval employed Brents to engineer a drive for the sale of stock for the stated purpose of securing funds to erect "a new Burritt College." Dr. Brents proved successful as a fund raiser, for within a few months he sold all the stock which the charter permitted.

A new administration building, the center of the proposed "new school," was completed in 1878. A magnificent structure, it was three stories high, contained seventeen rooms, and had a main hall eighty by fifty feet. Described as "large, commodious, and elegant, the edifice had a protruding tower centered in front, extending a full four stories, with a small portico attached on both sides for the first two floors. It clearly dominated the campus, being located at the very front with the smaller dormitories situated just to its right."

The building cost $12,000, whereas the old buildings, including the three small dormitories, were worth from $7,000 to $8,000. In addition to the new building, fifteen acres of ground were added to the ten acres which composed the campus.

The expanded campus was to be the nucleus of a "brotherhood school." In order to facilitate more efficient efforts toward this end, Elijah Denton deeded one-half of his stock in Burritt to Brents so that Brents could personally direct the fund drive. To persuade more people to contribute to this drive Brents proposed to make Burritt a religious school. This strategy paid off, for more than $25,000 was raised in cash and pledges from members of the Church of Christ in Middle Tennessee and elsewhere.

When the new building was completed in 1878, Brents, who now had a controlling interest in Burritt, demanded that Carnes resign and that he take Carnes' place. This caused a great sensation among Burritt supporters, for Brents' administrative experience was at best limited. Carnes' friends were shocked "with astonishment and indignation" at Brents' demands. Many openly protested to Brents, while a few of the trustees expressed their opposition by resigning their positions.

Finding himself in a quandary, Brents attempted a reconciliation with Carnes' faction by proposing that Carnes remain on at Burritt in a teaching capacity. Carnes declined the offer, however, and severed all ties with the school at the end of the spring session in 1878 to become president of Waters and Walling College, a new school at McMinnville supported by members of the Church of Christ. Pop Carnes was a life-long member of the church and he labored to advance it's causes in every situation in which he found himself. Brents was eager to see his children educated in a "religious" school.

With Carnes' resignation, Brents seized the presidency for himself. The man whom he replaced had made important contributions to the school which he had served so well and which in turn had served him. Besides establishing the academic and moral quality of Burritt, Carnes also helped to perpetuate the thoroughness of the educational process. It was said of his terms as president that "gradu-

15

ates were not turned off...as fast as some would desire;" however, "a diploma signed by him meant something." At the same time he pointed "to the nobility of the right," and appealed to the nobler sentiments of youth, which, connected with his own example, "inspired the student with aspirations after that kind of greatness that comes from purity and usefulness."

Dr. Brents' chief contribution, on the other hand, lay in establishing Burritt's financial and operative foundation. The highlight of his association with the institution was raising the funds to build the new college building as well as expanding the scope of the school into a religiously-oriented institution.

In keeping with his purpose to build "a new Burritt," Dr. Brents reorganized and expanded the curriculum. Whereas the curriculum had followed the traditional pattern, Brents, being a physician, stressed the scientific field, and during his tenure as president he made it a special object to interest students in such subjects as anatomy, physiology, and botany. The curriculum was divided into ten departments, including such subjects as English, science, mathematics, history and political economy, and foreign languages.

Burritt College prospered during Dr. Brents' term more than at any other time since its reopening. In the academic year 1879-1880, 213 students were enrolled. Prior to that time the largest enrollment was in 1876, when Burritt recorded seventy-nine students for the first day of classes.

Dr. Brents resigned in 1882 to devote himself to writing and preaching. He became widely known for his book, ***The Gospel Plan of Salvation,*** and a collection of sermons entitled ***Gospel Sermons***.[3] In 1884 he established a bank at

---

[3] *Gospel Sermons* has recently been reprinted by Cobb Publishing.

Lewisburg, Tennessee, where he lived until his death in 1905.

Dr. Brents was followed by Aaron Tillman Seitz, a native of Warren County and a lawyer by profession. Seitz was educated at Burritt, having graduated from there in 1854. While a student at Burritt he was baptized into the Church of Christ by President Carnes, and during the Civil War served in Company I, Sixteenth Regiment, Tennessee Volunteers.[4]

Brents' association with Burritt College lasted as long as his children were attending the institution. After they graduated, he cut his association with Burritt College and made his way back to Marshall County where he began the area of his life which he personally enjoyed and in which he labored the most. It is during this time that his most famous labors were held. It is here, now that his family was cared of, that he would begin to do his work as a gospel preacher.

HIS RELIGION

All religion has a philosophy of life but it isn't just mere philosophy. God must be the center of it and it must be above man. Dr. Brents believed fully in the Father God of the Bible as was revealed in Jesus Christ. He was of the philosophic type and this was what made a theologian of him. Theology was the warp and woof of the religion which was his. It followed the principles that could only come from the Bible and it alone. He was not the creator of his philosophy and theology but the discoverer of both. Those who philosophize tend to be free thinkers, so they have a problem with the Bible. It is full of commands and precepts so free-thinkers have a problem with it. Dr. Brents

---

[4] Burritt College Historical Website

claimed no originality nor independence in his religion but held to the commands and precepts as were laid out by the Word of God.

He was motivated by many different ideas but by far the greatest motivator was his idea of what religion was. The key to Dr. Brents' mature life was his religion.

In his youth, he labored as a blacksmith to support his family and provide for the necessities of life. He then labored night and day for an education but this was only a means to an end. In his mature years, he used that education to be a good minister to those of the Lord's flock under his charge. He liked money but not for its possession alone. He had no pleasure in dissipation. His love of his religion is the only explanation for the life that he led. The earlier part of his life seemed sane and successful and people expected him to carry on in the same manner as he had begun. People were shocked when he turned his back on both medicine and collegiate education because that wasn't what most people would do. We know though, that he had his eyes on the bigger prize when he left both medicine and education. He had been a man of wisdom and purpose and what he did was just not what the vast majority of people would do. He had gone to great expense of time, effort and money in his study and trial of life and his life was now half-way spent. It is a hazardous thing to change professions at any age but especially so between the ages of forty and fifty. He had changed twice and now proposed a third. This must have perplexed his family greatly.

It seems that he had conferred with no one in making his decision but it appears that he had no doubts as to what he intended to do. The only possible explanation comes back to what we have earlier mentioned: it was his religion that caused his tremendous change in life and purpose.

To begin with, after his two careers had finished, he returned to Marshall County where he was born and reared. He wasn't in search of honor and glory but after the will of

18

God. It was now time for him to undertake his third and final career. That career was in the service of His Lord and Master.

At another time, Dr. Brents claimed that his ministry covered fifty years. A little math takes him back to his young manhood and also includes the time when he was practicing medicine as well as during his time as a college president. He was teaching at both Macon Medical College as well as at Burritt Christian College. This was in fact a part-time ministry as he was teaching full-time. A little more math tells us that his conversion was either in his youth or young manhood. This is probably while he was teaching himself Latin and especially Koine Greek. The New Testament is written in Koine Greek and it was probably what he was studying while learning that language.

Looking at another time and another place, the Campbell's unity movement was still in its infancy while Dr. Brents was a young man. As he matured and learned to teach, it is highly likely that he saw the primitive situations in the churches around where he taught. Pioneer conditions died hard and the primitiveness of the churches probably urged him on to both learn the scriptures as well as try to teach them. At that point of time, there were a lot more evangelists than congregational preachers to teach, feed and nurture all the young believers. After he returned to Marshall county as an older and wiser man, he saw the plight of these young churches who were in desperate need of grounding, feeding and the nurturing that can only come from a well-grounded, well-taught and mature man familiar with the teacher's art. Dr. Brents had doubtless observed the need of both teaching and leadership in those churches through the many years and felt the need to nurture them, lest they die. All of his past years were preparative for this time.

Dr. Brents was a believer in the Campbells, but he was a disciple of Jesus Christ in the New Testament sense. He had joined the movement of the Campbells for Christian unity. But the first time that this message was preached in the state of Tennessee was by Barton W. Stone. This happened in 1811-13 while he was residing at Goodlettsville. Stone then gathered the saints together to form a church at Wilson Hill. They are still gathering to break bread in this early twenty-first century. This was the first church of the Lord in Tennessee. Near to Dr. Brents' home, Old Cane Creek Church, was established in 1823, the year of Brents' birth. We can be reasonably sure that he was not baptized by his Methodist parents as there would have been some record of this somewhere. That would have been rather ironic as he spent a good deal of his life exposing this error. He left no record of his conversion so we do not know when and by whom he was immersed. It is strongly probable that he was baptized by Reece Jones, who was a pioneer preacher of the Disciples movement in Tennessee. Later, in the *Gospel Advocate* of December, 1856, page 368, he is referred to as a "Timothy" to Reece Jones. This was in a gospel meeting held by the two that lasted nine days and resulted in fifteen baptisms. Jones' son, Dr. I.N. Jones followed Dr. Brents as president of Burritt College. The entire Jones family were known as noted teachers and preachers.

Dr. Brents' religion is seen best against the background of religious ideas of that day. Just like today, they are arguing and squabbling. Although there were squabbles, there were also searchers for truth who were seeking the Lord's will for themselves. These seekers for truth often were found by traveling evangelists such as Jacob Creath Jr. and were taught well and added to the church. These brethren did virtually little else than travel to places to teach those wanting to know the truth. After the teaching, came the repentance and finally immersion into Christ. Churches were being filled and there quite often was no preacher to take them in and teach the basics. Again, this was where Dr. Brents saw how he could step in and do something to save these congregations from falling away from spiritual weakness.

But, Dr. Brents found much in the creeds, teaching and practice of the various sects to oppose and cast off. The Campbells, tired out by religious warfare, conceived a peace and unity plan, which involved the rejection of divisive creeds and the dissolution of the sects, which caught the mind and heart of Dr. Brents. Brents agreed with the Campbells in everything they taught. The records contain many agreements with no disagreements as far as the earlier Editor could find. There were minor differences, of course, but they did not matter.

As to Dr. Brents' essential tenets of his religion, he wrote out no creed for himself but he had few items of faith that he insisted upon under all circumstances. First, the Bible, the spoken and written word of God and Jesus Christ, the incarnate word of God, as well as being the Son of God, the Savior of all men who will obey him, and the church established after the New Testament pattern. He was known as a real stickler for Bible Things, but not a dogmatist. His teaching was known to be plain and clear in all teaching but never offensive. In everything he accepted and followed this principle: "Where the Scriptures Speak we speak. Where the Scriptures are silent we are silent" and he is the only one that we know for sure followed it. Also, where the Scriptures are silent he granted liberty; but insisted on compliance where they spoke. This doesn't in any sense define Dr. Brents' religion. This is merely putting down markers to outline his religious boundaries.

Dr. Brents' religion of work and worship was written and preached by the good Dr. himself. He was his own theologian. There were few of his associates of which it could be said that this was the case. Some of his co-workers were John T. Johnson, Racoon John Smith, Philip H. Fall, Jacob Creath Sr & Jr., Benjamin Franklin, John Mulkey, Aylette Rains and Tolbert Fanning. Benjamin Franklin was the only one who also could be seen as a theologian. Franklin's books, along with Brents' books could be used by young gospel preachers trying to find out what they were supposed to believe and preach.

It is very difficult to make a brief statement about what T.W. Brents believed. It was so unique and personal that it could not be explained in a brief statement of facts. Everything that he spoke about, wrote about or acted upon was a statement of what his belief was. During this age, creeds abounded and virtually every church had one. They were held in the highest regards and most denominations would fight to uphold them. As was recorded by one little old lady, "I like the Bible for it backs up our creed." Regarding these creeds, Dr. Brent's religion caused him to take a long, hard look at these and, like the little old lady-this time to compare the creeds to what the Bible says to see to what extent they differed or agreed with the Scriptures. Being a Bible Theologian, requiring all items of faith and practice to be in harmony with the Bible and the Jesus Christ of the Bible. Having done this, he had determined right from wrong and was fully prepared to do and to teach God's precepts to everyone who would hear him. All this speaking and writing was voluminous and was an embodiment of his beliefs, which had been examined in the light of God's word. This covered fifty years of his life. His religion, therefore, could be examined and summarized. This was the theologian part of him.

Dr. Brents was a man of great thoughts, a real thinking man. He was not a man of emotions for as we examine his written works, we will never see a part where he was not fully in control of himself. Whereas many speakers, mostly denominational, would work themselves into a froth while speaking, Dr. Brents never did. In one of the debates that I was working on, you could see his denominational opponent doing just that-working himself up to a fever pitch during his speech. When Dr. Brents got up to speak, it was almost in a cold, disinterested manner. He arose and at the speaker's spot proceeded to coolly unload such a scriptural blast that so overtook his opponent to a point where he never quite recovered during the rest of the debate.

When it comes to out emotional makeup, we all are somewhere between intellectual and emotional. The scale runs between the two ends. Dr. Brents was by nature inclined to the intellectual. He had more intelligence than most folks and he used it well. He was largely influenced by the intellectual, but he did not deny or discredit the emotional facet. He had a guiding principle: "Prove all things, hold fast to that which is good." This was the first voice that he heard was reason, logic. There were at this time, some folks who knew Dr. Brents and their estimation of him was that he was cold and unfeeling. They were completely right in their judgment. When a man uses logic and intellect, it would appear to be cold and unfeeling. This wasn't necessarily a wrong or bad thing, just a *different* way of looking at things. Having made this judgment about Dr. Brents, they did still have to admit that he was right, in the long run. After having made his judgment, there were very little grounds left for protests and exceptions.

With Dr. Brents, justice came first. Regardless of the emphasis on the intellect or the emotions, let God be true and justice be done. But, there were complaints with some people that Dr. Brents was weak on the emotions; but he was so strong emotionally that he was highly moving in his speech. How or why these opposites could be in agreement, this writer can't explain.

That age was an age of forensic argumentation. There were some who would argue for the pure sport of the argument; but they tended to be more honest than does their offspring today. Today, agendas exist far away from those creeds of old. Today, very often it is a matter of pure power and not to determine truth. Today, each man "does that which is right in his own eyes." In Dr. Brents time it was a seeking after truth, or at least perceived truth. He kept digging for the truth while they just followed their creeds in their arguments. Brents was honor bound to show the truth and he was fully exonerated by it.

Back to theologians: They search for those grains of truth which are fundamental. But, some theologians end up as philosophers because they wander in their search for the truth. Brents didn't fall into that trap as he was always duty bound to hold to revealed truth. When you do that, that can't be tricked, or even dragged away from the truth. Dr. Brents was a Bible theologian, purposing to bring everything that he taught and practiced into harmony with the word of God as expressed on the pages of Holy Writ. The Bible is very old yet it appears to be very young and Jesus Christ, its main subject is the same each and every day. That was Dr. Brents' religion

The unity movement of the Campbells was right so from the early days. Dr. Brents wasn't such in favor as they were because in his debates he was so busy separating the wheat from the chaff that he had no time for expressing unity like the Campbells did. His dealings were with individual congregations so that he had very little time to express the idea of unity with other congregations. This did not mean that he wasn't interested in unity but his work was IN the local churches and that it gave him very little time to deal with extra-congregational matters. He applied most of the Scriptures to the local body and its internal workings therefore had little time for dealing with the universal church. His greatest concern was with the local bodies, their identity, organization, work and worship. This was because of the conditions that he found in the local churches. The Disciples had no sure pattern shown to them while evangelism. This "boot camp" was necessary in preparing them to deal with the denominational onslaught that they would possibly face. The whole denominational world was in chaos and the individual christian needed to know how to deal with these people when he did come across them.

The Campbells came to this country searching for a way to accomplish a unity of the church in a larger sense; but Dr. Brents seemed to be rather skeptical of any effort to this end. The earlier editor, who had spoken to Dr. Brents found nothing in opposition to this but just that he had not found a place in which to speak thus. Again, he was dealing with the machinery on an inner congregational level. To be more specific, these were items such as identity, organization, work and worship of those congregations.

Dr. Brents truly held to "where the scriptures speak, we speak", but also, "where the Scriptures are silent, we are silent." Because of this we have no way to gauge his views on issues like instrumental music or extra-congregational entities. One thing that I learned from his daughter was that he left all Christ's silences as items of Christian liberty. Unfortunately, there is no other way to verify this so it will remain in silence. He confined himself to teaching plainly stated things as there is more than enough to keep a teacher going for a great deal longer than the time he had with each congregation. He never would argue about untaught issues. Notwithstanding, the many silences of the Scriptures he claimed there was plenty given to constitute a full pattern for the church. In fact, all the inspired speakers and writers affirm that the Scriptures fully equip the church and individual Christians for all religious needs.

Dr. Brents laid aside two great professions, medicine and education, and then used his time and talents for building up the church after the New Testament pattern. He examined and rejected denominations because they were not constructed like the New Testament pattern. This was in regard to both essentials and non-essentials. It became his duty to illuminate the errors that he found. That led to days and nights of debating. It was in the realm of polemics that he sought to bring these errors out in the light of the New

Testament pattern. The first and greatest of these errors was the passive system of salvation. This will be discussed more in depth in another chapter.

Today, we have some that say that we can have "unity in diversity." It is also said that there is no blueprint pattern for the church. They also claim that there is so much difference that how can we see a pattern? This, of course, is said by those who want to make more changes. It is here that we need to take a stand upon the Scriptures and show decisively that there is a pattern, no matter how much change agents spout against it. Dr. Brents fought the same type of teacher for a great deal of the time that he labored among the churches. Every student of the scriptures can show you incidental non-essential difference in the New Testament churches which do not interfere with the identity of those congregations. The authors of the New Testament recognize this and clarify these essentials. Dr. Brents was far more concerned about how much-not how little the deity and authority of the Scriptures are being violated by some disciples, whose errors come not from the Bible but mostly from disciples' schools.

Now, the problem doesn't get any better if the Scriptures are ignored, which some do. There are humanists in the churches today as there were in the New Testament churches. They do not like the scriptural authority any more today than they did back then. Paul met them at Athens and accomplished nothing. Each individual had to have his own religion. It hasn't changed today except the pagans now inhabit the denominations where they can be comfortable. It never will stop until the day when the Lord returns and they will call the hills to fall on them. By then, it will be too late.

As Alexander Campbell was a leader, so was Dr. Brents. He broke fellowship with none of the churches that we know of. Again, the silence of the Scriptures prevails. He was more independent than was Campbell. Brents never

26

hesitated to state conclusions on what he felt were "doctrines of men." He never spoke disrespectfully of any; and he was always fair and friendly to all the true followers of Christ, however he never stated or defined his fellowship. Just as A. Campbell was never fully convinced on the subject of fellowship; but he practically fellowshipped everyone. The question of fellowship and church membership has been difficult since the beginning. Dr. Brents probably lost some fellowship because he did not speak on instrumental music or extra-biblical entities, where the silence of the scripture reigns. Brents' theological studies and work was largely to himself and his fellowship was "with the Father and his Son Jesus Christ." He fellowshipped many and we do not know if he disfellowshipped anyone. That will be looked in a future chapter.

HIS WORK

We don't have any information about the preparations he made before he entered any school. We do know that there must have been a great deal of time and effort made on his part to be able to function in the very first school that he entered, which was the Eclectic Medical School. The reason this is said is can you imagine any school, much less a school of medicine accepting anyone who claimed to be self-educated? Yet, there was something very special about Dr. Brents which somehow gained admission to the ultra-difficult school. Most likely there had been admission exams which would have weeded out all inferior candidates. He somehow managed to gain admission all through his studies alone. There was no one to speak for him except his test scores. Now, imagine this, an older man gaining access to the tests and doing so well that they had to admit him. That was T.W. Brents.

Before that success was untold hours of reading, studying, always looking for more. That drive was self-generated! We see the vision of the grease lamp and the filthy blacksmith's shop where a young Thomas Wesley Brents labored over the forge, swinging that horrible hammer over and over. One more hit and this will be complete, then back to my studies-I must not fall behind. The grease lamp and the tallow candle in the late hours of the night is telling to all who will look. The smutty, dirty hours of the daytime, leading to the dark and lonely hours of the night. All of this just to have time to study the classics, or perhaps a work on geometry or chemistry, or even better, a work on Koine Greek as used in the Scriptures. These are the prizes that Brents valued so highly in those formative days. Besides his young family, they were all that he had to keep himself going. To preach a sermon to the church-what a prize to be had!

Now, he studied and worked alone, which would tend to be discouraging. He had no helper, no Timothy or Titus, no helpers of any sort except his family, who were there when they could be. It was he who helped himself along the long, lonely path that leads to success. There was no one prepared to assist him in his religious studies. That included interpretation and application of the Bible to the pioneer folk of his area and time. There were also enemies who would discourage him from doing what was right. They were there just like they always are in every time and place. The churches had to be defended from the denominational threats that they faced. The most able and shrewdest minds of the day were intent upon destroying the new religious group that was there. Truth has to be defended! The crucial task of defense fell to Dr. Brents. The debates that he held saved the new religious work from sheer destruction. While he had previously done another type of work-that of a teacher-his teaching experience enabled him to face his opposers in the polemic ring where what one learned had better be right for they were to be tested by trials. If you had the truth you were unconquerable! The Sword of the Spirit was his and he very well knew how to use it in cutting his enemies down. There was many a debate where after it was finished his congregation had grown-from the denominational group he was opposing. Debates are the way that truth can more easily be seen by friend and foe alike. That is why there were often defections to the side of truth. People for the most part are not fools. If you show them truth and put it alongside that of error, it can be very clear to the one who has a pure heart. He isn't likely to stay in a group proven to be wrong. He will see the truth and will be drawn to it just like the moth is drawn to the flame! Truth, unveiled, is irresistible to one who has a pure heart.

The earlier editor made a statement which needs to be clarified. He claimed that Bro. Brents was with the Campbells in the beginning. This statement needs some explanation. Alexander Campbell began his first religious journal in 1827. Dr. Brents would have been four years of age so that won't work. The only other possibility was that they were both involved in the foundation work. The Campbell's *Christian Baptist* led the charge out of Babylon towards Jerusalem. Dr. Brents' lengthy studies led him to the deep things of Christ and because of this understanding he was able to work on the foundation. His knowledge was of the passive system of religion. What is the "Passive System" of religion? The passive system of religion was what was believed and practiced in the denominations as the church began to be restored. It would also come to be known as Calvinism.

Calvinism, with its five tenets was a system where you could not be born again except God calls you. You could not err as to lose your salvation, all babies be born in sin, etc.

The Disciples were forced to deal with Calvinism as it threatened everything that they believed was sacred. The earlier Disciples were hard pressed to deal with it in the start of the movement. But, fortunately, there were people like Dr. Brents who would study the scriptures and gain enough knowledge so as to be able to discern between truth and error. When Dr. Brents had reached the conclusion of his studies, he could see Calvinism and what a threat it was and he had the gumption to be willing to deal with these errors in such a way as to finally break them. And break them he did. As mentioned earlier, Dr. Brents' resolve took him far and wide debating or merely teaching congregations the truth.

The Disciples had an active plan, conceived by the Campbells and proclaimed by Walter Scott. This was taught by the earliest disciples in their own special way. Dr. Brents was more of a wrecking ball when dealing with the denominations and their special creeds. He put the hammer down, just like he had in his earlier days of blacksmithing. This made him a special enemy of the sects. They would try just about any way they could to silence him. Most activity took place on the polemical field though. The Disciples had an active system of salvation whereas the denominations were initially passive. The two systems could not live together. In each was a different force of conversion. The Disciples plan was new and invigorating. It set the religious world afire. But, it needed some foundation work done to withstand the assaults that would be launched upon it over the years. This work could only be done by theologians, and Dr. Brents was a theologian extraordinaire. He came onto the field of conflict prepared to do battle for the truth. He also was prepared to do the necessary groundwork to build up the lagging Disciples. This he would do day in and day out for many years. He began to preach and write day and night over those many years. In a few years he began to write his first book *The Gospel Plan of Salvation.* His next effort was a book of sermons named *Gospel Sermons.* Those two books are a complete refutation of the passive system of religion known as Calvinism. This was largely accomplished by Dr. Brents and accounts today for our modern progress toward Christian unity and a broader fellowship. Although some may reject the Campbell-Brents theology, they surely do have to respect the system and how well it works. The truth works well! Many of us, myself included, still accept and follow and advocate this Scriptural theology. In truth, we need another Dr. Brents to reopen this type of religion. But, it was Dr. Brents who slew the doctrinal giant of Calvinism by his preaching, books and multiple debates.

Dr. Brents' first work was Iconoclastic The church needed to be free from Calvinism which was on the back of the passive system of salvation, and which most of the churches believed and followed. The difference in the prevailing sects were wide and strong, most of which stemmed from the two theories of salvation and was all through the creeds. One held that man can do nothing for his salvation; the other held that there is much that he can and must do. Supposedly, there were Scriptures on both sides of the question with examples in both covenants. All of these depended upon a reasonable explanation and interpretation of each. Interpretation must be in harmony with the Bible, and the Bible in harmony with itself. If the passive theory is held to, the entire Bible must be in harmony with it; whereas the active theory was held to, there were seeming contradictions that must be removed. There were a number of phrases introduced "One can and one can't; he will and he won't, be damned if he does, and damned if he don't." The creeds were written to support the theory; instead of the theory being made to harmonize the whole Bible. It is old news now, but it wasn't then. Every item in the creeds were searched for error, exposed to criticism and defended on every step of the way.

Nearly all of the churches held to the passive theory and practiced it in their worship with all of its unusual tendency. Things such as the Mourner's Bench, divine call, etc. The new sect, the "Disciples" rejected it and opposed it in total. It was from this small "sect" that war would be unleashed against the passive system. They then proclaimed the active system having taken it from the Bible. This became the theological bone of the day; and Dr. Brents could be located only where the thickest of the fight lay. The Calvinists taught that man can do nothing to save himself; and Dr. Brents and associates declared that there are a number of things that man must do to save himself, which were clearly shown in the Bible. The strangest thing was that the Campbells were Calvinists themselves and sought the unity of all Calvinists; but, when they committed themselves to unity upon the Scriptures, they were brought to a new study of the Scriptures and found many barriers to it. Alexander Campbell began a new study of the Scriptures in their original language, which revealed many difficulties. Dr. Brents, with many years of studies of the languages, was equipped for this study and work. When he began to preach he found almost every item of the creeds based on the passive theory of salvation. After further study in Greek and Latin he was soon drawn into the thickest and fiercest of the religious warfare, for that it was. In his sermons, he began to dig up Calvinism up by the roots, showing from the original errors of the creeds, incorporated in harmony with the passive salvation, which he later set forth in more detail and fullness in his books. The combination of both preaching and writing broke the back of Calvinism and led finally to the rejection of the passive theory of salvation. Later, when the American Standard translation came out, it translated "turn" as the translation of "Be converted," all the churches have since done away with the Mourner's Bench and all other symbols of passive salvation. The errors that we call Calvinism, have mostly been done away with and we have a little more unity than before. Mind you, we have a long way to go to achieve the unity that Jesus prayed for, but it has at least gotten somewhat better.

The persons and history of this particular fellowship and unity need to be better understood. This came only after a thirty-year religious war of which Dr. Brents was the center. When we think of war, we think of evil, war is sometimes a necessary evil; and religion hasn't been made free from it. There are times when fighting, we must maintain true religion in the world. This is a perfect example of why the apostle Paul equipped us for warfare. This authorization can be found in Ephesians 6:10-20.

As the war between the two theories of salvation, the passive and the active, grew and spread, more and more people and churches as well as extra biblical entities became involved. The "fame" and prestige of Dr. Brents grew and enlarged. He saw that there was no place for the two theories to live next to each other in any area. One had to be victorious. Which one would it be-the passive that had grown so old in many areas, or the active theory which gathered strength from the living power of the word of God? The Campbells couldn't help as they were Calvinists and were still struggling with their own troubles. They desperately wanted unity among the churches but could expect nothing while the theories and their relations kept up the fight. Now, as to who it was to be cast out, mankind could do nothing to win the war as it had to come from the word of God itself. That must be the one making the decision, not weak, fallible man. Now, Dr. Brents, who saw the outcome of this battle began to act. Originally, he began crafting his work through the pages of a Gospel journal, the *Gospel Advocate*. This journal was started by William Lipscomb and Tolbert Fanning in 1855. It enjoyed widening distribution until the second half of the year 1861. The American Civil War caused a hiatus until the year 1866 when David Lipscomb joined Fanning as editor. They sought to call all wandering saints back from the backsliding that was a result of the unending blood spillage and raw carnage. There was peace and the call went out from the *Advocate*. Well, enough of that history. I'd best be getting back to the war of the theories. It continued when Dr. Brents got involved with the paper after many successful meetings were put in the paper. He felt that much good could be done through the pages of the *Advocate*. After some discussion, it was agreed that in a way to further evangelization, a regular "Department" called "The Alien's Dept." would appear in the paper, which it first did in the January 1867 issue, page 55. These articles were originally for evangelism but gradually the tone changed and the forerunner for all of Dr. Brents' work ended up this way. Apparently, the response was overwhelming so Dr. Brents started producing articles on Hereditary Depravity and other related topics. These articles were some twenty pages or so. The important thing is to remember the overwhelming response that T.W. Brents and David Lipscomb had to these articles. Many were cut out of the paper and handed around. When these were (expectedly) lost, many wrote in asking for more copies that they could pass around. David Lipscomb had one of those "lightbulb" moments and decided to reprint them and sell them as (giant) tracts. To be sure that he had enough, a liberal number of the tracts were printed. Like anything that was from Brents, they sold like hotcakes and DL soon found himself with two things. 1)no more tracts 2) Really angry folks when they could get no more tracts. Lipscomb should have had one main idea-get more tracts printed post haste. For some reason, he could get no more for a while and this caused him some real difficulties. People were sending him money for tracts but there was none to be had and he did not know who sent money so he could return it. This was not a good thing at all.

Dr. Brents came to Nashville relatively often and someone had another lightbulb moment and said AHA! A Book, a Book. Dr. Brents was encouraged to rework his tracts and write enough material to make it into a decent size book. He proceeded to do this. It took nearly two years but the **Gospel Plan of Salvation** was born.

The battle of the theories was a really strong war because people backed up each theory and fought for them. With his whole soul and body, he backed the active theory because it was scriptural and the passive could not be supported by the Word of God. In every congregation that would give him a hearing (and that was about all due to curiosity) he explained the two theories and why he felt the active was better, being supported by the Scriptures. With the double punch of the book and also his personal work, slowly the foundations of the passive began to weaken and then collapse. Preacher by preacher, congregation by congregation discontinued their support for the passive theory and practice and today we have practical unity on this issue. Some folks would call this fight "old straw" for the mills of the church. True, but one hundred years ago it was quite new and it was Dr. Brents who led the fight against it. The earlier editor felt that God used Dr. Brents to fight this battle and perhaps it was. Why did Foy Wallace lead the fight against premillennial interests? God called him to do it and that's that. Dr. Brents was the man for the job. He said "Here am I, Lord, send me." Now, don't misunderstand me, there were a lot of good men who were personally involved in the war, Brents wasn't alone by any means. But let's give him the credit that he rightly deserves.

After this war had been concluded and the giant lay on its back, Brents had more work to do. This time it was constructive. It was related to the Unity Movement. Brents wasn't an evangelist but a builder. No church could have done better than hosting him for a Gospel Meeting. These new converts would to be spiritually provided for and; otherwise they would weaken and die. Jesus provided the church for them to reside in. As Brents saw the myriads of pioneers, he was reminded to pressing into the church, he was reminded of his mission to teach and establish the churches for them.

Alexander Campbell could never make up his mind about whether it was a movement within the church or the church itself. If it were just a movement it would as well disappear into the church. Dr. Brents emphasized the local body over the universal. He also purposed a permanent institution, the Christian Church, These were his thoughts.

Dr. Brents followed the evangelists, teaching the converts the Christian way of life and organizing them into churches. He did produce converts, himself, if you had a chance to read in the *Gospel Advocate*. His was a work producing churches and building up the new converts that were produced during his meetings. Usually, in each issue would be a result of where he had been and how many converts there were. This never stopped him from his work of building up local churches but there definitely were usually any number of converts listed. I write this in differing from the early editor who stated that he never produced converts. Having searched the *Gospel Advocate* from 1855 to his death in 1905, I can unequivocally state that there were usually any number of conversions listed in each of his gospel meetings. He also, during his meetings, would teach new converts, for a few days the nature and forms of the church. It was left to him as well as others to establish the church, and to confirm them in their faith and to feed the babes their spiritual milk. As stated earlier, Dr. Brents was a real theologian and knew how to simplify his teaching to where it was easy to understand by those new to the Faith. In all of the churches he visited, he did strive to establish the churches according to the pattern laid out by the New Testament. Between he and the Campbells, this was more of an ideal than a firm idea. They would look through the pages of their New Testaments for the guidance needed in this realm. When we look back to the days of Paul and his co-workers, this step was much easier because they had the indwelling, miraculous Holy Spirit to assist them in building up these converts their earlier preaching had produced. Well, the hero of our story did not have the miraculous indwelling to assist him so he opened his Bible for all of the guidance that he could handle. We must remember that the Holy Spirit was also available through the pages of Holy Writ to Dr. Brents, as well as to the Campbells. Also, like as some insist that every "t" be crossed and every "I" be dotted, Dr. Brents did not operate like this. That fell to Moses and his instructions with the tabernacle. (see Brents' sermon on the tabernacle) Jesus, like Moses, was a lawgiver though not as minute as was Moses; and in the Letter to the Hebrews, the apostle was striving to get the new converts to abandon Jewish style worship, he retains them only the antitypes, such as the altar of prayer, which also Dr. Brents retains. In seeking to model the church, Brents sought out the requirements that Jesus and the apostles made. During his long ministry, he was urged to make the silences of both Jesus and the Apostles inclusive. This he refused to do. There is no place where this was successfully done; that is, successfully added into the foundation of the church. He resisted this in each and every place. If you will read his sermon on the establishment of the church, you will know the pattern and identities of the church.

Without a doubt, the single greatest achievement he accomplished was his exposure and discrediting of the denominational creeds. Each denomination conceived and propagated its own distinctive creed which they put into the foundation of each church. The rank and file members believed in these creeds much more than they believed the Bible. They were supposed to be taken from the Bible, but few or none of them were. Few or none of them were the same, in fact, they were opposite to the Bible in some respects. They were old and reverenced, and defended as the essential deposit of their faith and practice. They had become divisive issues and causes of division in themselves. They had become authoritarian within the denomination as rulings of the assembled church. The original authors of these creeds were the great theologians of the churches such as Luther, Calvin, Zwingli, Knox, Wesley, Edwards, et al, but they were being discredited when the Campbells came to this country. They had been skeptical of their authority and some came out in open opposition to their use; but, of course, with a sympathetic background which kept them from becoming radicals.

When Dr. Brents came on scene, he was intensely opposed. He had the correct background and maturity to be prepared for this negative mission. In Dr. Brents' eyes, unity in the Scriptures did away and all other extra-Biblical statements of faith were forbidden and excluded. In year after year he wrote and preached and debated, he attacked the validity and use of creeds. Welcome to the battleground of Theologians! To see what is being referred to, turn in **The Gospel Plan of Salvation** and read the chapters upon Predestination, Election, Reprobation, Depravity, Calvinistic Proofs examined, etc. Maybe you feel that Dr. Brents was not able to handle these subjects and the egregious errors, which were the live issues of that day. One thing that was clearly established was that the creeds were erroneous and totally useless and definitely harmful to the unity of the church!

With creeds discredited, he turned to the Calvinistic passive system of salvation and the establishment of the active plan of salvation instead, which was noted in an earlier chapter. With these dead items buried, the march of faith was able to be continued.

Dr. Brents was a tireless worker. He had to be. In a search of the *Gospel Advocate*, the agenda of Dr. Brents was printed from issue to issue. As an example, the following can be given: Fall, 1858-page 29 Meeting at Liberty, 25 additions, pg. 33, article: Is There No Other Way, Pg.43,

Oscaloosa, meeting 15 additions, pg.112 Visibles and Invisibles, pg261 Brents, Reece Jones mtg, 40 added. Pg.305 The Holy Spirit 9/17/58 Lewisburg, pg 318 Report from Marshall County Tenn. pg. 336 The Gifts of the Spirit, 366 The Reception and Operation of the HS, 10/26/58, This was mostly covered by his articles but other years can be shown to give his meeting schedules which was arduous. This particular time is while he was writing those articles that ended up being his first book. He must have been like Joshua, the son of Nun, who would never stop while there was work to be done. So was Dr. Brents. He would never hurry if there was some one who was seeking light. His dedication and loyalty to the Bible made him a trusted exegete and teacher. At one point there was a drive to get him to write a commentary on the entire Bible. If I look at my record of his works, I see this around the time that he was teaching at the Nashville Bible School which would put this around the late 1880's and into 1890. What a wonderful thing that would have been had he not been so busy to actually take the time to write that commentary. I tell you this not to exalt my knowledge of his daily life but to show you the confidence that the brotherhood held towards him.

The Disciples were accused of being the people of only one book. What a wonderful accusation! If only this were true today!! Dr. Brents was a man of many books. He was constantly acquiring them and studying various different ones. One thing that I feel is a downright shame is that no one knows where his library went to upon his death in June of 1905. It never made it to the Disciples of Christ Historical Society because when the earlier editor—John Cowden— "retired" he gave his entire library to DCHS, he asked them what they knew of Dr. Brents. The reply was that they one had one of his books—probably *The Gospel Plan of Salvation.* Other than that lonely tome, nothing whatsoever exists. Where did that library go? It could not have been small so no one snatched it away. Where did it go? Can you imagine what gems it held? Sorry, that was the daydream of a book worm!

Dr. Brents had no co-workers with whom he regularly worked. Few or none were prepared for this heavy task. Where would they have been when the shells from denominational guns began splashing around him? We don't know because there was no Timothy or Titus. No one to help bear the weight of the monumental work that he was endeavoring to do. He wasn't a recluse though he guarded his private life from nearly everyone. He could have been seen to be like Jesus, a man of public life. He lived the life of an early pioneer preacher, and went from place to place doing the work as only he could. The practical pioneer needs crowded out ideals and led him to look for and plan practical ends.

He was not an idealist but a pragmatist in his work. The South was settled much later than the East and North. It was this harsh environment that caused him to strive to meet local conditions as best as could be met. He was born in a one room dirt-floored cabin and knew its privations and needs; but he never lost his cherished ideals. Once all has been said and done, his approach was that of the common man. Benjamin Franklin was once referred to as the "Great Commoner" but T.W. Brents could just as easily shared that title. He was from common stock but through superhuman effort he was able to lift himself out of his humble beginnings to become a very great man. With him, it was Unity based upon the Scriptures and nothing else because anything else will not be in accord with God's Word. Today, there is a tendency among Disciples that because we can't unite on the Scriptures, unite off of them. The Scriptures can be a hindrance to unity but they are not a preventative when properly understood. In all of Dr. Brents' preaching and writing he sought unity on the Scriptures with the emphasis on the Scriptures; but today the emphasis is on union.

Dr. Brents could not be called a miracle worker as some style it. He labored under very difficult circumstances, far from home and family. Today, an evangelist is often set up at a local hotel and dines well at local restaurants. Travelling preachers of those days often stayed with local families and the fare was never guaranteed to be excellent, not even good in some circumstances. In a few cases it was considered awful and they had to take it all in without showing how they really felt. Most people don't even give that a thought. It goes without saying, but these men really were at the mercy-or rather ability-of local families. They lived out of a suitcase, they missed their homes and families and yet they took it all in good grace. I'll bet that Dr. Brents, if he could be asked, had some horror stories to share about the housing and food that was set before him. It gives me the shivers-thinking about how they fared at times and in different places...

He dealt well with all the circumstances that he was forced to deal with. He was a creative thinker and creative worker in the field. He first wanted to be a doctor, next a teacher and then a preacher of the Gospel. In all these jobs, he followed common sense and hard work and the light that he could get from any source possible. He was an original thinker and planner. When departing on any path he would research and study it. This was especially true when he started with his private studies. These were the first steps on a long journey which carried him through all the trials and tribulations of life. He, as they would say, kept his eyes on the prize. As a preacher, he recognized that he was under divine orders and he kept his feet on the ground and worked within available means. It wasn't his way to look for visions but for lost humanity and the divine way to effect man's salvation.

He was a disciple of the Campbells. He agreed with them in their essential teaching and work, often showing his approval for their leadership roles and for what they were teaching. But, there were differences. Dr. Brents did not mention them and neither did the Campbells. One area of difference was on the condition of the Christian Church. They were not sure if it was simply a movement and would pass away, or was it a church like other churches? The Campbells were unsure though Dr. Brents was pretty sure that it was in fact a church and should be seen in that light. That was the way that he treated it and especially the way that he taught in each and every opportunity that he had.

The work of all the above was more than merely a reformation but consisted in a revolution in that it had to do with changed fundamentals. Changing from the passive to the active plans of salvation changed everything theologically and caused changes in worship. Luther and Knox brought no great changes, the Campbells were reformers in their own minds and in the works that they did. Brents was a revolutionary because he held the passive system was fundamentally wrong and needed to be rejected and discontinued which led to a religious war. He was largely behind the defeat of the passive system and was involved with the rise of the active system of salvation. He threw himself into writing, preaching and debating over this issue and carried it through to completion. This isn't widely known but it is indeed the truth of the matter. This writer knew nothing of the issue and I have been a student of restoration history for a period of nearly thirty-three years. Only as I began to search the matter out in the *Gospel Advocate* did I find Dr. Brents' debates and writings. At the first reading of the Brents bio, which is the source material for this book, I was rather hesitant but in combination the evidence was convincing.

Another religious error of Calvinism, which was fought by the Campbells was infant baptism. As Calvinists, they had a personal problem with it. They had both been sprinkled in their infancy, which, after a study of the problem, caused them to be immersed. For some reason, this settled the matter so far as they were concerned; but it caused a furor within the denominations. Infant Baptism and original sin were a major issue with the sects. It also was a major foundation issue with them and caused them great trouble in their creeds which were left in an uproar. This new group of religious upstarts came in and messes everything up for all of these denominations which were ill at ease with each other in the best of circumstances. What a perfect ground for a religious war!! The Campbells fought this error on all occasions with all righteous means. When Dr. Brents joined them he was even more destructive of this evil in the innocent. In all of his preaching and in his book under the heading "Who should be baptized?" he openly opposed this error. It had to be maddening to the champions of orthodoxy! It also explains why Dr. Brents debated Jacob Ditzler (the champion of the Methodist Church) on seven occasions in different areas of the South. It was a veritable clash of the Titans. That just goes to show what a learned man and his Bible can accomplish when God is with them! In all good conscience, not all churches accepted the demise of the passive system until the American Standard Version came along with the words properly translated. That was the last straw.

There were other errors associated with Calvinism such as divine call, apostolic succession, close communion, the religious name, the work of the Holy Spirit, the clergy & the laity and a bunch of others that could be listed. Dr. Brents was the lone religious "wolf that huffed and puffed and blew religious houses down." That is, those that weren't properly grounded in the Scriptures and in truth in general, that is, not built according to the divine pattern. He had but one test of religious soundness, and that was, it must be in harmony with the Scriptures. Brents never was a disagreeable trouble maker although I am convinced that the sects saw him as one. Instead, he was a religious trouble shooter. He was positive and decisive and not willful and ugly, rather tolerant, in fact. However, he was a religious antagonist whenever challenged either in low or in high places, but not offensive. I have seen an area where it would be understandable to be an antagonist. That is behind the debater's bench. His opponents would be ranting and raving and he would get up for his turn being absolutely cold and composed. It would drive his opponents into a froth and he would just smile and calmly start his speech which would be delivered in such a cool, collected way. People at the debate would be shocked at the rage of his opponents and his kindness and composure. This was how he lived his life, in a calm, cool and collected way that would wreck his opponents.

Professionally, Dr. Brents lived and worked alone. All of his fields of study, medicine, teaching, and debate preparation left him isolated in the life of a student. Also, he was by nature a bit of a hermit which gave the appearance of being cold and independent a lot more so than he really was. He had few or no contacts that would draw him out. Though he was a writer, one thing that he did not do was to write about himself, which makes preparation of any sort of biography so very difficult. He didn't write down any times or dates by which his tracks could be traced. The one advantage that I have that his earlier biographer did not is that I possess the *Gospel Advocate* which does trace his steps over the years by his meeting announcements and articles. It has helped me immeasurably when it comes to a "where" and "When." He was continually asked to write for church papers but he would not, with the exception of the *Advocate* where he did do some. He finally did give his reason for not writing more because he said that a church paper was supposed to only give the views of the owner, not anyone else. He was also against representing large numbers of people because they would become a sect. A religious paper should be as representative of the owner, just like his sermon or book for that matter. This explains why there

44

were so few articles from Dr. Brents in the church press, which is a great loss to the past and the present. Besides, he said that so many church papers are mere propaganda for some sect. Another fact is that intellectuals have been notorious for being hard to communicate with. He was no exception to the rule.

Ministers of the word are prescribed and selected according to need and talent, not according to mere whims. The most important is the "ministry of the word." Acts 6:1-6 describes both preaching and teaching. The Word was two-fold, written and spoken word of God as given in the Scriptures. Dr. Brents preached and taught only "the unsearchable riches of Christ," a bottomless treasure of truth. Now, this was the general belief and practice of those days, but not so much today. A well-known elder recently was heard as saying, "If I had my life to live over, I would do more expository preaching." Dr. Brents did no other type. Some might think of him as an old fogey, but you do have to admit that his sermons are still relevant and interesting.

Alexander Campbell was a theological type of preacher, as was Dr. Brents. They both seem to have been naturals at religion, especially the philosophical part of it. He saw all parts of it and knew how they were interrelated. He dealt with the great realities of man's soul and the plain facts of the matter and only drew from the Bible as his source. Today, you find philosophy, humor and current events. Wonder why we are no longer "the people of one book?"

He visited churches that the evangelists had planted, deepening and broadening their spiritual knowledge and confirming their faith. He did not visit a church often but when he did he brought a load of spiritual blessings which can only come from the Word of God. He was an exhaustive preacher of both subjects and people. When he did preach, he declined to preach for less than two hours. He was, like the great Campbell and Tolbert Fanning, spellbinding in his approach to all things Biblical. Preachers

were scarce in those days (most were out in the field working) and having one, not to even mention Dr. Brents, was a
very special occasion in which the people took great pleasure. They would have all hands aboard for this occasion.

In his old age he moved to Lewisburg, where he often
supplied in the absence of the regular preacher, W.H. Shef-
fer. On one occasion, a traveling salesman stopped at the
hotel and went to hear him. As was his custom his sermon
was long and deep. Afterward, the salesman returned to the
hotel and said "That is a smart old man at that church; but
he does not know the difference between time and eternity." Dr. Brents usually warned the people that he did not
preach sermonettes. He gave "big-boy" sermons. The earlier editor, John Cowden, writes that: "When I was a small
boy I sat through those long sermons; and the people
seemed deeply interested, because he fed their souls on the
meat of the Gospel. He was an expository preacher, taking
some great text of the Bible and interpreting and applying it
for the people, which is the highest kind of preaching."
Something special happens when a great preacher and a
great Bible text meet in the pulpit. It is worth hearing and
people stayed to hear. Dr. Brents began to preach at age
twenty-seven. His studies over the years prepared him to
preach. Our faith in the Bible as the only true faith and
practice in religion was a tenet that most everyone had so it
was a popular with the people. It wasn't necessary then but
was still popular then. Today, unfortunately, not so much.
Brents declared for the Bible as "it came from the inspiring
Spirit of God:" and thus he preached it.

In those days, there were only two types of preachers;
the evangelistic and the doctrinal. Most churches had a
good number of new converts and was too small and weak
to afford a preacher, though they needed them desperately.
Middle Tennessee had two kinds: Dr. Brents and Billie
Dixon. They spent their entire life in the same county, Marshall. They were such opposite extremes that they never

46

could understand each other, yet they were fully coopera-
tive and successful in their respective lines, salvation and
doctrine. There was absolutely nothing that they had in
common. Dr. Brents, without schools, was highly educated;
and Billy Dixon with only two or three grades of before-
the-war schools; but, as a team they were par excellent and
invincible.

To start, Billie Dixon was a dismal failure. He had neither education nor talent. When he returned from the war
he failed in his first three efforts at preaching since he was
such a hopeless failure. Three times he had to take his seat
seeing as he forgot what he had to say; but it didn't phase
him. He loved Jesus Christ and his Gospel; and this caused
him to persist, but only by the Grace of God he made a
preacher. Only as a supplement to Dr. Brents is he worthy
of mention. While he was not the greatest preacher, he was
the greatest exhorter that Dr. Brents had ever heard. After a
short sermon he would be afire with his topic with more
fire than light. He would be waving his arms around as he
walked back and forth looking for sinners who might be
interested in coming forward to confess their sins, repent,
call on the Lord and be immersed. His eyes would be full
of tears as he did this. If there were sinners there, they either went forward or were deeply affected. He would even
go to their homes the next day to confer with them. There
was no way to escape him and his simple story of salvation.
He did most of his work at the Cane Creek congregation
and baptized over two hundred of their members. He held
one meeting where he baptized over one hundred. That is
mighty fine work for a dismal failure! There was much further work done by Bro. Dixon. At his funeral, it was told
that he was responsible for planting twenty-eight congregations in four surrounding counties! That goes to show what
can be accomplished if your heart is right with the Lord.
The possibilities are endless.

But that wasn't the type of preaching to be done by T.W. Brents. He would choose a text which he would define and followed through its Scriptural ramifications and applications which would take two or more hours or more. But, the people would be loaded with Gospel teaching which they would carry with them all their lives. As I have said before, Dr. Brents was a Bible Theologian, indoctrinating the people of the churches with great principles of Christianity, without the which, the people would die from the lack of nourishment. His attitude was: "Come now, let us reason together;" and his slogan was "Prove all things; hold to that which is good." Bro. Dixon preached without proof; but was no less sure. There is a doubt that he would have known the proof if he had given it; but he did convince more people than did Dr. Brents. That needs to be said in his honor. Dr. Brents revealed and confirmed them in their faith while Bro. Dixon brought them in so Dr. Brents could do his part. The two men made the perfect Gospel team!

While talking about great men, there is another great man from that area who deserves to be mentioned. His name was Prof. Hiram Leonard. His work left a permanent record. He was a teacher who became responsible for education. He stepped in to fill the gap that existed between the Darnell-Randolph Academy, which was going down, and the Public Schools. He was an education wonder. Former students still remember him with gladness. Not only was he a great teacher but he also was a Great Preacher. John Cowden says: "I have heard many preachers, but he preached the two greatest sermons I have ever heard. One was on David as the greatest product of Judaism, and Paul as the greatest product of Christianity. Yet, he wasn't known outside of the areas of his schools and the church. He seemed to have no interest beyond his school and church. I enrolled him as one of the World's Greatest Unknowns."

Brents never lost his interest in young preachers. While he was writing, speaking and debating, it seemed that he had them in mind. He constantly was on the lookout for promising young candidates for the ministry. There were not any schools of preaching nor seminaries so it was hard to find training. In the early years, there was only Bethany College as well as Burritt College but that was about all that could be called "training centers for Gospel Preachers." The existing academies really only taught "secular" knowledge. Later on, religion was introduced which helped but in the early days, times were hard. In the nineties Nashville Bible College, under David Lipscomb and J.A. Harding was a real effort to combine the two, being Bible knowledge and secular education. In the nineties, T.W. Brents was in his late sixties when he began teaching classes in the Scriptures and even some secular material. His goal was to prepare young talent for work in the church in the new century which was just dawning upon them. C.E.W. Dorris was a student in Dr. Brents' classes in the early days and he reported "Dr. Brents came to the school yearly for a course of lectures; and he was never the happier than when he was so engaged. This was in his old age, when he was not creating new sermons and lectures but using those of his books. Even then Dr. Brents had a full deep, strong, melodious voice that carried to the limits of any auditorium; and he was the most impressive preacher and teacher that we had heard; and he was an inspiration to all." Burritt College was at it's zenith at that time but for some reason it was putting out few preachers. David Lipscomb College was ministerial and grew into a great organization at the time. The course it has chosen is not what some would agree with but it still operates at this time.[5]

---

[5] 2017, Kyle Frank.

There is much that could be said about the venerable Reece Jones who was a pioneer preacher in Tennessee. It is thought that he was responsible for the conversion of a young T.W. Brents in either the forties or early fifties. If Dr. Brents had any equals in Tennessee and the south in his time it was in Reece Jones and his son Dr. I.N. Jones, president of Burritt College following Dr. Brents. These were the days of Giants and the histories of these men should have been written by a contemporary. They both labored and sacrificed in the churches at the beginning of the restoration movement in Tennessee. Although Dr. Brents worked alone, he had many co-workers formerly as well as contemporaries. His labor bore a lot of fruit but it was mostly in a lone-wolf manner. He did work alongside men such as those at the *Gospel Advocate* and the pages of the journal always had words of warmth for his visits. Men such as David Lipscomb, E.G. Sewell, James A. Harding were warm confidants of Dr. Brents. Although he often seemed to be cold and reserved, judging by what these men would write, some sort of close communication must have occurred.

In summation, his work was fundamental, doctrinal, congregational instruction, establishing the church as an institution of work and worship after the New Testament Pattern. He did this by preaching, writing and debating. He followed the evangelists, who had started the church and confirmed them in the form, faith and work. The congregations were small, and weak and needed teaching. He gave them the strong spiritual meat, which they never forgot. He was the only effective theologian in the field, who indoctrinated all the churches that he was able to reach.

DENOMINATIONAL MATTERS

Denominational matters did not mean what they do today. They were treated with less importance than they are now. In those days, everything centered on the creeds. If you were for or against them, your opinion mattered and many people were quick to tell you their opinion. The denominations were for the most part at peace with one another though there were debates from time to time. Some even held that denominations were even beneficial. Some today even hold this view "Visit the church of your choice." The Campbells and Dr. Brents came to a far different conclusion after a long and thorough search of the scriptures. Their conclusion was that the denominations were sinful and one of the reasons for this was the Lord's prayer in John 17. His prayer was for unity; for just one body, not the patchwork pattern across the land as we see today. The creeds and the denominations were inexorably yoked together; they stand or fall together.

The Campbells were not offensive in their teachings on this point. They were far more interested in a full and complete Bible ideology rather than any particular part. By the time Dr. Brents came upon the scene, there was considerable tension on the subject of baptism though he was not extreme on the topic.

Another issue was the millennium and in one of his sermons, he wrote: "Some think that the millennium will consist of breaking down of denominationalism and the universal acceptance of the pure Gospel of Christ, as taught by Mr. Campbell and his co-workers. However, desirable this may be, we see no prospect of this; nor can we find satisfactory evidence on which to base such a belief. Denominationalism is here, and it is here to stay. It will be here when Jesus comes, perhaps just as about as it is now. Some of the denominations that are here now will doubtless pass away. Some are dying and have been struggling in the throes of death for a number of years. The hand-writing is on the wall, and they must go; and he is a poor reader of the signs of the time who does not already see this; but perhaps other parties will rise up and take their place, and thus denominations will continue as long as time endures. All the world has not yet accepted the pure word of God, and never will. He is dreaming who expects the millennium to come about in this way."

Throughout Dr. Brents' long career as a preacher and debater, John Cowden found no expression of bitterness and offense by him. In his many debates in which he was protecting the Christian Church, when it needed the most defense, he found no criticism for being unfair, discourteous or abusive by any of his opponents in debate. Now, this could not be said about many of his contemporaries. As the church grew and opposition to it increased, tensions became worse, and feelings on both sides were embittered to the discredit of the Church. Many preachers/debaters became known as "fighters," which they really were. This type of behavior discredited the saints and caused increased denominational strife. As long as religious error exists, it must be exposed and rejected; but there is a Christian way to accomplish it.

It needs to be remembered that there are two or more sides to any issue. The Campbells and Dr. Brents gave full, free and courteous discussion of issues in the continued search to find the truth in any matter. This attitude was obvious and evident in all their preaching and teaching though it was not evident with some of their contemporaries. Dr. Brents struggled to maintain the right attitude even when it was not easy to do so. He was sure and positive but not dogmatic and intolerant. Furthermore, the denominations became far more antagonistic, which resulted in a "thirty-year" religious war, as it came to be known.

Denominational troubles from without were not all the difficulties and problems. Some issues came from within and were known "from Dan to Beersheba." Then, the denominations began to point the finger, saying, "Look, These people who were going to unite all, are divided themselves." But, it was many years later before this actually occurred. Brents was in agreement with the Campbells and often told them so. He was a real "Campbellite." He readily agreed with them on the essentials, and especially with them on their favorite topic, which was union on the Scriptures.

But Christian unity was not the only item which caused internal strife. Many other points of difference of less importance arose, hindering their progress. Congregational organization was another sore spot. Both A. Campbell and Dr. Brents wrote elaborate, agreeable treatises on the subject. The name also gave trouble. BW Stone, Dr. Brents and many others contended for the name "Christian"; but Campbell and others clung to the name "Disciple." That issue has come down to us even to this day unsolved. They were fully agreed upon the plan of salvation, which Brents put into book form and which became the guide and textbook for preachers of the reformation from the south and the west. All became in agreement on the active plan of salvation as deduced from the New Testament. But, finally someone dragged in Organized Missions as well as Instrumental Music in Worship out of the skeleton closet and THEN the real trouble started. The Campbells at first opposed both but later came to tolerate both. Dr. Brents, true to "Where the Bible Speaks, we speak, and where it is silent we are silent." Said nothing as far as I was able to locate in his *Gospel Advocate* writings. Jesus was silent so Dr. Brents was silent during his whole ministry.

His daughter, Mrs. Charles Dabney, asked him why he never expressed his views or preached on the subject. His answer to her put all such matters of the silence of the Scriptures in the realm of Christian Liberty, which the congregation could have or have not as they saw fit. The use of the silences of Jesus and the apostles was the great cross in the household of the Christian church. Some took the position that these silences excluded from the church everything on which they were silent; and the others took the position that all such were automatically put in the realm of Christian liberty, which the congregation could have, or have not as they saw fit. Dr. Brents did not argue the case but most others all did. The difference was never settled and finally in 1906 it led to division of the church one year after the death of Dr. Brents.

Church membership has also been a disturbing question from the beginning; but it never gave serious trouble until recent years, because nearly all held close membership views. Dr. Brents declared only membership to those only who comply with the Scriptural views. He was silent on the subject of fellowship, which was the only theological question on which he remained in silence. What is said is said through silence. Trouble has come from a confusion of church membership and Christian fellowship. Church membership is confined to the saved, which is in the hands of the Lord, and does not come in the jurisdiction, so either close membership or open membership is off of human bounds; but fellowship was fully treated by Jesus and is in the hands of his disciples. (The terms of fellowship prescribed by Jesus are, meeting in his name for work and worship. He not only states the terms but gives examples. Dr. Brents, I think, could not bring himself to accept and practice such an open fellowship. Like people today they were too sectarian; but Jesus never changed or repealed the above terms. They are clear and simple in execution. Anyone who meets in the name of Jesus for Christian work and worship may be received into the fellowship but not into the saved state of the Church. Nothing is said of salvation and the church membership. This fellowship places them only in the visible assembly for work and worship; but salvation and church membership are left with Jesus and the individual alone. See Romans 14:4) [6]

The problems of church membership and fellowship are part of the larger problem of Christian unity. The whole problem whole subject of unity has given trouble all through the years. The Campbells had a passion for unity, and they thought their plan on unity would solve the problem but it did not. Many of the people did not want unity. They wanted what they had, division, which they thought was the better polity. All could have their own Denomination as they liked. This was the lazy man's way as real unity takes good old-fashioned work. They love their denomination and worked to advance them. On the other hand, the Disciples, or Christians only, went their lone way protesting being called a denomination. There was a dormant difference between the Campbells and Dr. Brents on the matter; but it gave little or no trouble. It was a matter of emphasis. Dr. Brents thought the local bodies were necessary steps toward the universal body, the Kingdom of God; and he gave his time and attention largely to the congregations; and, whether or not the denominations ever united, the true church would be here.

All through his religious career he was more of an individualist than a co-operator. Independence is a commendable Christian possession of Christian Liberty; but we can have too much of both. Why is it that each one has to lean to liberty or license, one way or the other, when Jesus wants all to be balanced?

---

[6] John Cowden

HIS DEBATES

Dr. Brents was a debater at heart. It was work that he deeply enjoyed. Debating was one of his great talents. He cultivated this in every way he could. Nothing gave him as much enjoyment as the debater's bench. Everything else that he did would help him in his debating work. He was busy in his other work but he never really found himself until he found himself facing an opponent on the stage of public discussion. On that stage, all of his talents shone at their best as if he was "about his Father's business." Debating was the part of his religion which he could take to the people.

Dr. Brents lived in a forensic age, in which the syllogism was the pattern of thought. Logic and argumentation were intuitive with him. Debating was the art of able, strong full-grown men. He also had the ability to make public discussion interesting and understandable for all thinking people. A debate connotes something above and beyond the common people that requires clarification and proclamation. It calls for the highest form of thinking and discussion. The fundamental principles of both the State and the Church have been determined and established by public discussions, and most of our greatest men have been debaters. Men, such as Webster, Jefferson, Clay, and Calhoun were avid debaters. Others in the religious field were such as Luther, Calvin, Edwards and also A. Campbell, though he was opposed to debates, had often engaged in the same and thereby saved the truth for which he pled and established by public discussions. He declared for full and free discussion, which is still at the head of many restoration journals. But, for some reason, debating is in disrepute and under the anathema of many churches. A militant religion is a remnant from the past. This is partly because few or none are prepared to defend and proclaim truth. Debating has always required the highest intelligence and most

56

thorough preparation. In Dr. Brents' day, no one below the level of bishop or an informed specialist was called to debate. He was not a "bishop" but he sure was an informed specialist. Dr. Brents ate and slept debating.

He had the misfortune to get a late start but when he did get started, you could not make him stop. It was related that he was disinterested with anything else than his studies in his younger day, after he had gotten started on his education. It has been related that knowledge is power and it seems that he had a keen understanding of that statement. He was ready, prepared and able when the call rang out to "Put on the whole armor of God" and fight. No one knew the Word of God better or how to use "the sword of the Spirit" in public discussion. His favorite maxim, "Prove all things; hold fast to that which is good" was just to his liking. Perhaps at first, there was some doubt but soon enough he was taking on all comers. Back in the early days, the churches were on the march to drive out the new movement because it was against them all. The saints had antagonized their passive system of Calvinism. So, it was war and that "Sword of the Spirit" was needed at all junctures. Because of this warfare, many were exposed to the truth so evangelists were needed at all points of conflict. Dr. Brents was in his natural element. His talents allowed him to preach the truth while exposing that which was false. There was no escaping this warfare. Without an answer in kind to these Calvinists, the restoration theme would have been discredited and died an early death. Perhaps that was why Dr. Brents had his talents and used them so well.

Debating has some advantages over other methods of preaching. The debate curbs wild and extreme opinions when that individual knows that his speech will be reviewed and examined by his opponent. I have heard of it as being "truth distilled" Thus, the debaters often find themselves nearer in faith and doctrine than they had first believed. Truth is rarely, if ever extreme. In debates, assertions must be proved or defended. Rarely if ever does a debater find a regular "crackpot" because of the review of that one's ideas in subsequent speeches. Also, when viewed from a distance, some people religiously seem to be shrouded in mists and clouds. In the heat of battle those mists are burned off and men find one another closer that they might think. Many have come together hating one another and separate as at least holding respect for one another.

At that time, nearly all of the churches were engaged in debating. It was an age of doctrine with each church striving for orthodoxy, which ultimately resulted in debates. The Christian Church came into a troubled religious world. The infant church under the Campbells was hailed with challenges for debate. Each debate tested a man's strength and wisdom and called for strong men. Those years of study and preparation made Dr. Brents a very strong man indeed. He was ready to "Give an answer to everyone that asked a reason for the hope within him." Most preachers were thus engaged in defending and propagating the faith in the beginning. The two greatest debaters were Dr. Brents and John S. Sweeney of Kentucky. They were very much alike in body, personality, mind and method. They shook the foundations when they rose to speak. Now, the greatest opponent was Bishop Jacob Ditzler of the Southern Methodist Church. He ranked first as a theologian and debater. Soon, they (Brents and Ditzler) were recognized as the ablest church representatives. They were called upon every time there was a controversy. The Lexington and Louisville debates were regarded and treated as national affairs to which preachers from all corners came to see the clash of Titans. There was a book produced from the Louisville debate which I have been seeking high and low. It was my intention to have it published in an accompanying volume to this biography. I have been able to locate three other debates which will be appearing somewhere but the one that I want the most eludes me still.

After meeting in middle Tennessee, they met in a total of seven other sections of the South. There were several other opponents to Dr. Brents: Dr. Timothy Frogge, Presbyterian; Dr. J.B. Moody, Missionary Baptist; Dr. Herod, Primitive Baptist, and many others, but Bishop Ditzler was the ablest of them all. He was a national personality and had the reputation of knowing all the facts and tricks of the game. He knew individual and mass psychology. Having read a great deal of his "work" in the *Gospel Advocate*, this writer has no regard for Dr. Ditzler because he would often question a source's veracity and would jump back and forth quoting whatever he thought would help him get out of the trouble that he was in. He questioned people and sources and would outright lie to get out of a jam.

Now, to give the reader a taste of Bishop Ditzler's antics, here is a sample, the 1873 Volume of the *Gospel Advocate*, page 518...

...incompetent to give testimony in the case. And if he so misrepresented those lexicons that we could expose — how much worse must he misrepresent those to which he knows we have no access so as to expose.

Mr. D. insisted that the Hebrew word "*Taval*" meant to sprinkle or pour. Dr. B. read every instance of its use in the Bible and showed conclusively, that in every single instance it meant to dip or plunge and nothing else. He showed that the Lexicons defined it to dip, plunge, or immerse. Especially Schlousner's Lexicon, so much praised by D. so defined it.

Mr. D. insisted that baptize in the Syriac meant to sprinkle or pour, but failed utterly to explain how it is the whole religious people reading and studying the Syriac and receiving their religious ideas exclusively from this version, invariably immersed. Among them, baptism by any other means than immersion, is and ever has been, entirely unknown. The same is true of those who use the Arabic version. If they teach anything else than immersion to be baptism, it is strange that those who have read and studied these versions for almost two thousand years, in their own vernacular tongue, never learned it.

This discovery was reserved for Mr. Ditzler, a foreigner, of necessity having a limited acquaintance with the languages. Certainly, he may lay claim to a discoverer of no ordinary character in biblical lexicography. The Nestorians and Armenians of Persia and Arabia—all the denominations of Christians using these versions of the Scripture, even the corrupted forms of Christianity, who get their ideas of baptism from the Syriac and Arabic, recognize only immersion as baptism. They have never dreamed of baptism by effusion.

Mr. D. once asserted that the Greek church baptized by sprinkling. He said the subject was required to walk into the water, kneel so that the water reached the waist and then the water was sprinkled on the head three times.

Dr. B. read from Moses Stuart the celebrated Presbyterian that they were dipped three times in the water. So, this accords with the universal testimony of everybody except Mr. D.

On the Bible argument Mr. D. made scarcely an effort, although in the affirmative. He had promised on Saturday afternoon he would take up the Scripture argument on Monday morning- Dr. B. here led the way, took up Mr. D.'s own chosen cases, and before Mr. D. reached them, so completely turned them against him that he did not approach them at all. He took up the case of the Eunuch, the jailor, Paul, the cases which he hotly contested with bro. Wilkes, now he scarcely touched them. Bro. Brents was at home in the Scriptures. Mr. D. showed his timidity. The last days work of bro. Brents, especially his summing up in the closing speech was as well and forcibly put as you ever heard an argument. Mr. D. showed his chagrin and sense of defeat and humiliation, by the exhibition of more bitterness and ill-temper than I ever heard from the lips of a public speaker on any subject. On Monday night, he grossly closed the debate, after the brethren divided time with Mr. D.'s friends in the use of their meeting house for preaching at night, had yielded the house to them on Sunday night, after Mr. Ditzler had divided the congregation on Sunday morning, Mr. D. preached in the Cumberland Presbyterian house on Monday night and divided the congregation.

Supposing of course he must have something very important to proclaim, to justify in his mind, such a violation of obligation of honor and courtesy we went to hear him. We have heard bitter speeches on religion and politics, at the bar and on various subjects, but we never heard anything to equal this in vindictive denunciation and slanderous falsehood.

He started out to tell what religion is, what it has been in all ages. It did not come through ordinances, it was independent of all ordinances, it had nothing to do with ordinances, it was opposed to ordinances, it always had been— was his ascending scale of statements. Ordinances often corrupted the religion of God. In the best days of Judaism, ordinances were certainly neglected and the people of Israel were held blameless by God in the matter. Enoch observed no ordinances, yet was taken. Abraham observed none until he was justified without ordinances. Samuel, Elijah and Elisha, observed no ordinances. Ordinances hindered true religion. The observance of ordinances produced idolatry. This seeking blessing in ordinances is worse than bowing down because of the observance of ordinances. Men who seek blessings through ordinances always come to reject the truth. The people in our country who lay so much stress on the observance of ordinances as conditions of receiving the blessing, repudiate the whole of the Old Testament. They do not believe that a man ever had faith in God, ever repented of sin, ever had a purified heart or was regenerat-

61

ed or obtained the pardon of his sins before Pentecost. Well Moses and Elijah went to heaven whether their sins were forgiven or not. If they went to heaven without forgiveness of sins, what is the use of forgiving sins?

These believers in ordinances, are always very zealous in making converts to their party, but they care nothing for purity of heart or holiness of life. The Bible tells us of some of these ordinance men, compassing sea and earth to make a convert and when he was made he was sevenfold more the child of hell, than before. You and I have seen believers in ordinances compassing sea and land to make a convert, to get him to obey the ordinances, and he is seven times as bad a man as before He is seven-fold worse after, than he was before his baptism. He is more selfish, more bigoted, more high-tempered, more unneighborly and unjust in his dealings than before. He may have been a clever man of the world before, but after he is proselyted he is a very bad man. You and I have both seen such a people, both in your country and mine....

Dr. Brents had a way of dealing with him where he would calmly, coldly, follow Ditzler wherever he went answering him with sources and facts which would show Ditzler's lies and tricks. At another time, and not in debate, Ditzler admitted that Dr. Brents was his most difficult opponent. Coming from him, that is the highest compliment— if you could take it like that.

John Cowden writes of Dr. Brents: "Bishop Ditzler, I never met, but Dr. Brents made the greatest impression on me of any man that I have known. He was old but had lost none of his personality physically or mentally. He was six feet or more tall, large frame, broad shouldered, strongly muscled, having the largest head I ever saw on a man, wearing a high silk hat with a Prince Albert coat, which were the clerical robes of the day. He had a broad open, forceful countenance, his face carrying a long, heavy flowing beard, radiating virility, in all a handsome imposing, commanding personality with a poise and presence that filled the place. It was often said that Dr. Brents had the debate half won when he entered and took his place; and nothing disturbed or frustrated him."

Now, to imagine the scene of what was about to take place. The stage was set for a crowd and Dr. Brents was ready. There were piles of books and papers on the stage. Debates usually ran for between one and two weeks with two two-hour sessions daily, which held the interest to a fever pitch. Often, feelings would boil over and bitterness was expressed. Dr. Brents' strategy was courtesy and fairness always, which, for the most part held the debate on a high plane. Dr. Ditzler was not beyond trickery whenever he could. The first time he tried trickery he got Dr. Brents to depart home, since the debate was supposedly over. After he left, Ditzler took two days reviewing everything that Brents had said. That was the first-and last time that he ever pulled a trick over on Brents after that. In fact, Brents pursued him in a way that he surely did not like. Fair was fair after all.

Nearly all the debates were on the background of the Scriptures, which all held to be the Word of God which greatly simplified and magnified the discussions. Dr. Brents' way was to smother the opposition with multiple Scriptures, which he quoted and applied to the point at issue. Some felt that there was never a greater expositor and interpreter of the Scriptures. He was a theologian before he was a debater. No Scripture ever caught him without a sane explanation. Because he was self-educated, he spoke the language of the people and not the schools; so he led the people in understanding conviction. If you have any doubts about this, just read his books and you will understand. He sought to be understood and not admired.

It must be remembered that religious debates are militaristic in form and spirit. It must be that both Jesus and Paul approved of Spiritual warfare. If you examine Matt. 10:34-

39 as well as Eph. 6:10-20. In this warfare, no weapons are used except the "Sword of the Spirit, which is the Word of God." No artillery, no bullets but words, words that are Christian words. The only fatalities but in error itself. That is why this form of combat is approved of by God. Error must not be allowed to prevail but righteousness. The only real realm of existence is the spiritual realm. It existed before and will way outlast the physical realm. The principles by which we either live or die are spiritual and it is spiritual principles which underlie us all. When Satan came to pass, sin, or rather error came to pass and the war began. The extent of the war, we can't possibly know yet as we are still in the flesh. Someday, when all comes to pass and the war is over, we will then know. Back to debating; Dr. Brents never fired a gun in anger nor did his body bear the marks in material secular warfare but he certainly used the sword of the spirit in dealing with error as it was in the church. And, it was with the sword of the spirit that he dealt with error in both low and high places. He was a defender of the Christian faith in debates and as an establisher of the of the church as the Citadel of Christianity, he was a true and honored Christian soldier. He was blessed to have the talent and mind to serve, the preparation, knowledge and brilliance to succeed, so his honor and reward should be great.

They say that the proof of the pudding is in the eating and the proof of the debater is in his debate. His contemporaries are all dead so there isn't any first person reporting except that which I was able to find in the pages of the *Gospel Advocate.* These were written by those who were there and did report what was said. At this point I am undecided on whether these reports will be in this volume or in an accompanying volume. Either way, there is a lot of material that is now available that brings a lot of Bro. Brents' debating before the religious audience. As was mentioned in another part of this biography, the biggest debate of them all is missing. It was called *The Louisville Debate* between

Brents and Jacob Ditzler. This is THE debate that I will be seeking until I either find it or die. The debates that will be included are the Brents-Herod Debate, The Petersburg Debate—Brents-Pennington, and finally The Brents-Frogge Debate. Unfortunately, Dr. Brents kept no record of his debates and we have but a few that we know of. There was one with a Mr. Moody from the Baptist church. I do not know even what branch of the Baptists though I do understand that the preliminaries were printed but not the debate itself.

One of the saddest things when it comes to Dr. Brents was that upon his death in June, 1905, his magnificent library was not kept but allowed to be scattered to the winds. We have no record of which books they were or of who took them. Such a gem!!

But, debates have for the most part ceased, not because of a lack of difference but for lack of debaters themselves. Dr. Brents and Bishop Ditzler's debates settled a lot of the differences between the two. Those that are left, though, are more than enough to keep the two separate but are minor compared to before. This has changed the way in which the public sees debates. If there was one to arise and attack the church in any of the fundamentals, the Dr. Brents or Bishop Ditzlers in the churches would come forth to defend them.

HIS BOOKS

As has been stated earlier, Dr. Brents was a man of One Book. And as the reader would guess, the book was the Word of God. But in his reading, study and writing, he was a man of many books. Books were his only teachers; and they made a scholar of him. It was with the assistance of all his books that he was able to achieve all that he achieved. His studies came late but he made up for that in the intensity what he lost in time. Being so indebted to books it would only seem natural that he would want to write one himself. The question was to him of what type he would write. It was in 1874 that he arrived at his half-century mark and it was by this date that he knew what he would write.

The story of his first book begins back in 1867 while he was busy preaching around the area of his birth and nativity, that is in central Tennessee. David Lipscomb, in the *Gospel Advocate* of January 3, 1867 was beginning his New Year planning and on page 10 writes: "The very proposition to enlarge (the paper kdf) has called forth the promise of aid from one of the clearest headed of Bible Students and most cogent reasoners in this or any other State, I mean Dr. Brents. We wish to give opportunity for the development and cultivation of talent that is now lying idle and dormant." Now, a tremendous amount can be drawn from that statement but since we are discussing his books, the story will stay there. It was at this time or thereabouts that a promise was made to David Lipscomb by T.W. Brents that he (Brents) was going to help build up the *Advocate* by writing for its pages. This was a promise that Dr. Brents was willing and quite able to keep. Lipscomb writes on page 18: "We have also secured the promises of Bro. J. T. Walsh, of North Carolina; Bro. Jacob Creath, of Missouri; Bro. Dr. Brents, of Tennessee, and a promise of Bro. C. Kendrick, of Texas, provided certain former arrangements could be satisfactorily adjusted, to aid us as regular contributors."

Apparently, Dr. Brents was concerned about the lost because the regular contribution was to be known as "The Alien Department." That is a rather unusual title but we must remember that it meant far different in those days as it does now. We see the use of "alien" in several places in the KJV Old Testament of the Holy Scriptures.

Having shown the promise of Dr. Brents, on page 53 he begins his "Aliens Department" with his trademark cognizance and clarity. The first article was on "Election and

Reprobation." The articles continued off and on up until the #13 issue, 3/31/1870. That article was on "The Reception of the Holy Spirit." These articles were wildly popular with those who read the *Gospel Advocate*. Without overwhelming the reader with dates, times and places from which letters came to David Lipscomb asking for back issues which contained these articles so that they could use them for evangelism as well as whatever else they could be used. The *Advocate* of those particular times was run much differently than we would see these days as there was not a run of extra copies to answer the call by these readers. Within a very short time the extras were gone and Lipscomb could not get any more copies to answer calls. He became very frustrated while many ended up being aggravated.

After many letters of complaint were received at the GA offices, the decision was finally made to make a printing run of various different tracts which could be purchased and circulated among members of the church and especially among the "aliens" who were originally being addressed. This continued until they ran out of tracts and started getting those angry letters of complaint again. Something needed to be done but what would they possibly do? I don't know whose bright idea it was to turn the tracts and articles into a book but someone floated the idea to T.W. Brents who accepted the challenge. It was up to him to take these tracts and somehow create a book which could be used by one and all. The year 1874 had come and he was called upon to write his book which he willingly did. He wanted to leave some of his thinking on record for posterity. (not to mention everyone who was after him for the book!) He had been in the thickest of the fight over the passive system of religion, (Calvinism) and he felt that the church would profit greatly with this material in human hands. He was also concerned that these errors might resurrect to trouble the church again. Because of this he also felt that he would need to write on the active system of salvation, which was still a live issue of that day. He took up these errors one by one and as follows: Predestination, Election and Reprobation, Calvinistic proofs, Foreknowledge of God, Heredity and Depravity, devoting a chapter to each.

Dr. Brents shows that there is a divine predestination but not that of the individual but of certain classes. Also, that there was an election before the foundation of the world but this is also of a definite class: those "in Christ," who were saved, and those in the Devil, who were eternally damned. The righteous Christians, are elected to eternal life and the wicked to eternal death, but Jesus Christ never abandoned any individual as reprobate. He, in depth and in detail examines the Calvinistic proofs, showing the glowing error of each and giving the Scriptural teaching on each.

With the ground cleared of Calvinistic errors, which were hindering issues of the day, Brents proceeds with the opposite theory, the active theory of salvation; but before commencing this, he gives a summary of the refutation, on which he proposes to build Christian salvation. His statements had behind them decades of study, meditation, and debating, which broke the back of Calvinism.

Having finished the negative portion of his book, he begins to build up that which had been torn down. He was not an iconoclast, that is to tear things down. He tore them down to clear the ground and to build better positive structures. Having completed the destruction, he begins to build up the church of the Lord Jesus Christ. Following Jesus' teaching, he knew that no religion could be lasting until a concrete institution, which Jesus called the kingdom of God, or the church. Dr. Brents had sure positive views about the church, so his first affirmative item of his positive message was "The Establishment of the Church." Step by step he follows the Scriptures in tracing the church from the birth of Jesus Christ to the close of the Day of Pentecost and afterward with the Apostles to their deaths. He drew on the scriptures for every item of the church.

Dr. Brents devotes the next chapter of his book to The New Birth and so treats first things first. All of life begins with generation and birth. Bro. Brents, being both a medical doctor and gospel preacher knew both the physical and spiritual life better. He had studied both. In fact, he knew spiritual life better than Nicodemus, to whom Jesus explained spiritual birth and life by an analogy with physical birth. Both Jesus and Paul used such analogies. Both contain mystery, but not quite the same as those to Nicodemus and the people of Dr. Brents' day.

The next chapter is on faith, which is normally treated as first by brethren of the restoration movement. It was not quite as big a battle back then as it is to be found today. He treated the subject fully but not antagonistically. He then shows how faith in God is received, coming by the word of God. All goes well till he comes to the statement that faith is the gift of God and salvation is by faith alone, or rather by grace alone. At this point Dr. Brents shows impatience. He outlines the faith that saves, that Jesus is the Christ the Son of the Living God. He goes to great lengths and rids Christian faith of the passive errors and showing that it is an active faith principle of the Gospel.

Repentance is the next subjective act in the active plan of salvation. This term is more difficult to define yet it can be found in the literature of all churches. It changes the heart of a man. People in the time of Dr. Brents, it was attempted to be made passive-that is, God does it for you. This, of course, is a wrongful use of this term. It was preached by John the Baptist with great effect. Jesus also used the term in Luke 13:3 in such a way as it cannot be explained away. People who say that they cannot repent are in the error of total depravity, which was a roadblock in Dr. Brents' day. Repentance is psychologically deep and every genuine Christian knows intimately.

69

Next, confession is called for in the active plan of salvation. Sometimes it proceeds and sometimes it follows repentance. There are many confessions but the main, most important is the "Jesus is the Christ, the Son of God." Jesus said that he would confess us before God if we confess him before men.

The last act, according to Dr. Brents and the Campbells, is baptism. This has been the most controversial; but regardless of all that has been spoken or written, Dr. Brents still devotes a great deal of time and space dealing with the subject. No topic is as thoroughly researched and spoken upon in any other book such as Dr. Brents does in his book. Surely this is the last work on the topic.

Dr. Brents wrote **The Gospel Plan of Salvation** for evangelists although he was no evangelist. He was a theologian who sought to build up both churches and individual Christians in his Gospel Meetings. This was far different than the "average" evangelist. That is also why he wrote his two books. They were designed to speak for him when he could no longer speak for himself.

Throughout this book I have written what I gathered from his short biography as well as the Gospel Advocate and other sources. I would like to write briefly on the literary form of his two books. Brents lived during the Victorian age and this the King James Version was virtually the only version used. He read and studied the text so much and so well that it became difficult to figure where Brents started and stopped. That is, where the reading of the Bible ended and his comments began. His expression was exact, words precise, his meanings were clear. His writings are models of the Victorian form of speech. It was remarkable that he maintained his high standard of excellence throughout his long and fruitful life. While he did have a talent for language he must have toiled, like he did on everything else in his life.

Dr. Brents wrote few books for a church writer; but the two that he did write embodied the full system of Christianity. You might disagree with his views but you will most certainly understand them very clearly. Fifty years he was a preacher of the ancient gospel and he wrote two books, leaving his favorite sermons so that the reader can know him better as a preacher.

HIS DECLINING YEARS

(by John B. Cowden)

Dr. Brents lost the first two decades of his life in getting a late start. He was twenty-one years of age before he seemed to have any direction to his life. No one now knows what became of this period of his life; and few people know what became of his youth. These years fly by like birds of passage, seeking pleasure and fancy. While this period appears unimportant, wise men tell us this is the time for acquiring a knowledge of self and our world. In fact, without this knowledge of ourselves and our world, we would be helpless creatures, not even good jelly fish.

After it is all over they tell us we learn more from that period than from all the remaining periods. Dr. Brents acquired his knowledge of himself and his world in the schools of Nature and Experience. In his childhood and youth, he found nothing worth recording except he was a member of a large pioneer wilderness family. At least, he faced life with a strong mind in a strong body.

After having drained three professions he came up to old age in vigor. Having returned to Marshall County and bought a large farm about ten miles East of his old home on a hill overlooking Liberty Valley and near Old Liberty Christian Church and also near Cowden's father's home a mile over Elk Ridge to the South. From the time that they lived in Liberty Valley he must have bought the farm also as a home for the family while he preached and debated. He attended Old Liberty Church and preached when there. He built or bought a large home. I do not know how many of the nine children were at home at this time. It appears from the time after their return to Marshall County that they spent 28 years in this home, covering the time of his religious work.

One of Dr. Brents' greatest achievements was his family. He raised nine children, four boys and five girls. The first mother died early leaving five young children. The second mother soon stepped into the breach to meet the need, which was an act of heroism and love; and the crisis was met. There followed the four children of the second marriage, which made a heavy load in itself. These two mothers were heroines of the highest order. The first, Angilina Scott, came to him in his blind, foolish frivolous youth, when he had no ambition or direction in his life. She taught him to read and write; and perhaps secured the old English grammar for him, which was an Aladdin's lamp to him. With her influence and the appeal of the children, he was soon on his way to fame and fortune. All praise to Angilina Scott. But no less a heroine was Elizabeth Jane Taylor, the second mother, a widow, who took up the labor of love. She was a step and a real mother at the same time, which was a difficult situation.

Dr. Brents was a devoted family man, having the interest of the children in mind and sacrificing for them. I think that he must have resigned the presidency of the Medical College to go to Spencer, Burritt College, to give the children an education, where most of them graduated. Also, doubtless he had the children in mind when he bought the farm and country home. He produced a family of great credit and worth.

All are now dead and made honorable and useful careers; but it is a great loss to his history to have none of their tributes and memories of their father. No one else knew him so well or loved more. His real and true history is known fully to no one else; and usually children die with this history sealed within them, which seems true in this case.

While Dr. Brents did not trace the name back to its historical origin, one of his relatives, Chester Horton Brent did do so, tracing the family back to Hugh Brent, of Va., Ky., Tenn.; and the descendants of Dr. Brents have preserved a genealogy of the immediate family, written by a grandson, Wm. Rufus Brents, of Sherman, Texas, and now in possession of another grandson, R. L. McBride, Jr. of Lewisburg, Tenn., which is continuous and correct, running back to the days and family of king Edward. The following genealogies are taken from this record.

Thomas Brents, Sr 1775-1837, wife Margurett McQuirter had the following children: Alpheus; William; James, wife, Rhoda Davis Cowden; Elizabeth, husband, Steven Talley; Mary Lucinda, husband, Hill; Jane, husband, Flemming; Matilda,

Dr. Thomas Wesley Brents, 1823-1905, Wife, Angilina Scott, Children, Dr. Thomas Elias; Marguert; Alexander Campbell; Mollie; John. Second wife, Elizabeth Jane Taylor, children, Clemma; Ella, husband, Dabney; James; Ida, husband, McBride.

But this is the history of Dr. Brents and not his family; and space forbids an account of the family; but there must be credit and honor that are due. Like most families of the great, they had too much father. They could not start from or reach the level of their father. There was just one Dr. Brents, one in ten thousand; and he was above them as he was above his other contemporaries, which was embarrassing and a handicap. However, one, James, broke through this handicap and became the editor of the *Louisville Post,* one of the great papers of the nation; but he ran into a bigger handicap in his competitor, Hon. Henry Waterson, who was a handicap to all the other editors; but he held his way with Marse Henry and became a great editor. I had a brush off with James in my early days. I started to school under him in the country school. He reported to my mother that she would have to take me in charge or suffer the consequences. She took me in charge; but I am not trying to get even.

His grandson, Rufus, reached fame and fortune in Sherman, Texas; but deaths interfered and ended all. Personally, I knew only one of the family, Mrs. Ella Dabney, who was a cultured and brilliant woman, the wife of Charles Dabney, a Nashville insurance head. All the children are now dead; and the grandchildren are on the stage of action. I have met four of this generation, namely Rev. James Brents, (nephew), Nashville, Christian preacher and author; Thomas W. Brents, Tuscaloosa, Ala. business; R. L. McBride, Jr., Vice-President of First National Bank, Lewisburg; and Brents McBride, Nashville, head of the Conservation Department of the State. Genetists tell us that we do not inherit from our mothers and fathers but from our grandparents. This seems to be true of the above Brents in both body and mind. The McBrides bear a striking resemblance to Dr. Brents. They lack only his whiskers to being the old Dr. Brents incarnate. All of the first generation have passed to their rewards with their father, Dr. Brents. One of the girls, Clemma, I think, married Victor Dorris, one of the great preachers of Tennessee and Missouri.

Dr. Brents came to old age in strength and vigor. While he had the infirmities of old age, he had many interests and ways of spending his time. He was not of the type to take a rest when he was not tired. He had many avocations as well as vocations in his long active life, to which he could turn in his old age. There was no such thing in that age as Retirement, or Emeritus; and, if there had been, he would not have availed himself of it; but he became too old for any of his vocations or avocations. He held on to farming to the

74

last. For many years he had superintended the large rich cotton plantation (650 acres) on horseback or sitting in his large white home on a hill, from which the level fields were all visible. Here in this large two-story white frame house, which overlooked the whole of Liberty Valley, he did most of his reading, study and writing. This was his home for twenty-eight years. This house since burned and was replaced by a brick after his death. When the time of "the Sear and yellow leaf" came in his old age, the wear and tear of a long crowded hectic life were manifest in his body but not in his mind, so he moved to Lewisburg, the County seat town ten miles Northwest. I have no memory of this moving day. My father's home was over Elk Ridge one mile to the South; but there was a great vacancy left after they moved out. He built a large white house in Lewisburg on Farmington St. patterned after the farm house, which showed his attachment to the country home, where they had lived so long. This hermitage gave him an opportunity for reading and study that enabled him to do the great work that he did. I believe that the hand of God is thus plainly traceable throughout the long life of Dr. Brents. Any way, like Joshua the son of Nun "he never would stop until the work was done." Dr. Brents' work was done, so he moved into town for a rest in his old days; but he was restive with nothing to do, so before he bowed completely off of the stage of action, he planned a venture in a new field, banking. There was no bank in Marshall County. It was before the day of Banks. Banking was carried on by rich individuals. Dr. Brents was the best-known man in the County and knew most people. He conceived a public individual bank or a stock company bank, I do not know which. Anyway, the bank was started with Dr. Brents as president in charge. I do not know where the money came from; but it was there. Dr. Brents never appeared to have much money; but, when it was needed, he had it or got it. He operated the bank for four years successfully; and it is today one of the

75

great banks of Middle Tennessee. Not that Dr. Brents alone made it so. After him there have been other great men back of it and leading it, namely, Dr. Sam Hardison, W. D. Fox, "Uncle Willie," who gave it life and immortality, and present executives, Lee Moss, and R. L. McBride, the grandson of Dr. Brents. The wealth, the stability, the security, the trust, and above all, the intelligence of old Dr. Brents still hovers over this institution, making it known and trusted.

Dr. Brents made only one failure in his life, a marriage in his old age, which seems to be irresistible and inevitable for old men. The mistake was soon manifest; and separation was effected. Dr. Brents never lost any of his great faculties in his old age. He was the same to the end. A young preacher came to town and issued a challenge to meet Dr. Brents in debate, which Dr. Brents ignored; and he published Dr. Brents as deserting the cause. Like an old warhorse, he said that he would meet him and "teach this jack-a-nape some sense."

Throughout this whole study I have tried to avoid being fulsome, which Dr. Brents himself hated; but in all races of men there is "One in ten thousand," a man that stands out above and beyond all others, whom you can not portray without being fulsome with respect to others. There is no doubt about Dr. Brents being such a man. (and Cowden made no apologies for so portraying him.kdf) He can not be accounted for on any other grounds. This does not mean that he was faultless. What such a man does with his talents, life and character is his own affair and responsibility. Dr. Brents had his faults, some of which I have gathered from tradition, which I feel obligated to mention in the interest of the balanced truth of the man. He was egotistic, but with his talents, who would not be? He was a ten-talent man that received the praise of his Lord. Apparently, he was unsympathetic, proud and cold, domineering, critical, exacting, a big eater, which is the common fault of most preachers. With praise for his virtues and charity for his faults, we write this record of the

life of Dr. Brents with a feeling of incompleteness, that there is much in his great life that has allowed to be forgotten, because his contemporaries are all dead and no one kept a record; but enough is known to make him the leading and greatest citizen of Marshall County and far beyond through the South. Religiously, his parish covered the whole South in laying the foundations of the Christian Church and the church of Christ.

He lived to a mature old age of 82 and came to a natural end. He was born into a small world and died in the same. At the time of his death his world had greatly shrunk to Lewisburg and Marshall County; but formerly it had covered the area of the whole South; and the fruits of his labors still cover the same area. If life did not have its fruits that ripen and spread beyond the grave, life would not be worth the candle that lights it. No one in the Christian Church and the church of Christ has had a greater post-mortem fruitage than Dr. Brents. Ask the preachers past and present, the young evangelists and the elders in the churches. The simple story of his book, ***The Gospel Plan of Salvation***, has convinced and converted thousands all over the South and West and doctrinally armed the members of the churches. As a young minister, that book helped me as no other did, also, I was in the ministerial succession from Dr. Brents. All churches have profited from his exposure of the error of the passive system of salvation and his emptying the churches of all passive symbols. We have unity today where they had division. Dr. Brents' personal vine is still bearing fruit in the churches today. "By this my Father *is* glorified, that you bear much fruit, and so prove to be my disciples." Jno. 15: 8. Dr. Brents' vine had a rich fruitage during his life, which has continued beyond the grave, a good fortune that has come to few. But with his death and burial in the lifetime fields of his labors the sun of his life set beyond the hills of time to rise on eternal life.

He was known as a great man and he did not have to leave home to be great. With the exception of several years service in medical college and a few years in a church college, in both of which he achieved preeminence, he spent his whole life in the County in which he was born, serving neighbors and friends. When the religious giants threatened the young Disciple cause and church, the elders did not have to leave home for a defender and proclaimer. He met and defeated every enemy and contender. His fame soon spread to far sections of the South; and he was called to meet the national religious Goliaths. He proved to be one of the greatest debaters this country has produced. While he has been long dead, his teaching has "run and been glorified."

When Cowden went to Nashville first in 1898, there were two Christian churches and one Church of Christ, College Street. Today there are eight Christian churches and near a hundred Churches of Christ in the County (estimated, statistics not known), many of which are large and costly and located at advantageous points. They have built churches here, yonder and everywhere there was *a* need or an opening for a church; whereas the Christian Church has grown very little. There are many causes and factors in this difference; but I speak of only one that has to do with Dr. Brents. He formerly wrote and published the book, *The Gospel Plan of Salvation,* which he deduced from the Scriptures.

This book had wide circulation in Tennessee and other states. In this book, he exalts the Bible as the written and spoken word of God and the New Testament as containing the divine pattern of the church. This teaching had much to do with the above statistics and achievements.

Also before his books, Dr. Brents preached and debated constantly in this and all other sections. It was an instance of the Gospel's "running and being glorified." In the two thousand years since the Day of Pentecost, the Gospel has been and still is God's power to save; but its propagation is in the hands and hearts of the people who believe and work for it. It is the active plan of salvation, which Dr. Brents and others labored to establish. I wish that Dr. Brents could have lived to see this demonstration of this plan of salvation; but with this re-establishment of this way of salvation; his work was done; and "the rest" promised the people of God awaited him.

When Dr. Brents was born the Christian Church, including the Church of Christ, was estimated by the hundreds; when he died, it was estimated by the thousands; but today it is estimated by the millions.

What part of this growth and increase is due to Dr. Brents, I do not know. I would say, in the North and East, little or none; but in the South and Southwest, much. Dr. Brents was a great preacher, a powerful debater, a wise theologian and a superb writer, whose work and influence were far reaching in his day and generation and has been continuous since his death. I have been a roving evangelist in the interest of Christian unity; and I have had wide personal contacts with elders, preachers and evangelists. Many of them especially evangelists spoke gratefully of their indebtedness to Dr. Brents. Some made lay preachers with the aid of his books. These books circulated freely and widely throughout the South and passed from one generation to another. My copies came from my father's possession. While Dr. Brents was not personally active in much of this work, no one known to me was more helpful in the long run. All of us can truthfully say, "Others have labored; and we have entered into their labors," especially the labors of Dr. Brents.

It is too late to interview friends and neighbors and other contemporaries of Dr. Brents to get their estimate of him, because they are all dead. I doubt that they could fully and correctly appraise his worth and merits. The friends and neighbors of Jesus thought that he was just one of Joseph's family and were surprised and bewildered by his words and deeds. This was true of Dr. Brents. While he was "not without honor in his home" he was not fully known; and his home people did not fully understand and appreciate his work. They were doubtless surprised and awed by his achievements; but he was beyond their understanding. It has now been over a century since he began his work. It takes time for a man's record to mature for historical use. In the light of the Church of Christ today, we are the better able to appraise his worth and merits. This growth and progress are not due to Dr. Brents alone. Hundreds of others spent and were spent in this foundation work. He did a great doctrinal and theological work, which is still evident from his writings and influence; and he put up a superb defence of the faith in his debates.

After a long and useful life Dr. Brents came to a peaceful and natural end in his home in Lewisburg, Tenn., June 28th, 1905, at the age of 82 and was buried in the cemetery at Lewisburg, with R. Lin Cave, of Nashville, and Dr. Sam Hardison officiating, who were lifetime friends and coworkers in the ministry and medicine. "Like a story that is told," said David, man goes to his rest and reward. Every man's life is interesting when known and told, and Dr. Brents' especially so. This is written to make him better known and honored. The influence and lessons of his life will abide with us long after he has gone from the earth. As I linger at his tomb, many lessons of his life crowd my mind and heart as follows: While youth lasts, it is never too late to get an education. Religion, truth, is worth any sacrifice; it is worth fighting for. God has a plan for everyone's life, which must be found, followed and worked out. If anyone uses to the full all that God has given him, he will get more and succeed. The end must be kept in mind along the hard road of preparation and hard work. There is no royal road to learning, and achievement.

HIS EPITAPH :

Here lies
A GREAT HEALER OF THE BODY
A WISE TRAINER OF THE MIND
A STRONG PREACHER OF THE GOSPEL
A POWERFUL DEFENDER OF THE FAITH
A WRITER OF VICTORIAN ENGLISH,
DR. THOMAS WESLEY BRENTS, M.D.: D.D.
1823-1905

Dr. Brents has been long dead; but the cause for which he lived and worked has made great progress. This is a living, moving world. Man stops at the grave; but the tide moves on into the unpredictable future.

Some doubtless think that I have been fulsome in his portrayal; but he was a man apart and above his contemporaries, so none but superlatives can contain and reveal him. Under his leadership the Church of Christ made great progress. At his death the church was numbered in thousands; now they are estimated in the millions. They have followed the religious ideals deduced from the Bible by the Campbells and Dr. Brents. They have followed these prophets as they followed Jesus and his Apostles. Their words have "run and been glorified," the Church of Christ making the greatest growth of any church.

But we are living in a changed world. Those that are in or coming into these two churches today find a far different world to the frontier conditions, which the Campbells and Dr. Brents found and worked. We no longer have a land and home frontier, which the inhabitants sought and found. Our frontier today is people threatened with war, not trees and land; and many of them have no homes except nomadic shelters and government owned houses. We are no longer a rural people. Christianity has become a world religion with world responsibilities and problems. The pioneer church

81

under the Campbells and Dr. Brents met and fulfilled its mission. Can or will we fill ours?

We do not need to reform their work nor adopt their program. We have the same Bible, the same Gospel, the same Saviour, the same church, the same essential items of worship, the same freedom and the same hope. We have a rich heritage from our fathers. What will we do for the future? We start from where they left off, "following them as they followed Christ." No one can or needs to do the work of Dr. Brents. We need only Isaiah's dedication, "Here am I, Lord, send me."

Dr. Brents was a triple doctor in the original meaning of the word, teacher, in medicine, education and religion; and he reached preeminence in all three professions; but finally, it was religion, to which he gave his major study and effort, "the one thing" of his study, effort and purpose. He was a ten-talent man, whose absorbing theme and purpose of life was religion, for which he is credited, praised or blamed. If Dr. Brents were living today and could look back over the fields of his labor in the South and the West, where he sowed, cultivated and defended the seeds of the Christian Church he would behold a golden harvest from his planting. These four million people, though they never knew nor heard Dr. Brents, could testify to the rich heritage that we have in Dr. Brents, and as long as there is a Church of Christ in this area, he will share the credit of a pioneer "master builder" and be reverenced as a prophet of God.

The Alien's Department

THE STORY BEHIND THE ALIEN'S DEPARTMENT

The "Alien's Department" was T.W. Brents' idea for evangelizing the unsaved. David Lipscomb asked for help and this was Brents' idea. The series began in the January 17, 1867 issue of the *Gospel Advocate* and ran on and off until 1872. It began running as articles that people would use for evangelistic purposes. They then started asking the Gospel Advocate for copies so that they could circulate them. After hearing complaints David Lipscomb printed a number of these articles to circulate as tracts. This went over well until the supply ran out and no more could be procured. Then the complaints came again. People were sending money to pay for tracts that could not be had. Even after the GA printed articles to stop sending money, it still kept coming.

At this point someone had a EUREKA!! moment and the idea for a book was raised. Publishing a book was very difficult for Dr. Brents because he had to travel to Nashville to work on the manuscript in person. This trip was required several times imposing hardships each time it was required. In early 1874 the book was complete and ready to ship. It was an instant classic and has been in print the whole time of its existence

If you are familiar with **The Gospel Plan of Salvation**, you will recognize bits and pieces of these articles. There is some materials found here that aren't in the book so to me it was worth the extra work to produce these. I hope that you will be in agreement with me after you read these.

Kyle Frank

ELECTION AND REPROBATION

The brethren and sisters are presumed to understand the conditions upon which God proposes to save men from past sins, and have complied with them. To know the truth by which they were made free; delivered from the power of darkness and translated into the Kingdom of God's dear Son; it is not, therefore, especially for them, we propose writing a series of articles on THE GOSPEL PLAN OF SALVATION.

We propose to assist the alien in arriving at a knowledge of his duty, in order to his being made a citizen of God's government on the earth—a child of God's family—a member of Christ's body, the church. But while our essays are especially designed to benefit the alien, it is hoped a perusal of them will not be without interest to the "babes" in Christ. They should not regard themselves as fully grown when first born, and therefore cease their investigations, but they should feed upon the sincere milk of the word, that they may grow thereby. "Wherefore, I will not be negligent to put you always in remembrance of these things, though ye know them, and be established in the present truth. Yea, I think it meet, as long as I am in this tabernacle, to stir you up by putting you in remembrance; knowing that shortly I must put off this my tabernacle." 2 Peter i: 12 to 13.

But before we proceed with the alien to look for the conditions upon which he may secure the favor of our Heavenly Father, it is proper to enquire whether or not there is any thing he can do that will be conducive to this end. There are prominent doctrines taught by those for whose learning and piety we have the most profound respect, which, if true, render it wholly unnecessary, it seems to us, to spend time or labor in instructing the sinner with regard to his duty either to God or to man.

That we may have these doctrines properly before the mind of the reader without any chance, or at least probability of misrepresenting them, we beg permission to make a few quotations from the fountain-head from whence they flow.

"God, from all eternity did, by the most wise and holy counsel of his own will, freely and unchangeably ordain whatsoever comes to pass." Presbyterian Confession of Faith, chap. 3, sec. 1, page 21.

Now if the sentiment put forth in the foregoing paragraph be true, we think it impossible for man to err. Whatever he does is in keeping with God's foreordination, and therefore cannot be wrong. If he does anything, it matters not what, whether good or bad, if God has ordained everything, He has ordained that thing. If it come to pass that a man lies, God has ordained that he should lie. If it come to pass that a man steals, God has ordained that too. If it come to pass that a man kills his neighbor, God has ordained that also. God has said, "Thou shalt not steal; thou shall not commit adultery; Thou shalt not kill." Ex. xx: 13 to 15. As God has thus plainly forbidden things that do come to pass, it cannot be true that he has ordained them. That God should unchangeably ordain that a certain thing should come to pass, and at the same time positively forbid it, is an inconsistency entirely incompatible with His character, especially when we add to it; the thought that He threatens the guilty with endless punishment. When, therefore, the murderer stains his hands in the blood of his fellow, he cannot take shelter under the doctrine of the creed by saying that God, in ordaining everything that comes to pass, ordained that he should kill his neighbor, and thereby avoid the responsibility of the act and the punishment due his crime. If God has unchangeably ordained everything that comes to pass, man cannot change God's unchangeable ordination or decree, and hence there can no responsibility or blame attach to any person for anything he docs. If God unchangeably ordained or decreed that a man on a certain day should do a certain thing, there is no power left to man to avoid doing that thing, and If he fails to do the thing, it follows that the decree was not only changeable, but has been changed by man, and hence man becomes the superior power.

But again. This same high authority, on pages 23 and 24, says, "By the decree of God for the manifestation of His glory, some men and angels are predestinated unto everlasting life, and others foreordained to everlasting death. These angels and men, thus predestinated and foreordained, are particularly and unchangeably designed, and their number is so certain and definite that it cannot be either increased or diminished."

If this be true, why did Jesus commission his apostles to preach the Gospel to every creature, and promise that "He that believeth and is baptized shall be saved," elect or non-elect, and "He that believeth not shall be damned." Would it not have been more in keeping with the doctrine of the creed, if the commission had been something after the following style: "Go ye into all the world, preach the Gospel to the elect, that they may be made acquainted with the provision made for them before the world begun: but to the reprobate say nothing, for as they cannot by any possibility avert the awful doom that sorely awaits them, tis better to let them remain ignorant of their fate as long as possible."

If this be true, what is the use of all the expense and labor of printing Bibles, building meeting houses, and preaching the Gospel to either saint or sinner? If we are of the definite number elected and foreordained to eternal life, there is no chance for us to be lost, and if not, we cannot be saved. We have often heard this doctrine preached from the pulpit, and the sermon closed with an exhortation to sinners to come to the anxious seat to pray for pardon of sin.

What a mockery! Tell a man that God has unalterably fixed his destiny before time began, and then exhort him to make an effort to either change or confirm God's decree. Surely his efforts could do no good, nor could his negligence do any harm, for the same authority (sec. F,) tells us that "Those of mankind that are predestinated unto life, God, before the foundation of the world, was laid, according to his eternal and immutable purpose and the secret counsel and good pleasure of his will, hath chosen in Christ unto everlasting glory out of his free grace and love, without any foresight of faith or good works, or perseverance in either of them or any other thing in the creature as conditions or causes moving him thereunto." Thus, we see that neither faith, good works nor any other thing can avail, for the whole matter was not only unalterably fixed before the world began, but they go on to say (sec. G,) "Neither are any other redeemed by Christ, effectually called, justified, adopted, sanctified and saved but the elect only." If you are not of the elect, Christ never died for you—you have no interest in his blood or the atonement made by him. Though, you may consign your infant to the tomb while so young that it never could have had a wicked thought or done a wicked act, you have no assurance of its ever being raised in the image of Christ for the reason that you cannot tell whether it was one of the elect or not.

On page 64, chap. 10. sec. 3, the same book says, "Elect Infants dying in infancy are regenerated and saved by Christ through the Spirit who worketh when, and where, and how he pleaseth. So also, are all other elect persons who are incapable of being outwardly called by the ministry of the word." And what of the non-elect? Others not elected, though they may he called by the ministry of the word, and may have some common operations of the Spirit, yet they never truly come to Christ, and therefore cannot be saved."

The words "elect infants" clearly implies non-elect infants. Elect means to choose. There can be no choice where there is but one person or class of persons. The above quotation tells us that elect infants dying in Infancy are saved, and of course the non-elect infants dying in infancy, or in living to adult age, cannot be saved, as Christ never died for them or any but the elect.

Paul certainly did not so understand the doctrine of the atonement. Hear him. "We see Jesus, who was made a little lower than the angels for the suffering of death, crowned with glory and honor, that he, by the grace of God, should taste death for every man." Heb. ii: 9. And the beloved John says of Jesus, "He is the propitiation for our sins, and not for ours only, but also for the sins of the whole world." John ii: 2.

But we cannot pursue the subject further in these articles. We have said enough to call the attention of the reader to the doctrine as set forth authoritatively in the theological world. We conscientiously believe it antagonistic to the teaching of God's word, contrary to the spirit and genius of the Christian religion, and at war with the love, mercy and justice of God. He had the entire control of man's creation, and certainly would not have created him, having unalterably consigned the greater portion of his posterity to eternal misery, dishonor and wrath. How God could be glorified by the eternal punishment of man in order to carry out a decree made by Himself before the creation of man, is a matter incomprehensible to us. The doctrine makes God an embodiment of cruelty, tyranny and oppression too horrible to contemplate, and no one who believes it can acceptably obey God. "He that cometh to God must believe that he is and that he is the rewarder of them that diligently seek him."

How can he, who believes himself either one of the elect or one of the reprobate, and that there is nothing he can do that will in any way effect his salvation, ask such a question as "What must I do to be saved or in faith obey any command as a condition of salvation? We speak with all due reverence when we say we think such a thing impossible, until such persons can correct their faith on this subject. If we believed it we would never make another effort to persuade any person to seek to make his calling and election sure.

But our article is already too long and we must desist.

GA Vol.9, #3, 1/17/67 page 53.

HEREDITARY TOTAL DEPRAVITY.

Having previously disposed of unconditional Election and Reprobation as taught by the Presbyterian Confession we come now, to notice another doctrine taught by the same authority as well as by most of the denominations, which obtains much more general acceptance than the Calvinistic view of election and reprobation; but which is equally fatal to the obedience of faith required in the Gospel, to which we deem it proper to call attention before we set out to learn the duty of man in order to his adoption into the family of God. This is what is called by its advocates "hereditary total depravity."

We will make a few quotations from the Presbyterian Confession of Faith, as the highest authority of which we know that contains this doctrine, which will correctly set it before the reader. And we do not make these quotations for the purpose of following this doctrine into all its legitimate results in detail, but for the purpose of showing its bearing upon the subject of obedience to God.

"By this sin (eating the forbidden fruit) they (our first parents) fell from their original righteousness and communion with God, and so became dead in sin and wholly defiled in all the faculties and parts of soul and body. They being the root of all mankind, the guilt of this sin was imputed, and the same death in sin and corrupted nature conveyed to all their posterity descending from them by ordinary generation. From this original corruption, whereby we are utterly indisposed, disabled and made opposite to all good, and wholly inclined to all evil, do proceed all actual transgressions."

Now it seems to us that if this picture correctly represents the disposition of the human heart at birth, the Devil can be no worse. His Satanic majesty cannot be more than utterly indisposed, disabled, and opposite to all good and wholly inclined to all evil. Nor can we very well see how man can get any worse in the scale of moral turpitude. He cannot get worse than wholly defiled in all the faculties of soul and body; and this is his condition at birth, if the doctrine be true; yet Paul tells Timothy that "evil men and seducers shall wax worse and worse," 2 Tim. iii: 13. How can they get worse? Wholly defiled in-all the attributes of soul and body! Opposite to all good and wholly inclined to all evil, and still wax worse and worse? Does not the common observation of every man contradict this doctrine? The theory is, as we shall see directly, that this corrupt nature remain until the man is converted to Christianity, as some teach, while others insist that it remains through life even in those truly regenerated. Then we cannot be wholly defiled, opposite to all good by nature; for we see many men who make no pretension to Christianity at all, quite as ready to visit the sick and administer to the wants of the poor, as many who claim to have had their hearts cleansed by the Spirit of God. These persons are surely not opposed to all good while thus doing good; if they are, then their feelings and actions are strangely inconsistent.

But we are told that from this original corruption do proceed all actual transgressions. If this be true, how came Adam to sin? This corruption of nature is the cause of all actual transgression, and it was the consequence of Adam's sin but not the cause of it, according to the theory; and hence he was not under its influence until after he sinned. As this inherited corruption of nature is the source of all actual transgression now, what caused his transgression then? His transgression must have been caused by some other influence than the corruption of nature supposed to be the consequence of his sin, and if so, why may not the same or similar causes influence others now? We are now subject to many temptations from which he was then free. He could not have been tempted to steal from his neighbor for there was no one then living to be his neighbor, and no one owned any thing but himself. He could not have been tempted to kill, for there was no person to kill but his wife. He could not have had a temptation to adultery, for the only woman on the earth was his wife. Notwithstanding he was free from many sources of temptation that beset our pathway, he failed in the first trial he had of which we have a record. Then surely other causes than corruption, inherited from him on account of his sin, may cause transgression now.

But we are told that "this their sin God was pleased, according to his wise and holy counsel, to permit, having purposed to order it to his own glory." Chapter 6, Sec. 1. It does not seem to us that "permit" is exactly the word here. We have already been told that "God from all eternity did by the most wise and holy counsel of his own will, freely and unchangeably ordain whatsoever comes to pass." It did come to pass that they ate of the fruit whereof God commanded them not to eat. Then does it not follow that God not only permitted them to eat, but unchangeably ordained that they should eat the fruit, and violate the law he had given, having "purposed to order it to his own glory."

But how God could be glorified by this violation of his law, especially if we contemplate it's results in the light of this theory, we are not very well prepared to see. We have been accustomed to think that the best way to glorify God was to honor his authority by obedience to his commands. How could God be glorified by the direct violation of his positive command, when it made man wholly defiled in all the faculties of soul and body? Did he glory in man becoming opposite to all good and wholly inclined to all evil, that he might punish him in hell forever? Could there be any justice in placing man under a law which God had unchangeably ordained he should break? Was it not downright mockery for God to command him to obey when he had previously decreed that he should disobey?

But was God glorified by the corruption of his creature, man? Let us see. "And God saw that the wickedness of man was great in the earth, and that every imagination of the thoughts of his heart was only evil continually. And it repented the Lord that he had made man on the earth, and it grieved him at his heart." Gen. vi: 5,6. Did God grieve on account of his own glorification? If God was glorified by Adam's sin, the consequence of which was the entire corruption of the nature of his offspring, from whence flow all actual transgressions, the wickedness of the antediluvians was as much the result of it as the wickedness of any other people; hence, we cannot see how he would grieve over the result of an act which he had previously determined to order to his own glory, and which he had unchangeably ordained should come to pass.

Again : Would God have given man a command that he had unchangeably foreordained to be broken, that he might subject him to "death, with all miseries, spiritual, temporal, and eternal," then tell us that he "so loved the world that he gave his only begotten Son that whosoever believeth in him should not perish, but have everlasting life," John iii: 16; and at the same time restrict the benefits of his death to a few elect ones, and allow the Devil to have the many, and thus be glorified by their destruction —it being no fault of theirs? But if all actual transgressions proceed from this supposed corruption of nature, it is difficult to account for the difference of inclination to sin, which we see manifested by different persons. We are accustomed to expect the same cause when surrounded by the same circumstances, to produce the same effect on all occasions; yet we see persons, even in the same family, surrounded by as nearly the same circumstances as human beings can be in this life, somewhat differently inclined to sin, and as circumstances differ these differences increase until one is a moral, upright man, another a drunkard, another a thief, and another a murderer. Can any one tell, in keeping with this theory, why Cain killed his brother? They were both possessed of the same corrupt nature, and precisely to the same extent. Why, then, was one more vicious than the other? We cannot increase or intensify the meaning of such words as wholly, all, total, etc. We cannot say more wholly defiled, more all the faculties, more all evil, more all good. If all Adam's progeny are wholly defiled in all the faculties of soul and body, opposed to all good and wholly inclined to all evil. Cain could not have been more corrupt than Abel. And if this corrupt nature is the source of all actual transgressions, it was the cause of Cain's sin and Abel being possessed of this corruption of nature to the same extent, would have been just as much inclined to kill Cain, as Cain would have been to kill Abel. Men differ as widely in their inclinations to sin as it is possible for them to differ in anything; and they could not thus differ if the same corrupt nature influenced all, and was possessed by all to the same extent.

But worse still, from our stand point the theory necessarily damns every infant that dies in infancy. If all infants come into the world with natures inherited from our first parents, wholly defiled in all the faculties of soul and body, then those who die in infancy must go to Hell on account of this defilement, or go to Heaven in this defilement, or they must have it removed in some way unknown to the Bible. The makers of the creed plainly saw this difficulty, and attempted to provide for it. Chapter x : Sec. 3. They tell us that "elect infants, dying in infancy, are regenerated and saved by Christ through the Spirit, who worketh when and where and how he pleaseth." Thus they provide for elect infants dying in infancy; but they make no effort to save any but the elect, telling us plainly that Christ died for none others.

But the Calvinists are but a very small part of those who adopt this theory—how will the others escape?! The Cumberland Presbyterian Confession of Faith substitutes the word all for elect, thus "All infants dying in infancy are regenerated and saved by Christ, through the Spirit who worketh when, and where, and how he pleaseth," Chap, x: Sec. 3. And how did the authors know this? Where is the proof that Christ, by the Spirit removes this depravity from those dying in infancy and allows it to remain in the living ones? The creed refers us to Luke xviii: 15,16. "And they brought unto him also infants, that he would touch them; but when his disciples saw it, they rebuked them. But Jesus called them unto him, and said, "suffer little children to come unto me, and forbid them not: for of such is the Kingdom of God." "We have two objections to this proof, First; These were living, and not dead or dying children; how can it therefore prove anything about what the Spirit does for those dying in infancy. Second: It proves just the opposite of infantile depravity. If Jesus had said, "Suffer little children to come, and forbid them not, that the total depravity and corruption of their little defiled hearts may be removed by the Spirit; for of such as they will then be is the Kingdom of God"—then the text would have been appropriate. But as it is, it would fill the Kingdom of God with subjects wholly defiled in all the faculties of soul and body, opposed to all good, and wholly inclined to all evil. "Suffer little children to come unto me, and forbid them not, for of such (not as they will be, but are now) is the Kingdom of God"—that is, of such total depravity, and subjects wholly defiled in all the faculties of soul and body, is the Kingdom of God!! Mr. Jeter, the great Baptist luminary of Virginia, says: "Infants dying in infancy, must, by some process, known or unknown, be freed from depravity—morally renewed— or regenerated, or they can never be saved—never participate in the joys of Heaven." Jeter's **Campbellism Re-examined**, pages 51-2. And on page 49 he says: "I shall now proceed to show that in the case of dying infants and idiots, regeneration takes place by the agency of the Spirit without the word." Thus, we see that one error assumed and adopted creates the necessity for, perhaps many others. The false assumption that infants are wholly depraved has forced upon these authors and their ilk, the doctrine of infant regeneration and abstract spiritual influences. Nor is this all. The doctrine of infant baptism originated here.

Does any one demand proof? Dr. Wall, the most voluminous and authoritative writer that has ever wielded a pen in defence of Infant baptism, says: "And you will see in the following quotations that they often conclude the necessity of baptism for the forgiveness of sins, even of a child that, is but a day old." **Wall's History**, vol. 1, page 48. After making a quotation from Justin Martyr, who wrote about 40 years after the Apostles and about A. D. 140, our author says: "I recite this only to show that in these times, so very near the Apostles, they spoke of original sin affecting all mankind descended of Adam; and understood, that besides the actual sins of each particular person there is in our nature itself, since the fall, something that needs redemption and forgiveness by the merits of Christ. And that is ordinarily applied to every particular person by baptism." Ibid 64.

On pages 104-5, Dr. Wall quotes Origen as follows: "Besides all this, let it be considered, what is the reason that whereas the baptism of the Church is given for forgiveness of sins, infants also are by the usage of the Church baptized when if there were nothing in infants that wanted forgiveness and mercy, the grace of baptism would be needless to them.

Infants are baptized for the forgiveness of sins. Of what sins? Or when have they sinned? Or how can any reason of the latter in their case hold good, but according to that sense that we mentioned even now: none is free from pollution, though his life be but of the length of one day upon the earth? And it is for that reason because by the sacrament of baptism the pollution of our birth is taken away, that infants are baptized.

In the writings of Cyprian, bishop of Carthage, is a letter written by a council of sixty-six bishops to one Cnidus, about the close of the second century. Dr. Wall gives that part of this letter which pertains to the subject in hand; and says of it: "These bishops held, that to suffer the infant to die unbaptized was to endanger its salvation." **Wall's History**, vol. 1, page 139.

In support of infant baptism, Mr. Wesley says: "If infants are guilty of original sin, then they are proper subjects of baptism, seeing, in the ordinary way, they cannot be saved unless this be washed away by baptism. It has been already proved that this original stain cleaves to every child of man, and that hereby they are children of wrath, and liable to eternal damnation." This comes to us not only as written by Mr. Wesley but it was "Published by order of the General Conference in New York, in 1850. **Doctrinal Tracts** page 251. Many other quotations might be given from various authors held in high esteem by the various parties of these days; but surely these are sufficient to show that infant baptism grew out of the false assumption that infants are totally depraved in all the faculties and parts of soul and body—children of wrath, and liable to eternal damnation for Adam's sin unless baptized. We know that modern defenders of the practice are unwilling to admit this; but Dr. Wall, as a historian, gives authority for what he says; and historical facts, though ignored, can not be wiped out. They are events of the past and must so remain though erased from the pages of every book on earth. If, therefore, we have succeeded, or do succeed in showing that the dogma of hereditary total depravity is untrue we will have shown, not only that man has the power to believe and obey God, but also that the doctrine of abstract spiritual influences, infant regeneration, and infant baptism, as dependencies upon it, are necessarily untrue. Then let us continue our examination of it. If Adam's posterity inherited the corrupt nature described after the fall, then why do not children of Christians inherit their parent's purified natures after their conversion? Surely if God directly controlled the matter, he would have had as much pleasure in the transmission of purity of nature to the children of the faithful, as he would have had in entailing corruption of nature on the children of the disobedient. And if he had not specially controlled it, but left it to the laws of nature, we can see no reason why purity of heart would not have been as readily transmitted to the children of the Christian, as defilement of nature would have been to the children of the wicked. But the creed tells us that "This corruption of nature, during this life, doth remain in those that are regenerated." Presbyterian Confession Chapter 6, Sec. 5, page 41. Here, as usual, the creed and the Bible are in direct antagonism. When Peter addressed his fellow Apostles and elders, on one occasion, he said: "Men and brethren, ye know how that a good while ago God made choice among us that the Gentiles by my month should hear the Word of the Gospel and believe. And God, which knoweth the hearts, bare them witness, giving them the Holy Ghost even as unto us; and put no difference between us and them, purifying their hearts by faith." Acts xv : 7, 8, 9. In writing to his brethren he says: "Seeing you have purified your souls in obeying the truth." 1 Peter i: 22. Now if this corruption remains in those who are truly converted, how is it possible for persons to be wholly defiled in all the faculties and parts of soul and body, utterly indisposed, disabled, opposite to all good, and wholly inclined to all evil as described by the creed, and yet their hearts purified by faith, and their souls by obedience, as described by Peter, the converts to the creed are brethren of Peter; nor are they the blest of the

Lord for he says, " Blessed are the pure in heart for they shall see God." Matt, v: 8.

Jesus, in his explanation to the parable of the sower,— Luke viii: 15 says, "But that on the good ground are they which, in an honest and good heart, having heard the word, keep it, and bring forth fruit with patience." If there was not another passage of Scripture in the Bible bearing on the subject this one would be quite sufficient to spoil the whole theory. Had Jesus been educated in the theological schools of our day, he would not have spoken of honest and good hearts receiving the word, for he would have been therein taught that there are none such; but, on the contrary, all Adam's race are wholly defiled in all the faculties of soul and body, opposed to all good and wholly inclined to all evil. It seems to us that all speculative theorizing about doubtful interpretations of Scripture, to sustain our favorite dogma, should bend before such direct, plain, and positive statements of the Savior, as the above quoted.

But we are told in the creed that our natures are not only made totally corrupt by Adam's sin, but that the GUILT of it was imputed to all his descendants. This we regard as a fatal mistake growing out of a failure to discriminate between guilt and consequences. It is certainly, true that we suffer in consequence of Adam's sin but that ye are in any sense guilty of it, or morally accountable for it, is not exactly clear to us. To suffer the consequences of an act is one thing; but to be held guilty of it, by imputation or otherwise, is quite a different thing. A man, for illustration, may own an estate sufficient to abundantly supply the wants of his family for life; but by gambling he may have it all swept away in a single day. His wife and children may be reduced to poverty and want by his wickedness, and they are thus made to keenly feel the consequences of his act, but surely no one would regard them guilty in consequence of their misfortune. So, we suffer death as a consequence of Adam's sin, as we will more clearly see directly: but this is not quite sufficient to show that we are guilty of, or responsible for it. If we are guilty of, or responsible for his first sin why are we not accountable for all other sins committed by him? As he was childless when driven from the garden, and was an hundred and thirty years old when Seth, his third son, of which we have an account, was born, and was nine hundred and thirty years old when he died, it follows that he lived more than eight hundred years after eating the interdicted fruit. It is next to certain, therefore, that he did many things wrong during this long period. Is there any good reason why we are guilty of his first sin, and guilty of no other sin committed by him? And if we are responsible for, and guilty of Adam's sin are we not equally guilty of all the sins committed by our own father? He is much nearer us than Adam, and we can plainly see in ourselves some things inherited from him. If then we are guilty of the sins of Adam, we see no escape from the guilt of our father's sin. And as these are but two extremes in the long chain of parentage from us to Adam, we can see no reason why we may not be held guilty according to the same rule, of all the sins of every parent between them; if so, well may all ask "Lord who then can be saved?" When we do the best we can, we have quite enough in our own record to answer for; and if we are thus-charged with the sins of those who have lived before us, then the last lingering ray of hope for the salvation of man is forever extinguished. We are encouraged, however, by the fact that God has contradicted the whole theory, saying, "The soul that sinneth it shall die. The son shall not bear the iniquity of the father, neither shall the father bear the iniquity of the son: the righteousness of the righteous shall be upon him, and the wickedness of the wicked shall be upon him." Ezek. xviii: 20. It seems to us that the prophet intended to describe the false reasoners of our day, when he said, "The Gentiles shall come unto thee from the ends of the earth and shall say, surely our fathers have inherited his vanity, and things wherein there is no profit Jer. xvi: 10.

But is it possible, in the nature of things, that sin can be transmitted from parent to child? In order to arrive at a satisfactory solution of this question, it may be well to ascertain what sin is. And this we can do with great certainty, for we have a definition of it given by inspiration. John says: "Sin is the transgression of the law." 1 John iii:4. In the light of this definition, how is it possible that a transgression by one man may be transmitted to another, or from parent to child? God has said, "Thou shalt not kill." In violation of this law, a man thrusts a dagger to the heart of his neighbor. This is sin. Now this act, being the act of a father cannot possibly become the act of his child; nor can the child be made responsible for it. He may approve the act and for this approval may receive merited punishment; But it was the wicked approval that brought guilt to him, and not the act of the father. Without such approval, he may suffer in consequence of his father's act—may be made an orphan by it, but surely the act itself can not become his act. Sin is nowhere in God's word, defined to be a weakness, or hereditary but a transgression, or act of the guilty himself. "God is love," and cannot punish man for that which he has no power to prevent.

But we have said that we die as a consequence of Adam's sin. This is true, and yet we are not guilty of it. When Adam fell from the plastic hand of God, he was as mortal as he was after he ate of the interdicted fruit; how, then, is death a consequence of that act? He was placed in a garden, or orchard in which grew, among others, two trees respectively called the tree of life, and the tree of the knowledge of good and evil. For his government in this garden, God gave him a law saying, "Of every tree of the garden thou mayest freely eat: but of the tree of the knowledge of good and evil, thou shalt not eat of it: for in the day thou eatest thereof dying thou shalt die." Gen. ii; 16. 17. We have adopted the marginal reading of the Polyglot Bible, because it is agreed, by scholars, to be an improvement upon the king's translation. It will be seen, by an examination of this law, that Adam had access to the tree of life before he ate of the interdicted fruit, and the properties of the fruit of this tree were such as to counteract the mortal tendencies of his nature, and keep him alive as long as he had access to it. But when he violated God's law, it was only necessary that he should be driven from the garden, so that he might no longer have access to this life-giving fruit, that, under the laws of mortality to which his nature subjected him, he might suffer the penalty of the law which said, "dying thou shalt die." Hence God said, "Behold the man has become as one of us, to know good and evil: and now lest he put forth his hand, and take also of the tree of life and eat and live for ever: therefore the Lord God sent him forth from the garden of Eden to till the ground from whence he was taken. So, he drove out the man: and he placed at the east of the garden of Eden cherubim and a flaming sword which turned every way, to keep the way of the tree of life." Gen. iii: 22-3-4. Thus, we see how Adam died in consequence of his sin; and that he would not have died had he not sinned; hence says Paul, "By one man sin entered into the world, and death by sin." Rom. v: 12. Not that he possessed physical immortality before he sinned; for he did not: but he had a remedy for his mortality of which he was deprived after he sinned. We are sometimes asked whether or not the lower animals die as a consequence of Adam's sin? We answer they do not; but they die as a result of the common laws of mortality to which the whole animal creation is subject. They have been subject to these laws from the time they were created, not having had access to the fruit of the tree of life as Adam did before he sinned. From this stand-point it is easy to see how Adam's posterity die as a consequence of his sin. His children inherit from him just such an organization as he had, both before and after he sinned; and as they are born out of the garden of Eden, and away from the tree of life, they can not have its fruit to counteract the mortal tendencies of their nature, and hence, like him, dying they die. Shall we hence conclude that Adam's offspring are guilty of his sin? As well may we conclude that the African child, that falls a victim to cannibalism, sinned by being born in Africa. It was its misfortune to be born in a locality where men eat each other; so it is our misfortune to be born out of the garden of Eden, where, for a time, we can not get fruit from the tree of life; but if we do our Father's commandments there is coming a period when we will have a right to the tree of life and may enter through the gates into the city.

There is much speculation in the world with reference to the kind of death Adam and his posterity died as a consequence of his sin. Mr. Ewing, in his **Lectures**, page 63, tells us that, "By reason of our union with our federal head and representative, we sinned in him, and fell with him, and death is the consequence. Death spiritual, temporal, and eternal." If the death which Adam and the human race died was not only spiritual and temporal, but eternal, then we see no remedy that can reach such a case. Eternal must mean without end—of endless duration. Then if this death be eternal there can be no more life, and hence all our efforts to save those who are eternally dead can do no good, and the whole family of man is lost—hopelessly lost. If a single son of Adam be saved it follows that he was not eternally lost, for it matters not in what sense he died, if ever made alive that is an end to his death, and consequently his death could not have been eternal.

But Mr. Ewing further tells us, page 62, "The whole soul of man is entirely depraved, corrupt and alienated from God, a child of wrath, an heir of hell, going astray from the womb, conceived in sin, an enemy to God, having a heart deceitful above all things and desperately wicked; the understanding darkened, the affections earthly, and the whole

103

man sensual and devilish." Truly this is an appalling picture of our nature at birth, entailed upon us for no other reason than that we descended from Adam, with whom, by a single act of his we fell into his deplorable condition six thousand years before we were born. And when we add to this thought the language of the Presbyterian Confession, that "This corruption of nature, during this life, doth remain in those that are regenerated," we have a most ridiculous description of Christian character manufactured by this theory. Behold a Christian with a heart not only entirely depraved, sensual and devilish; but hating God, and an heir of hell! We do not suppose the authors of these books believed this monstrous absurdity themselves, or intended to teach it to others; but they were involved in it by the blinding influences of a false theory. Be this as it may, however, we can not admit that this is a correct picture of that "Holiness without which no man shall see the Lord." The mind of man is composed of numerous faculties which may be divided into two grand divisions, called respectively Animal, and Intellectual. By animal faculties we mean such as are possessed by man and beast; or we might simply say by animals; for man is only an intellectual animal. As examples of this class of faculties we may mention Alimentiveness, Combativeness, Destructiveness, Amativeness, Philoprogenitiveness, etc., etc. In man they are usually called propensities; but in lower animals they are called instincts. Paul calls them "The carnal mind" and tells us, "It is not subject to the law of God neither indeed can be," Rom. viii: 7. It would do but little good to read the ten commandments to a horse, as he would not be subject to them; neither indeed could he be; and it would do about as little good to read them to the purely carnal mind of man (if it were possible to do so) composed of similar constituents, which knows no law but animal gratification. But God has given to man an intellectuality capable of appreciating law, and has given him a law adapted to his organization by which his carnal propensities are to be exercised, and by which the whole man is to be governed. And while the whole man is governed by laws received from God, and applied by the intellectual man, all is harmony and order and without sin; but when these laws are superseded by animal propensities, such as appetite, passion, and lust, then come confusion, violence, and crime, and thus originated sin in the garden of Eden. God gave Adam a law for the government of his appetite, and while he obeyed it he had life and peace; but when law was supplanted by appetite, sin came, and death by sin. From the description of man's nature found in the creeds, it would seem that the authors regard these animal propensities as filling the entire measure of the human mind. But the duality of mind is well established by experience, observation, metaphysics, reason, and the Bible. The carnal mind we have seen already: the perceptive and reflective faculties, of which there are many, and the moral sentiments, such as benevolence, veneration, conscientiousness, firmness, hope, etc., make up the intellectual and moral nature of man, to which God's law is addressed; and Paul tells us "They that are after the flesh do mind the things of the flesh; but they that are after the Spirit, the things of the Spirit: for to be carnally minded is death; but to be spiritually minded is life and peace." Rom. viii: 5, 6. The antagonism of these two departments of man's nature is well shown in Paul's description of himself. "I find then," says he "a law, that, when I would do good, evil is present with me; for I delight in the law of God after the inward man: but I see another law in my members, warring against the law of my mind and bringing me into captivity to the law of sin which is in my members." Rom.vii: 2-3. Had this dual nature been displeased with in the creation of man, he must have been all animal, and therefore nothing more than a brute; or he must have been all intellectual and moral without any counter tendencies in his nature and therefore would have been a mere machine, acting as compelled to act, under one set of principles; and hence there would have been neither merit nor demerit in anything he did; nor could he have had the slightest freedom of will; and therefore could not have been in the slightest degree accountable to his Creator; who, in that event, would have been operating him, as a mechanic does his machine.

But if we can arrive at the meaning of the language "Dying thou shalt die," as connected with the law given to, and violated by Adam, then we think we may arrive at a knowledge of the kind of death he died. This we certainly can do with great clearness; as we have an exegesis of the language by God himself. After Adam violated the law, God adjudicated his case, and pronounced the sentence upon him. Both as the giver of the law and as God, he certainly knew what he meant by the language of the law; and he certainly pronounced the sentence in accordance therewith. What then was the sentence? "Dust thou art, and unto dust shalt thou return." Gen. iii: 19. Surely this must mean literal, physical death: nothing more, nothing less. Moses wrote the history of this affair about two thousand five hundred years after it occurred, when the word die, in all it's forms, was of no doubtful import, but had a well settled meaning in the current usage of that day. A few examples may not be out of place, here. In the 5th chap, Genesis, we have the word employed by the same writer no less than eight times as follow: "And all the days that Adam lived were nine hundred and thirty years; and he died." ver. 5. "And all the days of Seth were nine hundred and twelve years; and he died. ver.8. "And all the days of Enos were nine hundred and five years; and he died." ver. 11. "And all the days of Cainan were nine hundred and ten years; and he died." ver. 14. "And all-the days of Mahalaleel were eight hundred ninety and five years and he died." ver. 17. "And all the days of Jared were nine hundred sixty and two years; and He died." ver. 20. "And all the days of Methuselah were nine hundred sixty and nine years; and he died: ver.

27. "And all the days of Lamech were seven hundred seventy and seven years; and he died." ver. 31. These cases dearly show what Moses understood by the word die, and as he is the same writer that recorded the law violated by Adam, he must have meant the same by "die," in the law, that he meant in the other cases referred to. Again: The word die must certainly mean just the opposite of the word live. This word in its various forms occurs in the same chapter to indicate physical life. Had God afflicted Adam with greater punishment than the terms employed, indicated to him, then would he not have deceived him? And if He determined upon other, and greater punishment for him, after he committed the act, than that threatened in the law violated, then we insist that it was exposed to in its character, and therefore unjust. The circumstances under which Adam violated God's law would rather invoke a commutation of punishment, than an increase of it. He did not know good and evil, until he acquired a knowledge of it by eating the fruit of the tree of the knowledge of good and evil. This is evident from the language of God after he ate of it, "Behold the man is become as one of us, to know good and evil." Gen. iii: 22. He could only appreciate the law as a positive prohibition, but his moral obligation to obey God, as his Creator, he could not appreciate. He did not so much as know that he was naked; for God said, "Who told thee that thou wast naked? Hast thou eaten of the tree whereof I commanded thee that thou shouldest not eat?" Certainly, then if ignorance be a mitigating circumstance Adam was entitled to the full benefit of it.

From our stand-point such a thought as spiritual corruption by inheritance is utterly impossible. Paul says, "We have had fathers of our flesh which corrected us, and we gave them reverence: shall we not much rather be in subjection unto the Father of spirits and live?" Heb. 12: 9. Does not this passage plainly prove that the fathers of our flesh are not the fathers of our spirits? To our mind it shows that while our bodies are inherited from our parents, the Spirit is not so inherited but comes directly from God. Hence the style "Fathers of our flesh," "The Father of Spirits." Our bodies we inherit from our parents and consequently physical impurities may be transmitted from parent to child; but is the body the seat of moral depravity? We suppose all will agree that the mind, the spiritual, or inner man is the seat of moral depravity. If then we do not get our spirits by inheritance, it is impossible that we should inherit spiritual depravity from Adam. May we further examine the Scriptures on this subject? "The burden of the Word of the Lord for Israel saith the Lord, which stretcheth forth the Heavens, and layeth the foundation of the earth, and formeth the spirit of man within him." Zec. xii: 1. If God forms the spirit within man it seems improbable that he gets it by inheritance. Again: Solomon says, "Then shall the dust return to the earth as it was, and the spirit shall return to God who gave it." Eccl. xii: 7. By this we learn, not only that the spirit returns to God at death, but that God originally gave it. The words "returns to God" clearly imply that it had been there before. We can not say we returned to a place to which we had never been. In returning it did not go in or with the body, as the body returned to the ground as dust. As, therefore, the Spirit returns independent of the body, is it not likely that God gave it to man, not by of, through the body; but for the body? The words "God who gave it," have somewhat the same ring, too; nevertheless, they alone, would not be quite conclusive; for he gives us food, raiment, and many other things through means prepared to produce them. The question for us then is, does He give the spirit through means, or without means—does He give it directly, or indirectly—does He give it as we have seen that he takes it; or does He give it by procreation, organization, or some other means? Let us see. When Jesus restored the ruler's dead daughter to life, Luke says, "Her spirit came again, and she arose straightway." Luke viii: 55.

The spirit of the damsel came again. From whence did it come? Solomon says the spirit returns to God who gave it. Then it is clear that her spirit went to God when she died, and came directly from him when she was made alive. The words "came again" imply that it had done the same thing before; and as we have no account of her being miraculously made alive before, it follows that it was at the beginning of her existence that her spirit came directly from God the previous time.

But we are told that the spiritual man did not come directly from God; but is the Creature of the organization. We have not room for a thorough examination of this objection here, but we must notice it briefly; not by way of respect for materialistic infidelity of which it is the cornerstone; but in respect to our own argument, against which it may be presented. First then; if the spirit came not from God, how are the scriptures above quoted and the reasonings therefrom, to be met? And how can a material organization create an immaterial soul capable of existence separate from the organization after the latter has ceased to be? Or if the soul, created by materiality, is itself material why is it not subject to chemical analysis? The material organization is not only subject to chemical analysis, but has been analyzed repeatedly. The ultimate elements of it have been found, and if the soul is also material, why has it not been subjected to the same process? Surely the advocates of materialism have the ability to do it, if it were possible; and the defence of their theory would invoke the disposition to do it; if they, then, have not done it, it is clear that, because of the soul's immateriality, they can not do it. That the soul is capable of existence after the separation of soul and body, is clear from what we have already quoted from Solomon; that the body returns to the ground and the spirit returns to God who gave it. Not only so, but it is clear from numerous other passages. Paul says, "Therefore we are always confident, knowing that, whilst we are at home in the

109

body, we are absent from the Lord. We are confident, and willing rather to be absent from the body and to be present with the Lord." 2 Cor: 6, 8. John "Saw under the altar the souls of them that were slain for the Word of God." Rev. vi: 9. We might further quote Luke xvi: 24, 27, concerning the rich man and Lazarus, and many other Scriptures on this subject; but enough has been quoted to satisfy those who read and believe the Bible; and others will not likely read what we write about it. The body may be likened to a machine controlled by the mind or spiritual man. No machinery has ever been known, capable of generating its own motive power; hence the "Perpetual motion" has not been invented. If the human organism creates the soul, its own motive power, then it is an exception to all known law on the subject. If then our argument holds good and the spirit came, not by inheritance, but directly from God, it follows that when it is given it is not only good, but very good, and the whole theory of hereditary depravity is most certainly false. The child comes into the world with its infantile mind composed of numerous faculties susceptible of being cultivated, and developed by impressions made upon it through the senses; and when all its faculties are properly balanced, educated and governed they are calculated to make the man useful and happy; but if neglected, may make him vicious and miserable. And his inclinations to virtue or vice depend much upon the circumstances and influences surrounding him, hence inclinations to sin are as different persons, as the circumstances have been different by which they have been influenced from infancy to manhood. We most firmly believe that many men, who were raised under improper influences and became desperately wicked—perhaps terminated their being upon a scaffold, or suspended by a rope who, if they had been raised under wholesome influences, would have been useful members of society and finally saved in Heaven; and vice versa; Thus we see the importance of observing Solomon's admonition " Train up a child in the way he should go, and when he is old he will not depart from it;" with which Paul agrees, saying, "Bring up your children in the nurture and admonition of the Lord."

But there are differences of mental power, manifested by different persons growing out of a difference in the physical machinery inherited from our parents. This we not only admit, but firmly believe; but these do not affect our position in the least. An engine may run a vast amount of well-made and properly applied machinery and thus exhibit great power, but were we to apply the same engine to heavy, cumbersome, unwieldy unbalanced machinery it could do but little, though the same man operated it. So, a man who has inherited a fine organization, large and well balanced brain, of fine material, will exhibit much more mental power than one who has inherited an imperfect organization of coarse material. But inherited weakness, whether physical or mental, is not sin; no guilt can attach to it; and therefore, the differences in mental power spoken of, can not prove the doctrine of total depravity on the contrary, if they prove anything concerning it, they contradict it, for these differences, cannot be the result of total depravity because all who are totally depraved are, in this respect, exactly alike. There is no comparative degree in total depravity.

But we must briefly notice some: of the proof relied on to sustain the doctrine. First, we are told that; the infant gets angry as soon as born, and thus gives evidence of total depravity. If this proof be conclusive then God is totally depraved too. He said to Moses, when the people worshipped the calf made by Aaron, "Let me alone, that my wrath may wax hot against them." Ex. 32; 10. And again; "God is angry with the wicked every day." Ps. 7: 11. Does not the infant smile as well as cry? And does it not very soon divide it's toys and food with its associate thus exhibiting feelings of kindness as well as anger?

111

But we are referred to some Scriptures which we must notice. "As, it is written, There is none righteous, no, not one: there is none that understandeth; there is none that seeketh after God; they are all gone out of the way; they are together become I unprofitable; there is none that doeth good, no, not one. Their throat; is an open sepulcher; with their; tongues they have used deceit; the poison of asps is under their lips; whose mouth is full of cursing and bitterness; their feet are swift to shed blood; destruction and misery are in their ways, and the way of peace have they not known. There is no fear of God before their eyes." Rom. iii: 10-18. Now we only need to carefully read this quotation in order to see that it cannot apply to any inherited corruption of nature existing at birth, but to such as had corrupted themselves by wicked works. Infants are not expected to be righteous; for righteousness consists in doing right. Nor are they expected to understand—seek God—to have gone out of the way, or in the way—to have done good or evil. Their tongues have not used deceit, nor are their mouths full of cursing and bitterness, for they cannot talk at all. Their feet are not swift to shed blood, for they cannot hurt any one. And it will be borne in mind that the passage is relied upon to prove an inherited corruption of nature that comes into the world with us by ordinary generation. Paul makes this quotation from David, [Ps. 14] where he tells how they became corrupt. "They have done abominable works." hence their corruption came not by Adam's sin, but by their own wickedness.

Next we examine the language of David—Psalm li: 5. "Behold, I was shapen in iniquity, and in sin did my mother conceive me." Whatever may be the meaning of this passage it cannot be the imputation of sin to the child. In sin did my mother conceive me; that is, she acted wickedly when I was conceived. Were the wife to say, "in drunkenness my husband beat me" or the child that "in anger my father whipped me," surely no one would attribute drunkenness to the wife, or anger to the child; neither can they impute the sin of the mother to the child. We come now to notice the language of the prophet with regard to "Judah and Jerusalem." Is. i: 5, 6. "Why should ye be stricken any more? Ye will revolt more and more. The whole head is sick and the whole heart faint; from the sole of the foot even unto the head there is no soundness in it; but wounds and bruises and putrefying sores." This was not spoken with regard to any inherited defilement attaching to any one, but with regard to the Jews as a nation. As a nation they had become corrupt, not by inheritance, but by actual transgressions of their own. And God had scourged them, and afflicted them for their own wickedness, (not Adam's sin) until, as a nation, they were comparable to a man full of wounds and bruises and putrefying sores; and still they would not reform; hence by His Prophet, He asks, why should you be stricken any more? You will revolt more and more. As much as to say, I have sent fiery serpents to bite you, by which thousands have died—I have allowed you to go to war with the nations around you until multiplied thousands have been slain in battle; and in various ways I have chastened you as a father chasteneth his children; but all to no purpose. Why should I afflict you further? It will only make you worse and worse. "Your country is desolate; your cities are burned with fire; your land strangers devour it in your presence, and it is desolate as overthrown by strangers" — thus clearly speaking of national calamities that had befallen them as a nation. Not a word of allusion to Adam's sin or its consequences in the whole connection.

We are next referred to the language of David, Ps. lviii: 1-8, "Do ye indeed speak righteousness, O congregation? do ye judge uprightly O ye sons of men? Yea, in heart ye work wickedness; ye weigh the violence of your hands in the earth. The wicked are estranged from the womb: they go astray as soon as they are born, speaking lies. Their poison is like the poison of a serpent; they are like the deaf

113

adder that stoppeth her ear: which will not hearken to the voice of charmers, charming ever so wisely." Here, again, we need only read the passage carefully to see that it cannot apply to infants at birth. In heart they work wickedness: children at birth do not work wickedness.

The wicked are estranged from the womb: the theory says all are wicked and estranged. They go astray as soon as they are born; speaking lies: the theory says they are born astray. These persons spake lies: infants cannot speak at all. Shall we hear David's prayer for them? "Break their teeth O God, in their mouth." Do infants have teeth, in their mouth at birth? He continues, "Break out the great teeth of the young lions, O Lord. Let them melt away as waters which run continually: when he bendeth his bow to shoot his arrows, let them be as cut in pieces." Surely this was a singular prayer coming from David for the punishment and destruction of infants. This was simply strong language used to describe the Wickedness of the congregation and judge mentioned in the first verse.

We are next referred to the language of Paul to the Ephesians, chap, ii: 1-3, "And you hath he quickened who were dead in trespasses and sins." This does not fit the theory, for then it should read "dead in trespass or sin." But how came their death? "Wherein in time past ye walked according to the course of this world, according to the prince of the power of the air, the spirit that now worketh in the children of disobedience: among whom also we all had our conversation in times past in the lusts of our flesh, fulfilling the desires of the flesh and of the mind; and were by nature the children of wrath even as others." This shows us clearly how their nature became corrupt, which was by wicked works, or as Paul expresses it, fulfilling the desires of the flesh. Not a word about Adam's sin. They were dead in their own sins.

But we are referred to Rom. v :12. "Wherefore, as by one man sin entered into the world, and death by sin; and so death passed upon all men for that all have sinned." This passage does have reference to Adam's sin, and its consequences; but if falls very far short of proving that all men, or even Adam, became totally depraved. David sinned very grievously; yet his heart was perfect with the Lord his God (1 King. xv : 3.) in so much that he was a man after God's own heart. (1 Sam'l. xiii: 14. Acts xiii: 22.) If his sin left his heart perfect with God, how did a single sin of Adam totally deprave him and all his posterity. If a man were to commit a crime worthy of death, and were to have the sentence of death passed upon him, still, all this could not prove him totally depraved, opposed to all good and wholly inclined to all evil; he may have some good emotion yet. Here we might safely dismiss the passage having shown that it does not prove that for which it is introduced; but can we learn the meaning of it? The fact that almost every exponent of it has a theory of his own, derived from it, is quite enough to prove the import of it to be doubtful. A doubtful interpretation of an obscure passage must not come in contact with a plain passage about the meaning of which there can be no mistake. When the phrase "all have sinned" is interpreted to mean that the whole race of man sinned in Adam, it seems to us a plain contradiction of God's law which says, "The soul that sinneth it shall die. The son shall not bear the iniquity of the father, neither shall the father hear the iniquity of the son: the righteousness of the righteous shall be upon him, and the wickedness of the wicked shall be upon him." The theory says the children of Adam do bear his iniquity, and his wickedness is not only on him, but also on them. It is also antagonistic to John's definition of sin, that "it is the transgression of the law;" and also with the fact seen already that a transgression, or act (for sin is an act) of one man cannot be transmitted to, or become the act of another. We regard the passage as dearly metonymical. The consequences of Adam's sin being suffered by all, the sin is said to have been committed by all; the consequences being put for the act. The Apostle alludes to the sin of Adam, as a consequence of which all suffer death in accordance with the laws of their mortal nature inherited from Adam; they not having fruit from the tree of life with which to counter-act mortality as Adam had before he sinned; and thus "Death reigned from Adam to Moses, even over them that had not sinned after the similitude of Adam's transgres-sion." ver. 14.

It is some what strange to us that those who profess to disbelieve universalism can believe that the death here spo-ken of is spiritual death. If spiritual death passed upon all men because they all sinned in Adam, then universalism must be true; for the Apostle goes on to say, "If through the offence of one many be dead, much more the grace of God, and the gift by grace, which is by one man Jesus Christ hath abounded unto many." The grace of God and the gift by grace has abounded to just as many through Christ, the last Adam, as are dead by the offence of the first Adam. "Therefore, as by the offence of one, judgment came upon all men to condemnation, even so by the righteousness of one the free gift came upon all men unto justification of life." Verse 18. The same all who suffer by the offence of one, are made alive by the righteousness of another. This is not only the teaching of Paul here, but he communicates the same thought to his brethren at Corinth. The fifteenth chap-ter of his first letter to them is devoted to the resurrection of the dead; and in the twenty-second verse he has the follow-ing very significant language. "For as in Adam all die, even so in Christ shall all be made alive." As in Adam all die, not died back yonder in the garden; but die now, in Adam. And who dies in Adam? All men most certainly. Even so, in Christ shall the same all be made alive; the infant and the aged, the wicked and the just, all die and their "dust returns to the earth as it was;" but when the trump of God shall sound, they will be raised from the dead through Christ.

But every man in his own order: Christ the first fruits; afterward they that are Christ's at His coming." Ver. 23.

But we are sometimes told that if man is not guilty of Adam's sin, then Christ's mission and death were useless. Surely such persons have very narrow views of the subject. How shall we escape the punishment due us on account of our own sins? And how shall we be raised from the dead only through Christ? It is no where said in the word of the Lord, that Christ died to save man from Adam's sin; but we have abundant testimony proving that he came to save man from his own sins. Joseph was told by the Lord to call the infant Savior Jesus, because he should save his people from their sins, not Adam's sin. Peter commanded his hearers, when preaching from Solomon's porch "Repent ye therefore, and be converted, that your sins maybe blotted out." It was their sins which were to be blotted out, and not Adam's sin. God's promise, in the new covenant, to his people was, "And their sins and iniquities will I remember no more." The new covenant made no provision for Adam's sin, therefore if God ever remembered it against his people under this covenant, He is remembering it yet. Paul said to the Colossians, "You being dead in your sins and the uncircumcision of your flesh" They were not dead in Adam's sin, nor in the uncircumcision of his flesh. Under the Jewish law God made provisions for pardon of sins committed against it, and he mentions many sins for which offerings were to be made in a prescribed form; but he provided no remedy for Adam's sin, nor did he ever speak of it as chargeable to the Jews. Surely if God has Adam's sin in remembrance against Adam's posterity he would have mentioned it somewhere, or in some dispensation made provision for the pardon of it. Christ came, then, "Who his own self bear our sins in his own body on the tree," but he came not only that we might have pardon of our sins but, as we have already seen, that we may have a resurrection of the dead; hence the language of Paul, "If Christ be not raised your faith is vain; ye are yet in your sins. Then they also which are fallen asleep in Christ are perished." Surely these are objects sufficiently important to invoke the mission and sufferings of the Christ, the Son of God—salvation from sin, a resurrection from the grave and eternal life.

We come now to notice the practical bearing of the doctrine of total depravity, as an effect of Adam's sin, upon the reception of the Gospel as the power of God unto Salvation. The Presbyterian Confession of Faith tells us that "Man, by his fall into sin, hath wholly lost all ability of will to any spiritual good accompanying salvation. Man was not able, by his own strength, to convert himself or to prepare himself thereunto." Chap. 9, see. 3. Now if the man has lost all ability of will to any spiritual good, it follows that he cannot even will or desire his own salvation. What can he do, then? Just nothing at all! He is as passive as a block of marble in the hands of the sculptor. But "when God converts a sinner, and translates him into the state of grace, he freeth him from his natural bondage under sin, and by his grace alone enables him freely to will and to do that which is spiritually good." Ibid sec. 4. Thus, we see that this theory brings man into the world wholly defiled in all the faculties of soul and body, opposed to all good and wholly inclined to all evil, not even able to will any spiritual good accompanying salvation, until God converts and translates him into the state of grace, so as to free him from his natural bondage, and enable him freely to will and to do that which is spiritually good. Then, if God never converts him and he is finally lost, who is to blame for it? Surely not man, for he could not even will or desire his own salvation, or prepare himself thereunto. Why did Christ command that the Gospel be preached among all nations, and to every creature, promising salvation to those who would believe and obey it, when he must have known, if this theory be true, that they could neither believe nor obey it? nay, they could not even so much as will to desire their salvation, or any thing good connected therewith, to say nothing of doing anything to secure it. And why did he threaten them with damnation if they did not believe it? when, according to the theory, they have no more power to believe it than they have to make a world.

We insist that the doctrine is too monstrously absurd to be entertained by any one for a moment—antagonistic to the whole tenor of God's word and the spirit of the Christian religion—alike dishonoring to God and destructive to man. And when we remember that the world has been taught this doctrine for centuries, by the large majority of those who have spoken and written concerning it, we are made to wonder, not that infidelity is abroad in the land, but that there are not a hundred infidels where there is one. God never, at any time, commanded man to do that which he was unable to do and the very fact that he commands man to believe and obey him, is evidence, high as heaven, that he has the ability to do the things required of him. All things necessary for man's salvation and happiness, which he is unable to do for himself, God has done; or will do for him; but what he is able to do for himself, God requires of him, and will not do for him. These fundamental truths however, we must leave the reader to amplify for himself; we cannot pursue this branch of our subject further at present. Though we have not exhausted it, we fear we may exhaust his patience ere we get before him some remaining thoughts deemed important to our investigation.

If God charged Adam's posterity with the guilt of his sin, we wish to know when it was, or will be forgiven. Was it forgiven when Jesus made the atonement? If so, the whole theory of man's present guilt of that sin is destroyed, for he can not be guilty of a sin already pardoned. Is it pardoned when man is pardoned for his own sins? No, for the creed tells us that it remains through life in those who are regenerated and it also tells us that it is appointed unto all men once to die for that all have sinned. Surely, he would

119

not yet have to die: for a sin that had been pardoned. Is it forgiven at death? Where is the proof of it? And what are the conditions, if any, upon which it is to be done? Or, if unconditionally pardoned what are the means to accomplish it? Is it forgiven in the intermediate state between death and the judgment? If so why cannot all other sins be pardoned in that state? And if they can, why the necessity of having them pardoned in this life? Is it pardoned at the final judgment? so, then we will be judged according to the deeds done in Adam's body, and not every one according to the deeds done in his own body. Is it not pardoned at all? Then will the Christian be damned for the guilt of Adam's sin after having been pardoned for his own sins. If so, the sentence will not be "Depart from me ye workers of iniquity." but "Depart from me all ye that have washed your robes, and made them white in the blood of the Lamb. Though your sins have all been cancelled from the book of God's remembrance, in accordance with the provisions of the new covenant, and though your righteousness is as robes of linen, clean and white; there is one sin, which, though not committed by you, is imputed to, or charged against you, for which you must go with the devil that deceived you in Adam, into the lake of fire and brimstone, where the beast and the false prophet are, where you shall be tormented day and night forever and ever. Or if he does not go to hell on account of it, will he go to heaven with it still charged against him— with a nature totally depraved, wholly opposed to all good and inclined to all evil? We most confidently deny that any one of Adam's posterity ever has been, or will be sent to hell for Adam's sin. As we have stated more than once, all die as a consequence of it, and through Christ, will be raised from the dead. Those who are intelligent and therefore responsible, and who have heartily accepted and complied with the terms of pardon for their own sins, as offered them in the gospel through Christ, will be raised to the enjoyment of life eternal. Here they will gain even more in Christ than they lost in Adam. As saith the Poet:

"In him the tribes of Adam boast.
More blessings than their father lost."

They exchange not only temporal, for eternal life, but they exchange mortal, for immortal bodies, and for the first time will they have put on immortality. Having done the commandments they will have a right to the tree of life, and enter through the gates into the city. In these immortal and spiritual bodies they will not again be subject to temptation and sin. The devil, who seduced Adam will not be there; but they will have the society of God their Father, Jesus their elder brother and as saints of the most high they will join the angelic host in praising God and the Lamb for over and ever.

"There pain and sickness never come,
And grief no place obtains;
Health triumphs in immortal bloom,
And endless pleasure reigns
No cloud these blissful regions know.
For ever bright and fair!
For sin, the source of every woe.
Can never enter there.
There no alternate night is known.
Nor sun's faint sickly ray;
But glow from the sacred throne
Spreads over lasting day."

But what of the wicked? "As in Adam all die, even so in Christ shall all be made alive." The wicked die as a consequence of Adam's sin, without their volition or agency; so, without their volition or agency, they will be raised from death through the merits of the resurrection of Jesus, the Christ; but not to life eternal. "These shall go away into everlasting punishment: but the righteous into life eternal."

121

They will be judged, every man according to his works not Adam's works. They will be judged, not for his sin because they are not, never have been, nor can they ever be guilty of it, but for their own sins of which they are guilty. And having refused the terms of pardon offered them in the Gospel, by which they might have been pardoned, they will be condemned. "The fearful, and unbelieving, and the abominable, and murderers, and whoremongers, and sorcerers, and idolaters, and all liars, shall have their part in the lake which burneth with fire and brimstone." And how long will this awful inheritance be theirs? "They shall be tormented day and night forever and ever." Oh! friendly sinner, is this to be thy final doom?

> " *What could your redeemer do.*
> *More than he has done for you?*
> *To procure your peace with God,*
> *Could he more than shed his blood?*
> *After all this flow of love.*
> *All his drawings from above.*
> *Why will you your Lord deny?*
> *Why will you resolve to die?* "

But there is yet another class. Infants, idiots and other irresponsible persons die as a consequence of Adam's transgression; and will be raised from the dead by the same power and through the same means employed in the resurrection of others. We have seen, that sin is the violation of law; and as they have never been subject to any law requiring any obedience of them, it follows that they have violated no law, and are hence without sins of their own. And as Adam's sin was not committed by, and therefore never charged to them, there is no sin for which they need forgiveness, and therefore, for which they may be condemned to endless punishment. Jesus said, "Of such is the Kingdom of God;" and required others to be converted and become as they are in order to enter it; therefore, if their purity of heart and innocence of character were such as to constitute the standard of purity for those who would enter the Kingdom of God on earth, we think they will scarcely be refused admittance into Heaven by the same adorable Son of God who pronounced blessings on them here. In coming from the dead, however, they will exchange their natural, mortal bodies for spiritual, immortal bodies and will be thus prepared to enter

"Where the saints of all ages in harmony meet,
Their Savior and brethren transported to greet;
While the anthems of rapture unceasingly roll.
And the smile of the Lord is the feast of the soul."

11 GA vol.12, #3, 1-20-70, page 49

ESTABLISHMENT OF THE CHURCH

It has been abundantly shown, through the *Advocate* of last year, that God has an organized government on the earth. This government is variously called, in the New Testament, "The Kingdom of God," "the Kingdom of Heaven," "the Kingdom of God's dear Son," "Church of God," "the body of Christ," etc., etc.

As respects its laws, it is truly a kingdom, an absolute monarchy. All Its laws emanate from the king; and its subjects have no part in making them. There is no representative democracy connected with it, no council, convention, or Legislative assembly has power or authority to abolish, alter, or amend them. It is a kingdom, not a republic. As respects organization, it is called a body, of which Christ is the head, all Its subjects are members, and in which dwells the Spirit, by which it is vitalized or kept alive, and without which It would become a dead body. As respects relationship to the world, It Is fitly called a Church—"ecclesia," or called out of the world ; and is therefore not of the world. It was set up, established, organized, begun on the earth, In the city of Jerusalem, on the day of Pentecost, by the authority of the Lord Jesus Christ, under the immediate agency of the apostles, guided by the direct inspiration of the Holy Spirit. A brief examination of the teaching of the Scriptures on this subject is important to the development. of "the Gospel as the power of God unto salvation" and will repay the attentive.

That we may properly appreciate the importance of arriving at truth on this subject, it may not be amiss to state that there are several theories, differing from each other with regard to the time when this kingdom was set up; each one of which has its own doctrines growing out of its own theory. And if we are correct in the proposition stated as to time and place, it follows that all ties setting up the kingdom, organizing the body, or beginning the proclamation of the Gospel, and laying, first, the foundation of the Church at any other time, are not only wrong, but all doctrines growing out of such theories are false. And if we succeed in uprooting the trunk, all the branches drawing support from the parent trunk, fall with it. To be more specific: One theory begins the church in an eternal covenant, as its advocates call it, which is supposed to have been entered into between God and his Son before the foundation of the world was laid. It is ascertained that, in this covenant, the salvation of the elect was unconditionally secured; and the balance of the human race consigned to eternal misery. If God and his Son were the contracting parties to the covenant; and the final destiny of man the consideration about which the covenant was made, is it not passingly strange that the devil should be the largest beneficiary? He was not represented in the covenant at all, unless God represented him, or acted as his proxy. We are told that few go in at the strait gate, while the many go in at the wide gate that leadeth to destruction. If this be the result of such a covenant, why was

124

God so liberal to the devil, and so illiberal to his Son. But, we do not propose to discuss these theories here. We call the attention of the reader to them at the threshold of our investigation, for the purpose of awakening attention to the importance of arriving at the both of the promises. Passing from this theory, then, there is another which establishes the Kingdom or Church of God as the family of Abraham. The advocates of this theory insist that as infants were included in the provisions of the covenant made by God with Abraham, they are in the Church now, and hence comes the doctrine of infant church membership. They further assume that baptism came in the room of circumcision, and as infants were then circumcised, they must now be baptized; and thus, some of them think they have Divine authority for infant baptism.

Others set up the Kingdom in the days of John the Baptist; hence the name "Baptist Church;" etc. Thus, we see that the time when the Kingdom of God was set up on the earth is a most important matter; one that rightly understood would tend much to heal the wounds in the body, caused by the many unfortunate divisions among those professing to be the people of God.

It is said, "Behold, the days come, saith the Lord, when I will make a new covenant with the house of Israel and with the house of Judah; not according to the covenant that I made with their fathers in the day when I took them by the hand to lead them out of the land of Egypt; because they continued not in my covenant, and I regarded them not, saith the Lord." Heb. viii: 8, 9. Then we need not look to the covenant made at the time of the deliverance of God's people from Egyptian bondage, for the beginning of the covenant under which the Church of our day was established. It was to be a new covenant, and not according to that one. It was to be "a more excellent ministry," "a covenant which was established upon better promises." Verse 6. And wherein was it a better covenant? The old was "a figure for the time then present, in which were offered both gifts and sacrifices, that could not make him that did the service perfect as pertaining to the conscience; which stood only in meats and drinks, and divers washings and carnal ordinances, imposed on them until the time of reformation." Verse 9, 10. "But in those sacrifices there is a remembrance again made of sins every year; for it is not possible that the blood of bulls and of goats should take away sins." But, "in that he saith, a new covenant he hath made the first old. Now that which decayeth and waxeth old is ready to vanish away." This old covenant was ready to vanish away and give place to the new one. And what were to be its provisions? "This is the covenant that I will make with the house of Israel after those days, saith the Lord; I will put my laws in their mind, and write them in their hearts; and I will be to them a God, and they shall be to me a people; and they shall not teach every man his neighbor, and every man his brother, saying, know the Lord; for all shall know me, from the least to the greatest. For I will be merciful to their unrighteousness, and their sins and their iniquities will I remember no more." Ver 10-13. Under the old covenant sins were only pardoned a year at a time, and then were remembered again; but under the new and better covenant, God has promised to be merciful to their unrighteousness, and sins and iniquities once pardoned are to be remembered no more. All its subjects were to know the Lord, too. There are no infants among them.

But we did not come here to follow out the superior advantages of one, and the disadvantages of the other; but to learn, as we think we have, that we live, not under the same covenant that was made with the Jews, under which they offered sacrifices according to the law; but under a new covenant, superior in its provisions to the old. We have now arrived at the proper point to look for the beginning of this now and better order of things.

During the time the Jews were held captive by Nebu-chadnezzar, King of Babylon, God made known to him, in a dream—which was interpreted by Daniel, one of the Jewish captives—certain great national changes that were to take place, in which was foretold the destruction of his own government and three others which were to consecutively arise after it; and finally, the establishment of the Kingdom of God, which was never to be destroyed, but was to fill the whole earth and stand forever. As these kingdoms were to succeed each other in regular chronological order, we have only to follow them up, and see the rise and fall of each, noting carefully the dates as we proceed, in order to see when God established his Kingdom.

For a full account of this remarkable revelation from God, the reader is referred to the whole of the second chapter of Daniel. We have only room to transcribe the dream and the interpretation of it, contained in the 31st to the 45th inclusive.

"Thou, O king, sawest, and, behold, a great image, whose brightness was excellent, stood before thee; and the form thereof was terrible. This linage's head was of fine gold, his breast and his arms of silver, his belly and his thighs of brass, his legs of iron, his feet part or iron and part of clay. Thou sawest till that a stone was cut out without hands, which smote the image upon his feet, that were of iron and clay, and break them to pieces. Then was the iron, the clay, the brass, the silver and the gold broken to pieces together, and became like the chaff of the summer thresh-ing-floors; and the wind carried them away that no place was found for them: and the stone that smote the image be-came a great mountain, and filled the whole earth. This is the dream, and we will tell the interpretation thereof before the king. Thou, 0 king, art a king of kings; for the God of Heaven hath given thee a kingdom, power, and strength, and glory; and wheresoever the children of men dwell, the beasts of the field and the fowls of the Heaven hath he given into thine hand, and hath made thee ruler over them all. Thou art this head of gold. And "after thee shall arise another kingdom inferior to thee, and another third kingdom of brass, which shall bear rule over all the earth. And the fourth kingdom shall be strong as iron; forasmuch as iron breaketh in pieces and subdueth all things; and as iron that breaketh all these, shall it break in pieces and bruise. And whereas thou sawest the feet and toes part of potter's clay and part of iron; the kingdom shall be divided; but there shall be in it of the strength of the iron; forasmuch as thou sawest the iron mixed with the miry clay; and as the toes of the feet were part of iron and part of clay, so the kingdom shall be partly strong and partly broken. And whereas thou sawest iron mixed with the miry clay, they shall mingle themselves with the seed of men; but they shall not cleave one to another, even as iron is not mixed with clay. And in the days of these kings shall the God of Heaven set up a Kingdom which shall never be destroyed; and the Kingdom shall not be it to other people, but it shall break in pieces and consume all the kingdoms, and it shall stand forever. Forasmuch as thou sawest that the stone was cut out of the mountain without hands, and that it break in pieces the iron, the brass, the clay, the silver, and the gold; the great God hath made known to the king what shall come to pass hereafter: and the dream is certain, and the interpretation thereof sure."

Now it will be observed that the Lord here tells Nebuchadnezzar that he was the head of gold. This Kingdom embraced the countries of Chaldea, Assyria, Syria, Arabia, and Palestine, and ended with the death of Belshazzar, B. C. 538 years, when it was overthrown by Cyrus, King of Persia, and Darius. King of Media. These two kings were kinsmen; and after they had thus broken up the Chaldean or Babylonian empire, the government assumed the name of the Medo-Persian kingdom, and was represented by the breast and arms of the image, and was the second government in numerical or chronological order. It began, as we have seen, 538 B. C., and was overthrown by Alexander. (son of Philip,) King of Macedon, before Christ 331 years. But he died; B. C. 323 years, having reigned only a little more than seven years. But as the Macedonian Empire Is represented by the belly and thighs of the image, we must look for a division in it. Hence, after the death of Alexander, his government became divided among his generals. Cassander had Macedon and Greece; Lysimachus had Thrace, and those parts of Asia which lay on the Hellespont and Bosphorus. Ptolemy had Egypt, Lybia, Arabia, Palestine, and Syria. Seleucids had Babylon, Media, Persia, Susiana, Assyria, Bactria, Hyrcania, and all other provinces, even to the Ganges. Thus, this empire, founded on the ruins of the Medo-Persian, "had rule over all the earth." But as the thighs of brass in the image represent the divided state of the empire, the above four divisions are soon merged into two, those of the Lagida and Seleucide, reigning in Egypt and Syria. A distinguished historian says, "Their kingdom was no more a different kingdom than the parts differ from the whole. It was the same government still continued. They who governed were still Macedonians."

When did these thighs end? In the year B.C. 30, Octavius Caesar overturned the Lagidse and Egypt, one of the thighs, became a Roman province. Not many years from this, (we have forgotten the date, and have not the history by us just now to which to refer,) Pompey overthrew the Seluecide, dethroned Antiochus and Syria, the other thigh, became a Roman province. Thus, we find the Roman government succeeded the Macedonian, and is evidently the fourth kingdom represented by the feet and toes, of the image that stood before Nebuchadnezzar, composed of iron and clay.

Without going into a minute application of the Scriptures to each of these governments, it is sufficient to our present purpose to show, as we think we have done, that these governments did, in their order, overthrow and succeed each other. Then, as they are numbered first, second, third, and fourth, in the interpretation given by Daniel, it is certain that they, following in that numerical order; and each one consuming its predecessor, are the kingdoms indicated. And as they have all merged into the Roman government thirty years before the coming of Christ, it follows that some time after that period, and during the existence of the Roman government, we may look for the God of Heaven to set up a kingdom. We cannot go back behind the date of this dream to look for the kingdom, for it was to smite the image on its feet—that is, it was to be set up during the existence of, and come in contact with the government represented by the feet. And Daniel tells Nebuchadnezzar that the whole affair was designed to make "known to the king what shall come to pass hereafter"—not before the foundation of the world, or in the days of Abraham—but hereafter.

As this prophecy brings us down to within thirty years of the coming of Christ to establish the government—in the time of which the Kingdom of Heaven was to be set up—we may expect John, the harbinger of the Savior, soon to commence preaching about it. Accordingly Matthew says, "In those days came John the Baptist preaching in the wilderness of Judea, and saying, Repent ye, for the Kingdom of Heaven is at hand." Matt, iii: 1,2. Here we find John announcing the near approach of the Kingdom for the origin of which we have been looking. But we are sometimes told that John set up the Kingdom himself. Let us hear the Savior on this point. After John was cast into prison, and his labors were at an end, Jesus taught his disciples to pray as follows: "Our Father who art in Heaven, hallowed be thy name, thy Kingdom come," etc. Matt. Ch—9,10. Would Jesus have instructed his disciples to pray for the Kingdom to come if it had already come? It is true, many repeat this petition now who believe that the Kingdom has long since come; but surely such persons think little about what they are saying. Like the school-boy, they find it in their lesson, and must repeat It. We may pray for the Kingdom to be advanced in the earth, but cannot pray for it to come after it has come, any more than we may pray for God to send down the Spirit when it was sent from Heaven to the earth on the day of Pentecost, and has been here ever since. Once more: When John heard of Jesus, he sent to him to know if he were the Christ, or whether he should continue to look for another. After Jesus had answered and sent the messengers away, he said to those around him, "Verily, I say unto you, among them that are born of women, there hath not risen a greater than John the Baptist; notwithstanding, he that Is lcast in the Kingdom of Heaven is greater than he." Matt, xi: 11. Then, as he that was least in the Kingdom of Heaven was greater than John, it follows that he was not in it; and surely he did not set up the Kingdom and fail to enter it himself.

But we are not done with the Savior's teaching on this point yet. When he sent forth the twelve apostles under their restricted commission, he said for the Kingdom of Heaven is at hand." Matt, iii: 1,2. Here we find John announcing the near approach of the Kingdom for the origin of which we have been looking. But we are sometimes told that John set up the Kingdom himself. Let us hear the Savior on this point. After John was cast into prison, and his labors were at an end, Jesus taught his disciples to pray as follows: "Our Father who art in Heaven, hallowed be thy name, thy Kingdom come," etc. Matt. vi—9,10. Would Jesus have instructed his disciples to pray for the Kingdom to come if it had already come? It is true, many repeat this petition now who believe that the Kingdom has long since come; but surely such persons think little about what they are saying. Like the school-boy, they find it in their lesson, and must repeat It. We may pray for the Kingdom to be advanced in the earth; but cannot pray for it to come after It has come, any more than we may pray for God to send down the Spirit when it was sent from Heaven to the earth on the day of Pentecost, and has been here ever since. Once more: When John heard of Jesus, he sent to him to know if he were the Christ, or whether he should continue to look for another. After Jesus had answered and sent the messengers away, he said to those around him, "Verily, I say unto you, among them that are born of women, there hath not risen a greater than John the Baptist; notwithstanding, he that is least in the Kingdom of Heaven is greater than he." Matt, xi: 11. Then, as he that was least in the Kingdom of Heaven was greater than John, it follows that he was not in it; and surely he did not set up the Kingdom and fail to enter it himself.

It is worthy of remark that the language is verbatim the same used by John—"the Kingdom of Heaven is at hand." Matt, x: 7. When he sent out the seventy, he gave them, in substance, the same message— "the Kingdom of God is nigh unto you." Luke x: 10. Now it is very apparent that the object of all this teaching was to let the people know that the Kingdom was approaching, that they might be prepared for it- when it came. But when he came into the coasts of Caesarea Philippi, and learned, by inquiry, what was said of him—and Peter confessed him as "the Christ, the Son of the living God"—he said to Peter, "upon this rock I will build my church." Matt, xvi: 18. This language is too plain to admit of doubt. There would be no sense in saying, I will build my house in a certain place, if it had been built long years before; and there would have been just as little sense in the language used by the Savior if he had intended to teach that his Church or Kingdom had been built prior to that time. Then we must press our investigations still further—its erection is still later than the time he used this language-Six days before his transfiguration he said, "Verily I say unto you, that there be some of them that stand here, which shall not taste of death till they have seen the Kingdom of God come with power." Mark ix: 1. Here we not only find him teaching that the coming of Christ was yet future, but that it would come within the life of those then living. But still later, When Jesus instituted the supper, he said, "For I say unto you, I will not drink of the fruit of the vine until the Kingdom of God shall come." Luke xxii: 18. Thus we see that near the end of the Savior's journey on the earth, he still teaches the people to look ahead for the coming of the Kingdom; and we next propose to show that those to whom he spake so understood his teaching. "And as they heard these things, he added and spake a parable, because he was nigh to Jerusalem, and because they thought that the Kingdom of God should immediately appear." Luke xix: 11. Thus we see they understood it was yet future; but thought its approach nearer than it really was. Coming down now to the time of his death, "Joseph of Arimathea, an honorable counsellor, which also: waited for the Kingdom of God, came and went in boldly unto Pilate, and have the body of Jesus." Mark xv: 43; Luke xxiii: 51. Here was a man of capacity to understand the Savior's teaching, who waited for the Kingdom to come even when the Savior was dead.

Let us next examine a prediction made by the prophets: "And it shall come to pass in the last days that the mountain of the Lord's house shall be established; in the top of the mountains, and shall be exalted above the hills, and all nations shall flow unto it. And many people shall go and say, come ye, and let us go up to the mountain of the Lord, to the house of the God of Jacob; and he will teach us of his ways, and we will walk in his paths; for out of Zion shall go forth the law and the word of the Lord from Jerusalem." Isaiah ii: 2, 3. This very interesting prophecy was uttered by Micah, (iv: 1, 2,) in very nearly the same words, and gives us to know that the establishment of the mountain of the Lord's house was to take place in the last days and we can see no other last days that could have been intended, only the last days of the Jewish dispensation—the last days of that covenant which Paul tells us had waxed old and was ready to vanish away.

But we get another important item of information from this prophecy; and for the sake of it, we have delayed the introduction of the whole until the mind of the reader was prepared for it. The word of the Lord was to go forth from Jerusalem. Hence, when Jesus was instructing and preparing his apostles for the establishment of his Kingdom, he "said unto them, Thus, it is written, and thus it behooved Christ to suffer, and to rise from the dead the third day; and that repentance and remission of sins should be preached in his name among all nations, beginning at Jerusalem." Luke xxiv: 46, 47. Jerusalem is the place from which the word of the Lord was to go forth, and it consisted in preaching repentance and remission of sins among all nations and this was to begin there. Jerusalem is the place, beyond the possibility of doubt. But to establish a kingdom there; must be persons duly qualified for the work; hence, Jesus, at the beginning of his personal ministry, selected twelve and took them under his immediate care, and for three years and a half instructed them in the work they were to perform. Not only so, but he selected one of them to lead off as foreman in the opening of his Kingdom, and said to him, "Thou art Peter, and upon this rock I will build my Church, and the gates of hell shall not prevail against it; and I will give thee the keys of the Kingdom of Heaven; and whatsoever thou shalt bind on earth shall be bound in heaven; and whatsoever thou shalt loose on earth shall be loosed in Heaven." To Peter, then, was given the exalted privilege of first opening the Kingdom with power to bind and to loose on the earth, with the assurance that his acts would be recognized in Heaven. Notwithstanding, Peter had been the constant attendant upon the teaching of the Savior, this work was too important to be entrusted to unaided human frailty. Man is imperfect and forgetful. An important item of Instruction given by the Lord might be forgotten by Peter when the final destiny of the human race trembled in awful suspension upon his decision. Hence, says the Savior, "But the Comforter, which is the Holy Ghost, whom the Father will send in my name, he shall teach you all things and bring all things to your remembrance, whatsoever I have said unto you." John xiv: 26. Thus he is secured against the frailties and imperfection of human recollection; but operations are to begin at Jerusalem; therefore, he must go there and await the time appointed of the Father; hence Jesus says to him, with the other apostles, "Behold, I send the promise of my Father upon you; but tarry ye in the city of Jerusalem until ye be endued with power from on high." Luke xxiv:19. Jerusalem is the place you are to begin, Peter, therefore go there, and wait for the coronation of Jesus Christ as King of the Kingdom to be set up; then he will send you the promised aid from on high. Shall we go with him to the appointed place and wait the developments of the time, when Jesus is crowned King of kings and Lord of lords. Without a king, there cannot be a kingdom. "He led them out as far as Bethany, and he lifted up his hands and blessed them. And it came to pass while he blessed them, he was parted from them and carried up into Heaven." Luke xxiv: 50, 51. Angelic hosts escort him to the throne appointed of his Father. On nearing the portals of the Skies his attendants demand admittance, saying, "Lift up your heads, 0 ye gates, and be ye lifted up ye everlasting doors, and the King of glory shall come in. Before the porters of Heaven admit the parties demanding entrance, they ask, "Who is the King of glory?" The attendants answer, "The Lord, strong and mighty, the Lord, mighty in battle." And again, the demand is repeated, "Lift up your heads, 0 ye gates; even lift them up ye everlasting doors, and the King of glory shall come in." When the question again comes from within, "Who is the King of glory?" and the same announcement is made, "The Lord of hosts, he is the King of glory." Psalm xxiv. He is admitted, crowned King—angels, principalities and powers are made subject to him. The Holy Spirit is dispatched with the joyful tidings from Heaven to Jerusalem; "And they were all filled with the Holy Ghost, and began to speak with other tongues as the Spirit gave them utterance." And what did they say? Here is Peter, the proper person, at Jerusalem, the proper place, and Jesus, as King, is on his throne—surely all things are now ready. Among other things, he said, "Therefore being by the right hand of God exalted, and having received of the Father the promise of the Holy Ghost, he hath shed forth this which ye now see and hear; for David is not ascended into the heavens, but he saith himself, The Lord said unto my Lord, Sit thou on my right hand until I make thy foes thy footstool. Therefore, let all the house of Israel know assuredly that God hath made that same Jesus whom ye have crucified both Lord and Christ." Here for the first time, the grand fact announced to the denizens of earth that Jesus reigns in the Kingdom of Heaven.

Persons ask admittance. Peter uses the keys of the Kingdom. They enter and are added to them. Them, who? The disciples—the hundred and twenty. After this, the church being organized, the Lord added daily the saved to the church. Never before this do we read from the pages of inspiration that any were added to the Church. No such statement is made with reference to those baptized by John the Baptist; and why not? Simply for the very good reason that the Church did not then exist. If it had been then in existence it would have been a kingdom without a king, for Jesus was not then crowned king. The Holy Ghost was not then given, (John vii: 39,) because that Jesus was not yet glorified." Then it, the "body, which is the Church," (Col. i: 24,) had existed prior to the glorification of Jesus, and; descent of the Holy Spirit, it would have been a body without a spirit, and therefore a dead body, as the body without the spirit is dead." Jas. ii: 26. Again: He is the head of the body the Church." Col. i: 18. When did he become head of the body? "The eyes of your understanding being enlightened; that ye may know what is the hope of your calling, and what the riches of the glory of his inheritance in the saints, and what is the exceeding greatness of his power to usward who believe, according to the working of his mighty power, which he wrought in Christ when he raised him from the dead, and set him at his own right hand in Heavenly places, far above all principality, and power, and might, and dominion, and every name that is named, not only in this world but also in that which is to come: and hath put all things under his feet, and gave him to be the head over all things to the Church." Eph. i: 18-22. Then as he was never given to be the head of the Church until he was set at his Father's right hand, and obtained his exalted name, it follows that if the Church or body existed prior to that time it was body without head. And for the very same reason, if the Kingdom, Church or body was not then set up, Jesus was a king without a kingdom, and a head without a body, and the Spirit was upon the earth without a habitation or dwelling place.

One more point and we are done on this branch of the subject. When Peter was making his defense before his brethren for going down to the house of Cornelius, In speaking of the events that occurred there, he says: "And as I began to speak, the Holy Ghost fell on them, as on us at the beginning." Acts xi: 15. Here we have the very word beginning referring to the time when the Holy Ghost fell on the disciples on the day of Pentecost. The Holy Ghost fell on them on that day, and Peter refers to it as at the beginning. Beginning of what? Let him, who thinks the Kingdom or Church began some time prior to the day of Pentecost, answer.

In our next we have some things to present with regard to the unity and identity of the Church, after which we will endeavor to and the way into it

GA Vol. 9, #2/27/67, page 148

THE IDENTITY OF THE CHURCH

We have found that the church of God was organized in the city of Jerusalem on the day of Pentecost, and it is worthy of note that all the forms of speech used to indicate it are in the singular number, thus: Kingdom of Heaven, Kingdom of God. Church of God, The Body, etc., etc. Where the word "churches" occurs in the plural number it has reference to the congregations worshiping at particular places and not to the Kingdom, Body or Church, which has been the object of our search. Paul tells the Ephesian brethren, that "there is one body, and one Spirit, even as ye are called in one hope of your calling; one Lord, one faith, one baptism, one God and Father of all." Eph. iv: 4. The connection in which we here have the phrase, "one body," as clearly shows that there is but one body, as does the language "one God" show; that there is but one God. But, in Rom. xii: 4,5, we are told, that "As we have many members in one body, and all members have not the same office, so we, being many, are one body in Christ." And again: "But now are they many members, yet but one body." (1 Cor. x ii: 21). Language cannot more clearly indicate any thing than that Christ has but one organized body on the earth. What constitutes this one body? With reference to Christ, Paul says: "He that is head of the body, the church." Col. i: 18. And again, verse 24, he says: "Who now rejoice in my sufferings for you, and fill up that which is behind of the afflictions of Christ in my flesh for his body's sake, which is the church." Here we are expressly told that the body is the church. And observe how definite the language, The Church. Not a church, some church, or any church; but the Church. There being but one body, and that being the church, it follows that there is but one church. Now, in kindness, we may be plain and candid without being offensive, we would like to enquire how it now comes to pass that there is, a Catholic Church, an Episcopalian Church,

138

several kinds of Presbyterian Churches, several kinds of Methodist Churches, several kinds of Baptist Churches, each claiming Divine authority for Its existence, and acknowledging the Bible to be true? My dear friends, is there not something wrong along here? We hear Paul addressing "The Church of God at Corinth," but he never speaks to, or instructs, the Baptist Church, the Presbyterian Church, the Methodist Church, nor does he ever address any class of persons as a church at all only those who compose the one body or Kingdom, of which Christ is the head and King.

But we are told that all these sectarian organizations are branches of the one church or body of which Paul speaks. This makes the matter no better, but rather worse. Paul no where addresses the Baptist branch of the church, the Presbyterian branch of the church, or the Methodist branch of the church. In order to sensibly speak of the branches of the church, one of three figures must be before the mind, viz: a tree, with trunk and branches; a vine, with its stem and branches, or a stream, with its tributaries. A tree and its branches, a vine and its branches, are so nearly alike in their illustrative character that we may consider them together, and suppose them to represent the church. When did these branch organizations shoot forth? We do not know that we can correctly date the origin of all of them; nor is it necessary that we should go back to the birth of the Roman Catholic and Greek Churches, for those who advocate the branch church doctrine, do not admit these as sister branches with them. Then we cannot get one of these branches further back than the fifteenth century. Was the church without branches for the first fifteen hundred years of her existence, and did she bring no fruit during that time? Neither tree nor vine can maintain its life, and bring forth fruit without branches, yet if these organizations are the branches, the church was a branchless, fruitless, lifeless trunk until they came into being. Since then, in one-third of that time, it has shot forth a host of branches, and branches of branches; and branches of branches of branches, until they have become so thick that we are inclined to think the pruning hook is necessary. And each of these branches differ in constitution, character, and fruit from all the rest. Such a tree! Such a tree! What a monstrosity!!! A tree bearing apples, pears, peaches, apricots, quinces, plums, cherries, berries, nuts of all kinds, "hard shell and soft," melons, pumpkins, squashes, etc., etc., and yet all came from the same "incorruptible seed"—the word of God. Strange as such a sight would appear, it would take a tree with more different kinds of branches and fruits than we have mentioned to represent the Church of God if she has as many branch churches growing out of her as there are denominations claiming to be branches of her at present. But we may be told that this variety is produced by grafting. If so the grafting was not done by Paul, or in accordance with his formula. He speaks of branches that were "cut out of the olive-tree, which is wild by nature, and grafted, contrary to nature, into a good olive-tree." Rom. xi: 2-1. Naturally, branches bear fruit like that of the tree from whence they are taken; but Paul's grafts bore fruit, contrary to nature, like the natural branches of the tree into which his grafts were inserted—-they were taken from the world and were engrafted into the church, and whether they were Jews or Gentiles, Christianity, or pure and undefiled religion was the fruit. And, therefore, if these sectarian parties were grafted branches of the one Church of God, they would all partake of its "root and fatness," and there would be no difference in them or their fruit. One could not bear sprinkling as baptism; another pouring; another immersion; another all three; another one of them; another vicarious atonement, total depravity, abstract, spiritual operations, unconditional election and reprobation, and many other doctrines differing as widely as these do.

Once more: Men usually take branches for grafting from other trees than the one into which they are to be inserted.

It is true, Paul tells us that these natural branches, that were taken out because of unbelief, might be grafted in again if they abode not in unbelief; out when they were broken off, they were as foreign as the unnatural branches. Now, as the one Church of God is made up of these branch churches, where is the trunk into which they are grafted, and where is the tree from whence they were taken before grafting? Is this great tree representing the church all branches? And from what were the branches taken before grafting? These branches are churches and not individuals; then from whence came they? They were not taken from the Church of God, for there would not be any use in taking a branch from a tree and grafting it back into the same tree. Then from what tree or vine were they taken? Or, to speak without a figure, from what church did these branch churches come, before they became part and parcel of the church made up of them? It will not do to say they were taken from the world, for they came from there as individuals, not as organizations.

And if we look at it under the figure of a great stream and its branches or tributaries, the same difficulties are in the way. As all these organizations are branches, where is the main stream and from whence do they come? They come not from Christ, the fountain of living water, for all the branches making up a great stream come not from the same spring, for then they would not be branches at all. If they come not from the innumerable fountains of the human imagination, we know not whence their source. We prefer the pure, limpid stream of living water, of which he that drinks shall thirst no more; but have a well of water springing up in him unto eternal life.

But we do read of branches, and we will now try to find what a branch is. Jesus says: "I am the vine, ye are the branches." John xv: 5. Here Jesus speaks of his disciples as branches of him and in him. "Abide in me," says he, verse 4. Paul speaks of himself and brethren as having been "bap-

141

tized into Christ." Rom. vi:1. His baptism did not give him a literal entrance into Christ; but it gave him entrance into his body, or the body organized by his authority, by which a relationship was created like that of a vine and its branches, or his body and its members. The same writer tells us, 1 Cor. xii: 13, that "by one spirit are we all baptized into one body." Here Paul tells us, that by baptism we enter into the one body or church, and become members of it; and when speaking to the Romans, with regard to the same relationship, he says, by baptism we enter into Christ, and thus individual as such, become branches of him the true vine; but an organized church, or body of persons, as such, cannot be termed a branch of the one body or Church of God. Hence when asked, as we frequently are, to what branch of the Church we belong, we answer, that we claim to be a humble branch our self, but know nothing about belonging to branches.

Jesus, as King, has but one Kingdom— that as head, has but one body; his bridegroom, has but one bride, and is the author of but one church, and his people should be one people, and no divisions among them. But we have heard persons, preachers too, thank God that there are divisions, that the people may be without excuse. "Thank God," say they, "that there are so many different denominations, each holding a different; doctrine, that all can be suited. If our church doesn't suit you, in the multitude of others you can find one suited to your fancy." Such persons, to say the least; of it, have a different view of things to that entertained by the Savior, for he considered unity among his people as of the utmost importance, and prayed for it in his most solemn prayer to his Father. "Neither pray I for these alone, but for them also which shall believe on me through their word, that they all may be one, as thou, Father, art in me, and I in thee, that they also may be one in us: that the world may believe that thou hast sent me." John xvii: 20, 21. Thus, we see that Jesus considered divisions among those claiming to be his people; a most fruitful source of infidelity, and he was not mistaken. We verily believe divisions among those professing to be the people of God have made more infidels than all the writings of Voltaire, Paine, Gibbon, Hume and every other infidel that has ever wielded a pen on the earth. A celebrated Indian chief, when asked by a missionary what he thought of religion, said: 'Go home and agree among yourselves, and then come to me and I will consider the matter." Hence Paul, unlike those who love and create divisions, said: "I beseech you brethren, by the name of our Lord Jesus Christ, that you speak the same thing, and that there be no divisions among you." 1 Cor. 1:10. But we have been asked why the Lord's people are not one, if such be the Import of his prayer. It is said that his Father always heard him when he prayed; and not only heard him, but granted his petitions: why then are his people divided? The class of persons for whom he prayed are all one. He prayed for unity among those who believed on him through the records of his apostles he did not pray for such as might believe on him through the traditions of their fathers, or the teachings of men, as put forth in Disciplines, Confessions of Faith, Catechisms, etc., which might be taught them from childhood. These are the sources of much of the faith that is in the world, and such come not within the range of the prayer made by the Savior.

Not unfrequently do we hear persons say, when asked to obey the Gospel, that "There are so many denominations, differing from each other, that I know not which is the right one. They all teach different doctrine, "and if the trumpet give an uncertain sound who shall repair himself to battle." Truly this is a difficulty; but we propose to assist the reader in recognizing the one body or Church of God. And we think it has certain marks, features, and other means of recognition, which, if subjected to the criteria by which we try the identity of persons and things, will enable us to Identify the Church with great certainty.

143

If you were hunting for a man who was personally a stranger to you, whose name was Martin Luther, and you were to find a man named John Wesley, you would know at once that he was not the man for whom you were hunting; if you knew him to bear the diameter of an honest man, you would continue your search until you found a man wearing the name of the man you desired to see. Then, if you wish to find "The Church of God," 2 Cor. 1:1, and you find a church calling herself The Roman Catholic Church, The Episcopalian Church, The Baptist Church, The Presbyterian Church, The Methodist Church, or, in a word, any other unscriptural name, is it not enough to cause you to suspect that you have not found the true Church; and will you not continue your search a little farther? There are, doubtless, many good persons in each of these sectarian organizations; but this proves not that any one of them, or all of them together, is the Church or God. God had a people in Babylon; but he admonished them to come out of her, that they partake not of her sins, and receive not of her plagues. Rev. xvi: 4.

But we are told that there is nothing in names. Then why not as well expect salvation through one name as another? Peter says of Christ's name, "Neither Is their salvation in any other, for there is none other name under Heaven given among men whereby we must be saved." Acts iv:12. But if there is nothing in names we may as well expect salvation through the name of Beelzebub as through the name of the Lord. If there is nothing in these denominational names, why think so much of them as to prefer to wear them rather than the name that honors our head? Do they not tend to keep up divisions and strife among good people, and if there is nothing in them why not give them up?

The Church is said to be "The Bride, the Lamb's wife," Rev. xxi: 9, and as such she should wear the name of her bridegroom. "The head of the woman is the man, and hence she honors her head by wearing his name, and she dishonors her head when she refuses to wear his name and assumes another. Suppose a citizen of your neighborhood were to marry a wife and when she is called by his name, she refuses, saving, "There are so many branches of my husband's family that, for the sake of distinction, I prefer to be called by some other name, and thereupon assumes another, perhaps the name of some other man of her acquaintance. What would you think of her? How would you treat her if she were your wife? Would she not have dishonored you, as her husband; dishonored him whose name she wished to assume, and dishonored and disgraced herself and would you not regard her as unworthy to be your wife, or enjoy the privileges of your house? Would she not have placed a foul blot upon her character, that would render her unworthy; the confidence and respect of the virtuous and good of every age and clime; and would you not feel a little like telling her to go and live with him whose name she preferred to wear? What say you? Then if the wife of a citizen would so far dishonor her husband, and degrade and debase herself, by refusing to wear the name of her husband, will it be less dishonoring to Christ for his bride to refuse to wear and be called by his name; and will it be less a blight upon the character of his bride for her to assume other names than his? Will he own that organization as a bride, before his Father, in the great day of the marriage that has, and was, some other name than his? Will he say, "My wife hath made herself ready, and to her was granted that she should be arrayed in fine linen, clean and white; or the fine linen is the righteousness of saints." Rev. xix: 7,8. Is the assumption of other names than that of the husband the righteousness of the saints that is comparable to fine linen, clean and white, with which the Church is to be clad as a bride adorned for her husband when he comes to receive her?

By the way, what will our Baptist friends do for a name now? They adopted the official name of John the Baptist as their denominational name, and the Bible Union, to which, as a church, they are fully committed, wiped the word Baptist from the revised edition of the New Testament, giving us "Immerser" instead thereof; thus, John the Immerser. Will they keep pace with the translation, and adopt the name "Immerser" Church? This would be rather wanting in euphony, to say the least of it; but the word, Baptist, is not in the revised Scriptures put forth by the Union at all.

Another means of knowing persons and things is by their age. If you wish to find a man known to be forty years old and you meet a lad of ten or twenty years of age; or a man whose whitened locks, furrowed cheeks, and bowed frame betoken that the weight of many years is upon him, in either case, you will know that this is not the man you wished to see; and this assurance will be made doubly sure if he wears not the proper name. The Church of God has its age; and as the age of a man is reckoned from the time of his birth, so the age of the Church is computed from the time of its organization. We have seen that this took place on the first Pentecost after the crucifixion of the Messiah; any organization, therefore, which begins the Church at any other time, either before or since, is not the Church of God.

Again: The record says Jesus was born in Bethlehem of Judea, and had any one appeared at the time he did, claiming to be the Messiah, who was born any where else, he would have been known to be an imposter. We have seen that the Church of God was organized in Jerusalem, by organization, therefore, that began at any other place is not the Church of God.

Once more: The Church established in the city of Jerusalem on the day of Pentecost admitted persons to membership in a certain way, and it could be entered in no other way; an organization that admits members in a different way, cannot be the Church of God. This we will endeavor to find in our next.

GA vol 9, #13, 3-28-67, page 250

THE NEW BIRTH.

We have said that persons enter the Church of God in one way, and only one way. In this we are sustained by the positive statement of Jesus himself. In a conversation with Nicodemus on this subject, he said: "Except a man be born again, he cannot see the Kingdom of God." John 3. And in the 5th verse he said: "Except a man be born of water, and of the Spirit, he cannot enter into the Kingdom of God." By the phrase Kingdom of God here, is meant the Church of God, or system of government established by God's authority on the earth. To this, we believe all agree When we speak of entering the Kingdom of God, then, we do not mean Heaven, the holiest of all into which Jesus, our adorable High Priest, hath for us entered; but the Kingdom established on the earth on the day of Pentecost. Into this Kingdom or Church, he that is not born again, cannot enter. This Kingdom is a system of government, and those who enter it must be subjects of government, capable of understanding and obeying its laws. Infants, idiots and irresponsible persons are not such; it was not, therefore, established for them; and their salvation is not suspended upon an entrance into it. Jesus says: "Of such is the Kingdom of Heaven," that is, of such as they are not without being born again.

Having seen that a man must be born again in order to enter the Kingdom, and that it is the office of the new birth to introduce the party born, into the Kingdom, it follows that a more important subject never engaged the attention of man; we will, therefore, examine the subject carefully and somewhat in detail, in the hope that the class of persons for whom we write may ponder well what may be said, and that some good may be done in the name of Jesus.

The first thing necessary to a birth is parentage. There must be a father and a mother, or then; can be nothing born. Who, then, are our spiritual parents? Paul salutes the brethren to whom he wrote, thus: "Grace to you, and peace from God our Father, and the Lord Jesus Christ." Rom. i: 7 ; 1 Cor. i: 3; 2 Cor. i: 2; Eph.i: 2; Phil, i: 2; Col. i: 2; 1 Thes. i: 1; 2 Thes. 1:2; 1 Tim. i: 2; Philemon 3. In all these places Paul in the same words recognizes God as our Father, and Jesus taught his disciples to address God, in prayer, as "Our Father who art in Heaven." Mat. vi: 9. John says: "Behold what manner of love the Father hath bestowed upon us, that we should he called the sons of God." And again: "Beloved, now are we the sons of God." 1 John iii: 1-2. Other Scriptures might be quoted, but these are sufficient to identify our Father with great clearness. Paul, in his allegory with reference to the two covenants, tells us that "Jerusalem which is above is free, which is the mother of us all." Gal. iv: 26. This Heavenly Jerusalem, answering in the allegory, to the free woman is our spiritual mother, hence to the 31st verse he says: "So then, brethren, we are not children of the bond-woman, but of the free." But before there can be a spiritual birth the subject must have been begotten. Man is begotten of his father and born of his mother, both physically and spiritually. He is not born of the father at all; either at the same time when born of the mother, or at any other time. The father may have been in his grave long ere the child is born; and how he is born of his father when born of his mother is not very clear to us. John says: "Whosoever believeth that Jesus Is the Christ, is begotten of God: and every one that loveth him that begat, loveth him also that is begotten of him." 1 John v : 1. Also, verse 18th, it is said: We know that whosoever is begotten of God, sinneth not; but he that is begotten of God, keepeth himself." In keeping with the Bible Union and Bro. Anderson's translations, we have exchanged the word born for begotten, in each of the verses quoted; and we venture to state further, that there is not a place in the New Testament where the words "born of God" occurs, that a faithful translation would not render "begotten of God." In no place will the

Spirit's teaching, faithfully translated, represent us as born of God; born of our Father. Such a thought is absurd in the very nature of things.

But to proceed. Peter speaks of his brethren as "being born [begotten] again, not of corruptible seed, but of incorruptible, by the word of God, which liveth and abideth forever." Here we learn that the word of God is the spiritual seed with which persons are spiritually begotten. And in order that we may be begotten of this incorruptible seed, our Father has ordained that human agents shall preach it to the world. Hence, in this sense, Paul calls Timothy and Titus his sons in the common faith; and also to the Corinthians he said: "In Christ Jesus I have begotten you through the Gospel." 1Cor. iv: 15. Then when Paul preached the word of God, Gospel or incorruptible seed to the Corinthians, and they believed and received it, they were begotten of God, and Paul speaks of them as having been begotten by him through the Gospel, because he was the person through whom God made known the Gospel to them. The Gospel is the power of God unto salvation only to those who believe it; but "How shall they believe in him of whom they have not heard? and how shall they hear without a preacher?" Rom. x: 14. So then "It pleased God by the foolishness of preaching to save them that believe." 1 Cor. i: 21. Then when a man believes the Gospel, is he not born again? "Devils believe and tremble." Jas. vi: 19. They also acknowledge Jesus as the Son of God. (Mark iii: 2) Were they born again? "Among the chief rulers also many believed on him; but because of the Pharisees they did not confess him, lest they should be put out of the synagogue: for they loved the praise of men more than the praise of God." John xi: 32-3. There are now many such as these chief rulers were then; are they born again? If a man be born again when he first believed the Gospel, where is he begotten, and where are the elements of birth, water and spirit, of which Jesus said he should be born? John says Je-

149

sus "Came unto his own, and his own received him not; but to as many as received him to them gave he power to become the sons of God, even to them that believe on his name." John i: 11-12. Jesus came to his own country, and his own people (the Jews) did not receive him or believe on him, but to as many of them as did receive him by believing on his name, he gave the power or privilege of becoming sons of God. Believing on his name, then, did not make them sons, but prepared them to become sons. When a man believes the Gospel, and with meekness receives it into a good and honest heart, he is then begotten of God, and is prepared to be born. The vital principle is then implanted in the heart; but he is no more born again at that time than he was physically born the moment he was conceived. As it is not the office of a birth to give life, but to bring the subject to the enjoyment of life previously possessed in a different state, so without being begotten by the Father through the Gospel, and thus having the principle of life implanted in the heart, the subject born would be dead when born, if it were possible for him to be born at all. When he is spiritually begotten, he may avail himself of the means of God's appointment for a birth and be born in the Kingdom, or he may refuse them as he may elect. In this particular, there is no analogy between a physical and a spiritual birth. In the former we have no agency in being begotten or born, nor is either, in the least, under our control; in the latter both are, to a considerable extent, under the control of the subject. He may (as many do) refuse to hear the Gospel at all, or he may refuse to believe it after he has heard it, if he believes it not his doom was pronounced by Jesus when he said: "he that believeth not shall be damned." He may also refuse to obey it after he has believed it; if so, he "believes in vain," and his faith is dead, not having been made perfect by obedience.

Faith causes us to love and fear God and desire to do His will; it also causes us to hate sin because it is contrary to his will; hence, Peter, in speaking of the conversion of the Gentiles, said that God "That no difference between us and them, purifying their hearts by faith." Acts xv: 9. This, the effect of faith, is what is called a change of heart, and must precede the new birth. A change of heart is one thing—the new birth a different thing. The conversion of Saul of Tarsus will make apparent the truth of this position. While he was "yet breathing out threatening and slaughter against the disciples of the Lord, went unto the high priest, and desired of him letters to Damascus to the synagogues, that if he found any of this way, whether they were men or women, he might bring them bound unto Jerusalem. And as he journeyed, he came near Damascus: and suddenly there shined round about him a light from Heaven: and he fell to the earth, and heard a voice saying unto him, Saul, Saul, why persecutest thou me? And he said, Who art thou, Lord? And the Lord said, I am Jesus whom thou persecutest" Acts ix: 1 to 5. It will be seen that Saul set out on his journey with his heart filled with bitterness toward the disciples, and thought he was doing right to persecute and punish them. Jesus convinced him by a miracle, that he was what he professed to be. Saul's faith is changed from believing that Jesus was an imposter to the belief of the truth, that he was the Son of God. This change in his faith produced a corresponding change in his heart, and he abandoned his errand of persecution and is willing to become a disciple himself, he is now begotten of God, but is he born again yet? If this is the birth, when and where was he begotten, and where are the elements of birth with which he had then come in contact? Three days hence he was born of water and of the Spirit in obedience to a Divine command given him by Ananias, "Arise, and be baptized, and wash away thy sins, calling on the name of the Lord." Acts xxii: 16. His heart was changed by the way, but he was born again three days afterward.

Faith produces repentance and repentance changes the practice of the subject —causes him to cease doing evil and commence doing right, but he is not born again yet. His heart may be as submissive to God's will as it can ever get to be; yes, he may be a worshiper of God to the best of his knowledge, and still not be born again. The new birth does not consist in a reformation of life. An examination of the character of Cornelius will give proof of this. "There was a certain man in Caesarea, called Cornelius, a Centurion of the band called the Italian band, a devout man, and one that feared God with all his house, which gave much alms to the people, and prayed to God always. He saw in a vision evidently, about the ninth hour of the day, an angel of God coming in to him, and saying unto him, Cornelius. And when he looked on him. he was afraid, and said, What is it, Lord? And he said unto him, Thy prayers and thine alms are come up for a memorial before God." Acts x: 1 to 4. Here was a devoted, charitable, praying and God-fearing man, quite as good as the best of our day, as far as reformation of life can make them good, and yet he was not born again. But, says an objector, "He was born again for he saw an angel that told him so." Not exactly: he did see and converse with an angel that told him his prayers and alms were come up for a memorial before God, and he told him more than this, "Send men to Joppa, and call for Simon, whose sir name is Peter, who shall tell thee words, whereby thou and all thy house shall be saved." Acts xi: 13-14. Was he born again and still unsaved? The promise "Shall be saved," clearly shows that he was then unsaved; and not only so, but he was to hear words of Peter by which he was to be saved. Was he saved by the words before he heard them? If so, why did not the angel shape the language thus: "Who shall tell thee words by which you are, or have been saved." If he was at that time born again, it follows that there is no salvation in being born again, for it is as clear as language can make any thing, that he was not then

saved in the Gospel sense of that word. If he was born
again when the angel appeared to him, he was born again
without ever having heard the Gospel, and, therefore, without Gospel faith. Peter, in alluding to this very matter, said
that "God made choice among us, that the Gentiles, by my
mouth, should hear the word of the Gospel, and believe."
Acts xv: 7. Then Cornelius had neither heard the Gospel
nor believed it until Peter preached it to him, and surely a
cause must be desperate that could assume that he was born
again prior to that time. Then as his conduct was as good
before birth as after it, it follows that the birth did not consist in a reformation of life in his case.

But the impatient reader is ready to conclude that we are
preparing to say that baptism is the new birth. Be not deceived. Baptism is not the new birth, or any part of it. Baptism is a means of birth, but not the birth itself. Is the womb
of a mother the birth of her offspring? Baptism is the means
which God has given our spiritual mother with which to
make increase of her family. A birth contemplates a change
of state; a transition or passing from one state to another. A
change of state, then, is the thought conveyed by the language born again, and we have the same thought presented
by Paul, in his epistles, by other figures, varied to suit the
circumstances under which he wrote. He expresses it by the
figure of marriage, Rom. vii: 11; by the figure of grafting,
Rom. xi, by the figure of adoption, Rom. viii: 15, Gal. iv: 5,
and by the figure of translation from one government to
another. Col. i: 13. If an individual be married to Christ, his
state is changed, he is born again. If he be taken from the
wild olive tree and grafted into the tame olive tree, or from
the world and grafted into Christ, the true vine, his state is
changed, he is born again. If he be taken as a child of one
family and adopted into another, the family of God, his
state is changed, he is born again. If he renounces his alle-
giance to one government, the Devil's, and be legally translated into another, the Kingdom of God's dear Son, his state

is changed, he is born again. We might amplify each of these figures of speech and show the correctness of the position assumed; but our space will only allow us to use a single one of the illustrations given.

A gentleman visits and seeks the hand of a lady under unfavorable circumstances, and is rejected. There may be a single cause or many causes co-operating to produce his rejection. She may be unfavorably impressed with his character, or she may worship at the shrine of another whose heart she hopes to win, or both causes may co-operate in producing his rejection. Circumstances change, however, and she finds her first suitor an unworthy man, and she becomes disgusted with him; meanwhile she learns more of the character of the man she rejected, and finds him chaste in his conversation, courteous, polite and accomplished in his manners—that a social, warm and undissembling heart controls him—that he has a mind well stored with valuable information—that he has descended from a good family, and above all, that he is possessed of inexhaustible wealth. A knowledge of these facts changes her heart, and she now admires and loves the man she once rejected. She receives him gladly, and is willing to become the sharer of his prosperity or adversity through life, but she is not yet his wife. Though her heart is changed, her state is not—she was in the single or unmarried state at first and is so yet. The parents may consent, the license be secured, the proper officer be present for the solemnization of the nuptials, the supper prepared and the wedding furnished with guests, and still she is not married, and were the process here arrested, she would not be entitled to the privileges of his house, to wear his name, or inherit his estate. When she is married and her state legally changed, then, and not till then, is she entitled to all these privileges growing out of her new relation. Now for the application. The Gospel is preached to the sinner— he is in love with the transient pleasures afforded in the service of the Devil. The carpenter's son, born in Bethlehem and cradled in a manger, has no charms for him. By-and- by he finds that the pleasures of sin are deceptive, and that the Devil, in whose service he delighted, has nothing with which to reward him but misery and woe—meanwhile he learns more of him who proposes to save all who will come to God by him. He finds him so chaste in conversation that guile is not found in his mouth; so amiable in disposition that when he is reviled he reviles not again, and yet so powerful that the furious winds and boisterous waves are calm at his bidding, the grave yields up the dead to live again, and devils tremble at his word, the waters of the sea are firm as a pavement beneath his majestic tread, God is his Father, and he the only Son and heir to all things—he is the chief among ten thousand and altogether lovely. With a faith like this he cannot fail to feel grieved that he ever loved the Devil or his service, because he is the enemy of him he now loves supremely. Surely his heart is now changed; is he born again? If so, there is no fitness in the figure, for he is not married yet. Though his heart is changed his state is not; and if he stops at this point he can no more claim the Christian name and character than can the unmarried woman claim the name and patrimony of him to whom she is espoused. But it is insisted that this change of heart is the new birth, and strange enough, too, the same persons insist that can have no change of heart, and deny the importance of it, when in reality we have their new birth in our change of heart. We insist that we must not only love our betrothed, but we must be married to the bridegroom according to law, before we can claim the privileges of his bride, he will not permit us to live with him in adultery if we were so disposed. A change of heart, then, is not a change of state; it must precede the new birth, but it is not the new birth.

The language "born again," was unique when used by Christ to Nicodemus. No inspired man had used such language before; is there any reason for Its use then? The Jews believed that Jesus had come to re-establish the Kingdom of David and literally sit on his throne on the earth; hence, when he entered Jerusalem on one occasion, "They that went before, and they that followed, cried, saying, Hosanna: Blessed is he that cometh in the name of the Lord. Blessed be the Kingdom of our Father David, that cometh in the name of the Lord." Mark ix: 9-10. And even his apostles did not fully understand the nature of his Kingdom until after they received the Holy Spirit on the day of Pentecost, and was by it guided into all truth. "When they therefore were come together, they asked of him, saying, Lord wilt thou at this time restore again the Kingdom to Israel." Acts i: 16. It is not unreasonable that Nicodemus had the same mistaken views of the Kingdom, and he knew well that he was born into that Kingdom, and had a right to citizenship in it by virtue of Abrahamic parentage; and being "A ruler of the Jews." "A master of Israel," he may have expected to be entitled to an office in Christ's Kingdom on that account. Jesus corrects this mistake by telling him, how that the Kingdom of God was not to be entered in that way, but as a birth of the flesh gave him entrance into that, he must be born again to enter this. There is much speculation about the import of this language; but as Jesus attempted to explain the matter to Nicodemus, and then asked, "Art thou a master of Israel and knoweth not these things?" we are encouraged to approach the examination of the subject in the belief that he intended to be understood, and as "A teacher come from God," he was competent to make clear what he attempted to explain. Let us then look up the language in which the conversation is recorded, and see whether or not we may understand it. "There was a man of the Pharisees named Nicodemus, a ruler of the Jews." So, reads the first verse, and from it we learn that at one time in the world's history there lived a man whose name was Nicodemus—that he belonged to the sect, of the Jews' religion, called the Pharisees, and that he was a distinguished personage or ruler among the Jews. 2nd verse, "The same [Nicodemus] came to Jesus by night, [not in day light] and said unto him, Rabbi, we know that thou art a teacher come from God: for no man can do these miracles that thou doest, except God be with him." Here we are convinced that Nicodemus was convinced by the miracles Jesus did that he was really a teacher; come from God. This is all plain, let us try again. 3rd verse, "Jesus answered and said unto him, Verily, verily, I say unto thee, except a man be born again, he cannot see the Kingdom of God." Here we learn, not how a man may be born again, but the indispensable necessity of being born again in order to see or enjoy the privileges and blessings of the Kingdom of God. 4th verse, "Nicodemus saith unto him, "How can a man be born when he is old? can he enter the second into his mother's womb, and be born?" Here we find that Nicodemus knew nothing of but one birth, and that was a birth of the flesh, and that he could not understand how a man. when old, could be born in this way, he, therefore, asks an explanation, how can a man be born when he is old? Jesus attempts to tell him how it can be, hence the 5th verse. "Jesus answered, born of water, and of the Spirit, he cannot enter into the Kingdom of God." Here we learn that the elements of birth are water and Spirit, and that a man must be born of both to be born again, not born of water and begotten by the Spirit, as some translations would indicate, but he must be born of both to be born at all. How is he born of water and of the Spirit? One answers that he must get religion in the altar, grove or elsewhere, and being then baptized with the Spirit, he is born of the Spirit, and after a time he is baptized of water and is then born of water. Well, this theory makes baptism in water indispensable to entering the Kingdom. Will they think of this? It also makes two births where there should be but one. The language is born again, not again and again or twice more; once at the altar and once at the creek. This is not all; the order is transposed.

157

Jesus said," Born of water and of the Spirit;" this theory says, Born of the Spirit and of water. It is out of joint at every angle. Another theory says, born of water when we are born into the world, and born of the Spirit when we "get religion." This will provoke a smile on the face of many, but it is taught by men of lofty pretensions. This makes the answer of Jesus wholly inapplicable to the question asked. he was not asked how a man was born into the world in infancy, but "How can a man be born again he is old? The answer was not that you have once been born of water and must be born again of the Spirit; but you must be born again; how? of water and of the Spirit.

But our question is yet unanswered, how is a man born of water and of the Spirit? He is born of water as taught by the Spirit. Shall we illustrate? Suppose a man born of water according to the teaching of John Wesley; he is in that sense born of water and Wesley. Is he born of water according to the teaching of the Spirit? then he is in that sense born of water and of the Spirit. To be, if possible, more plain: To be born contemplates a delivery, a coming forth from one state to another; then were we to immerse a man in water without faith, repentance or anything else (as we are often accused of doing) when he is delivered from the water, he would be born of water, but not of water and of the Spirit, because the process was not in accordance with the teaching of the Spirit; and it is equally clear that if born of water as taught by the Spirit, he is born of water and of the Spirit. But we are told that the word water, in the sentence, water and of the Spirit, does not mean water, and one quibbler will say it means grace, another that it means Spirit, and a third will say that he does not know what it means; but it cannot mean water, for then he must be baptized, or into the Kingdom of God he cannot go, and his theory tells him baptism is a non-essential. So, the word of the Lord is made to bend to suit the theory instead of giving shape to the theory. But we are told that the Greek particle, Kai, here rendered and, is sometimes rendered "even," and that this sentence should read thus, "Except a man be born of water, even of the Spirit, &c." It is true that the word is sometimes so rendered, but can it be rendered "even" in this connection? And, is the primary meaning of the word, and the rules of translation give preference to the primary meaning, unless the sense requires its removal. Does the sense require that and should give place to even in the sentence before us? Theories may require such a change, but the sense does not either require or allow it. The word water has no qualifying term, and wherever we find water, whether in the Jordan or elsewhere, we have the proper element; but not so of the Spirit. It is made definite, the Spirit, not spirit, a spirit, some spirit, or any spirit, but the Spirit. Born of water and of the Spirit —immersed in and born of water according to the teaching of the Spirit—how perfect the sense? But another tells us that the word water is exegetical of the word Spirit, hence to be born of water and of the Spirit is to be born of the Spirit like an overflow of water. Who ever saw an exegesis given in advance of the word explained. We feel ashamed that it is necessary to notice such quibbles as these. Suppose a man, living at the time the Savior was on the earth, who had witnessed the many immersions performed in those days, had heard Jesus say: "Except a man be born of water and of the Spirit, he cannot enter into the Kingdom of God," and he had no theory or prepossessions to give shape to his conclusions; but had to form them only by the language used, would he conclude that the word water meant grace, spirit or anything else but water? Would he not more likely conclude, with Wesley, Clark and others, that it had reference to water baptism. Is there a man out of the lunatic asylum who can believe that any one of these quibbles would ever have been thought of had it not been necessary to devise some means to save some theory from being destroyed by the obvious meaning of the Savior's language?

159

There were two questions asked by Nicodemus, in the fourth verse; the first, How can a man be born when he is old? Jesus answered, as we have seen, in the 5th verse. The second question, Can he enter the second time into his mother's womb and be born? shows that he had entirely mistaken the kind of birth required. This mistake Jesus corrects in the 6th verse by saying: "That which is born of the flesh is flesh; and that which is born of the Spirit is spirit. As much as to say to him, "You are thinking of a birth of the flesh, and a second birth of this character would indeed be impossible, but I am speaking of a moral transition of the spiritual or inner man. The man born again is the same physical man that he was before; but the temper and disposition of the inner man are not like they were before. "That which is born of the Spirit is spirit; marvel not that I said unto thee, ye must be born again." Seeing your difficulty grows out of a failure to recognize the existence of an invisible or "inner man," Eph. iii: 10, dwelling in "our earthly house of this tabernacle," 2 Cor. v:l,. and which is the subject of the change produced by the new birth, I will use an illustration which will make plain the fact just stated that, That which is born of the Spirit is spirit, hence the fifth verse, "The wind bloweth where it listeth, and thou hearest the sound thereof, but canst not tell whence it cometh; and whither it goeth; so is every one that is born of the Spirit." The mist and fog that men have thrown around this verse envelop it in darkness thick as that with which God cursed the land of Egypt. And we are of the opinion that most of it has grown out of a failure to keep before the mind the difficulty under which Nicodemus was laboring, for the removal of which Jesus introduced the illustration, and failing to get the point in the comparison at the right place. We once listened to a very eloquent man, through a labored effort to explain the new birth, at the close of which he said that this verse was designed to teach us that the new birth is incomprehensible to all finite minds.

Others can see that it teaches the doctrine of abstract and mysterious spiritual operations—others say that as the wind blows down a large oak, and leaves others standing around it, so the Spirit is partial in its operations, converting one or two out of the many who were with him or them at the mourner's bench. Jesus did not say, So, is the Spirit, or so is the operation of the Spirit—no such comparison was made or intended. Others say that the language was addressed to Nicodemus, and is not applicable to us at all, because we can tell where the wind comes from and where it goes to "he bringeth the wind out of his treasures." Psalm cxxxv: 7. " Who hath gathered the wind in his fist." Prov. xxx : 4. And what is gained by these quotations? Where are God's treasures from whence the wind comes? and where are his fists in which it is gathered? But suppose we can tell where the wind comes from and goes to, what light has been thrown on the new birth by the discovery? We confess our self unable to see any at all. If we go back to the fourth verse and see the difficulty on the mind of Nicodemus to be a second birth of the flesh; then come to the correction given to this mistake in the sixth verse, "That which is born of the Spirit is spirit;" and then regard the eighth verse as an illustration used to illustrate the existence of an invisible principle or spiritual man which is changed by the new birth, then, it seems to us there need be no difficulty in understanding the matter. We have seen several translations of this verse, six of which we have before us at this writing; one, each, by Bros. Campbell, Anderson, Fanning and Lard, one by the Bible Union, and one in the common version, and it is worthy of note, that whether the Greek *pneuma* rendered wind or spirit, the illustrative qualities of the figure are still the same, they are both invisible, recognized by sound and not by sight, "So is every one that is born of the Spirit," it being spirit that is so born.

While the Kingdom was yet in prospect, Jesus taught the people by parables and figures, but after its establishment figures gave place to facts, commands and promises. Jesus commissioned his apostles to preach the Gospel to every creature, promising salvation to those who would believe and obey it. He also promised them the Holy Spirit to guide them into all truth, and enable them to unerringly perform the work he had assigned them. When it came they began to preach as it inspired them—persons were cut to the heart and made to cry out, "Men and brethren, what shall we do?" Peter did not tell them to be born again, because the time for figures had past; he, therefore, told them to "Repent, and be baptized every one of them in the name of Jesus Christ, for the remission of sins." Acts ii: 38. Thus he told them plainly, without a figure, to do that which would translate them into the Kingdom of God's dear Son, and produce that change of state indicated by the figurative language of Jesus as used in the conversation with Nicodemus when he said: "Except a man be born of water, and of the Spirit, he cannot enter into the Kingdom of God." When Peter thus addressed them, "They that gladly received his word were baptized, and the same day there were added unto them about three thousand souls." Now are they born again? Surely, they are. When were they born again? Just when they did what Peter commanded them to do. Then if they were born again when they were baptized in the name of Jesus Christ, for the remission of sins, will you not be born again when you do as they did, and if it took this to introduce them into the Kingdom of God then, will anything less do you now? More anon.

GA vol. 9, #17, 4-25-67, page 221

REPENTANCE

Dear Alien: This is the last day of the year 1867; and while the earth is carpeted with snow and ice, and the fierce north wind still drives the falling sleet against the window glass by my side, my shattered lungs admonish me to keep within my room; may I not relieve the tedium of confinement in jotting down a few thoughts for your consideration.

Another year of our short lives, with its cares, anxieties, troubles, pain, sorrows, joys, responsibilities, privileges and blessings has past, forever past. We are one year's Journey nearer the grave, the cold charnel house of death; yea, and one year's journey nearer the great day of judgment than we were one year ago. Oh, the solemn thought, we can not change the record we have made! It may be read by ourselves and our friends while memory may serve to call up its events before us, and yes, it, perchance, may be read by Him who shall sit upon the great white throne when from his face the Earth and the Heaven shall have fled away; but we can not change it if we would. Is it just such a record as we should have made. If not, we can not live over again the precious hours of the past or re-embrace the opportunities we have had. Have we, then, improved all the opportunities for doing good, and avoided all the temptations to evil that have come in our way. If not, though, we cannot undo the past, may we not profit by the lives of experience it contains? True, the children of God have privileges which, as yet, are not yours. If they see where they might have done good and have not; when they have done things they should not; where they might have been more spiritually minded, more humble before God and devoted to Him than they have been, It is their privilege to confess their wrongs and ask their Heavenly Father to forgive the past, and sustain and aid them in the future. To assist you in putting yourselves in position to make these gracious privileges yours, is the object for which we write. While you cannot substitute a new record for the one you have made, God has promised that, on certain conditions he would forgive the wrongs it contains. "Blessed are they that do his commandments that they may have right to the tree of life, and may enter in through the gates into the city; for without are dogs, and sorcerers, and whoremongers, and murderers, and idolaters, and whosoever loveth and believeth a lie. I, Jesus have sent mine angel to testify unto you these things." Rev. 22:14, 15, 16:

In our previous articles we found what faith was, how it came and what it did. Among the first results of faith we found a change of heart produced; and we found what this was, and its office in the plan of salvation. Thus, we arrived at a proper stand-point from which to consider the subject of Repentance and to it we invite your attention for the present.

We find that the word "Repent" occurs in our common English Bible forty-two times, Repented thirty times, Repentance twenty-six times, Repenteth five times and Repentest, Repenting and Repentings one time each; in all one hundred and seven times. Repent, is used with reference to God sixteen times and with reference to man twenty-six times. It is used to indicate sorrow eleven times, a change of mind fourteen times, and includes the idea of a change or reformation of life eighteen times. Repented Is used with reference to God thirteen times and with reference to man seventeen times. It is used to indicate sorrow twelve times, a change of mind eight times, and includes a change of life ten times. Repentance is used with reference to God twice, and with reference to man twenty-four times. It is used to indicate sorrow twice, a change of mind once, and extends to reformation of life twenty-three times. Repenteth is used with reference to God three times, and with reference to man twice. Twice it Indicates sorrow, once a change of mind, and twice includes a change or reformation of life. Repenting and Repentest, are each used once with reference to God to indicate a change of mind. Repentings is once used with reference to God to indicate Sorrow. With reference to God the word is sometimes used in a negative sense, as "God is not a man that he should repent." Num. 23: 19. "The Lord hath sworn and will not repent." Psalm

110: 4. Heb. 7: 21. Sometimes it is used, with reference to God, affirmatively, as "It repented the Lord that he had made man on the earth." And again, "It repenteth me that I have made them." 'Gen. 6:6 and 7. At other times it is used with reference to God (conditionally) as "If that nation against whom I have pronounced turn from their evil, I will repent of the evil I thought to do unto them, if it do evil in my sight that it obey not my voice then I will repent of the good wherewith I said I would benefit them." Jer. 18: 8, 10. Again, it is sometimes used in petition to God, and "Turn from thy fierce wrath, and repent of this evil against thy people." Ex. 32: 12. In all the forms in which the word is used, it refers to God thirty-seven times and with reference to man sixty-nine times. It is used to indicate sorrow or re- gret twenty-eight times, a change of mind twenty-five times, and a change of mind resulting in change or refor- mation of life fifty-three times. When used with reference to God it is always used to indicate sorrow, regret, change of mind or purpose; and never extends to reformation, in the current use of that term. Much caution is necessary in an example notion of this term as applied to Jehovah. When used with reference to God it is often used in accommoda- tion to the use made of the word in its application to men. It is used to indicate a change in the mind or purpose of God when really there is no such change. For example, when God, through Jonah, said to the Ninevites: "Yet forty days and Nineveh shall be overthrown," they turned from their evil works and it is said, that "God repented of the evil that he had said that he would add unto them; and he did it not." Jonah 3:10. Here the word is used indicating a change in the mind or purpose of God.; but was there really such a change; or is this an accommodated use of the term? To simplify the thought, we will illustrate a circumstance common to the practice of medicine. The physician visits his patient and finds him with a high fever and all, its at- tendant symptoms. He bleeds him copiously and prescribes relaxants. The next day he visits him again and finds that the febrile excitement is gone and a complete state of collapse has taken its place. The hot skin of yesterday is today cold and clammy. The full and bounding pulse of yesterday is to-day thready and flickering. What is to be done now? Will the physician repeat the blood-letting and relaxants of yesterday? No, any old woman would have more sense than to do so. He will now prescribe stimulants and tonics. But why will he not repeat the prescription of the day before? Has his mind changed? He, he would have prescribed the same yesterday that he did to-day had the condition of his patient been then as now. His purpose was, all the time, to cure his patient, but without any change of mind he changed his prescription to suit the changed condition of his patient. So, when God failed to visit the threatened punishment upon the Ninevites it was not because his mind had changed, but because they had changed-turned from the wickedness for which he threatened to punish them.

When used in the New Testament as a command to the Alien in order to remission of sins, it always indicates such a change of mind as produces a change or reformation of life, under circumstances warranting the conclusion that sorrow for the past would or had preceded it. When so used, it is invariably derived from *metaswio*, and, when used to indicate sorrow or regret, it is invariably from *metasvslomai,* a different word though improperly rendered the same in English. A striking illustration of this difference in the import of the word repent, when derived from these different Greek words, will be found in 2 Cor. 7: 8, 9,10. "For though I made you sorry with a letter I do not repent [regret] though I did repent: (*inetemelomen*, regret) For I perceive that the same epistle hath made you sorry, though it were but for a season. Now I rejoice, not that ye were made sorry, but that ye sorrowed to repentance [meta-oolan, reformation] for ye were made sorry after a godly manner that ye might, receive damage by as in nothing; for

godly sorrow worketh repentance [*motanoian*, refor-
mation], to salvation not to be repented [*metsmeletou*, regretted.] Barely nothing could be more apparent than the
difference in the use which Paul here makes of these two
Greek words though both rendered repent in our common
translation. Now we wish to state that the words "Repentance" in the common version, Luke 24: 47; "Repent" Acts
2:38, and 3:49, are from the word *metanoio* and not from
metamelomai. Many seem to understand by these words
(Repentance in the Commission and Repent as emanating
from Peter; to mean nothing more than sorrow for their past
sins. If this were the measure of their import it seems to us
that it would be fully embraced in our idea of a change of
heart. It is difficult to understand how the heart may be
changed from a love of sin to the love of God without sorrow for the sins committed. When the Jews at Jerusalem,
on the day of Pentecost, heard Peter's preaching and by it
were convinced that they had truly crucified and slain the
son of God they were pierced in their hearts and cried out,
"men and brethren what shall we do?" Acts 2: 37. Can we
conclude that the hearts of those who asked this soul-
stirring question were not filled with sorrow for the sins
from which they desired salvation? Yet they were required
to "repent and be baptized." Surely then this command was
extended to indicate something more than sorrow for their
sins for this they had done before they were commanded to
repent. But it may be said that the sorrow they had was not
godly sorrow, and this is the reason why it was not repentance. It was the product of their faith: and their faith was
produced by Peter's preaching, and it was dictated by the
Holy Spirit sent that day from Heaven by him who sat at
God's right hand. If this was not godly sorrow then there
can be no such thing connected with conversion. But is
godly sorrow repentance? Paul did not so think. He says:
"Now I rejoice, not that ye were made sorry but that ye sorrowed to repentance for ye were made sorry after a godly

manner that ye might receive damage by us in nothing. For godly sorrow worketh repentance onto salvation not to be repented of; but the sorrow of the world worketh death." 2 Cor. 7: 9,10. Here we learn that godly sorrow precedes repentance but is not repentance. Godly sorrow is produced by respect for God and his violated law, and produces a reformation or change of life while the sorrow of the world may be produced by the fact that the party has been detected in crime—is subjected to the frowns of men, or the punishment inflicted by human laws per chance because his schemes have proven unprofitable and have resulted in loss to him. Such is the sorrow of the world, and makes no man better, but ends in death. The repentance contemplated is the commission and required by Peter of those to whom he spake, began where they gladly received his words, with a fixed purpose to reform their lives in accordance therewith; and it was preceded by deep sorrow-for the wrongs they had done.

But we have a definition of repentance given us in the words of inspiration that will make the matter, if possible, more plain. Jesus, on one occasion, said: "The men of Nineveh shall rise in judgment with this generation and shall condemn it, because they repented at the preaching of Jonas; and behold a greater than Jonas is here." Mat.12: 41. Jesus here says that the men of Nineveh repented at the preaching of Jonas, if, therefore, we can learn what the Ninevites did, we can, thence, learn what Jesus meant by repentance. Let us hear the record: "And God saw their works that they turned from their evil way; and God repented of the evil that he had said that he would do unto them; and he did it not." Jonah 3: 10. Then the turning, of the Ninevites, from their evil ways constituted their repentance, after deep sorrow for what they had done.

We have taken this view of the subject not unaware of the fact that great and good him have taught to the contrary. And in view of the fact, too, that others from whom we do not essentially differ have been unfortunate to the use of the terms employed by them. In the **Christian System**, pg. 255 it is said: "Genuine repentance does not always issue in reformation of life." Had the author said that genuine sorrow does not always issue in repentance or reformation of life, it would have been more consonant with the sentence immediately following viz: "Judas was sorrowful even unto death but could not reform." On page 259, the same work has the following: "Repentance is not reformation but is necessary to it." Had he said sorrow is not reformation but is necessary to it" the thought would have been more tangible to as sorrow must precede repentance which begins in a fixed determination to reform the life. This determination must be such a one as will lead the party to a reparation of injuries done to others, as far as may be in his power to make restitution. In vain may any one tell me that he repents slandering me while he refuses to correct his false statements concerning me; or that he repents stealing my horse while he continues to ride him without my consent. A circumstance recorded on page 256 **Ch. Syst.**, which, whether real or imaginary, so aptly illustrates our view of this subject that we feel constrained to transcribe it. "Peccator wounded the reputation of his neighbor, Hermis, and on another occasion defrauded him of ten pounds. Some of the neighborhood were apprized that he had done both. Peccator was converted under the preaching of Panlinus, and, on giving in a relation of his sorrow for his sins spoke of the depth of his convictions, and of his abhorrence of his transgressions. He was received into the congregation, and sat down with the faithful to commemorate the great sin-offering. Hermis and his neighbors were witnesses of all this. They saw that Peccator was penitent, and much reformed in his behavior; but they could not believe him sincere, because he had made no restitution. They regarded him either as a hypocrite or self-deceived because, having it in his power, he repaid not the ten pounds, nor once contradicted the slanders he had propagated. Peccator, however, felt little enjoyment in his profession, and soon fell back into his former habits. He became again penitent, and, on examining the grounds of his falling off; discovered that he had never cordially turned away from his sins. Overwhelmed in sorrow for the past, he resolved on giving himself up to the Lord; and, reflecting on his past life, set about the work of reformation in earnest. He called on Hermis, paid him his ten pounds, and the interest for every day he had kept it back, went to all the persons to whom he had slandered him, told them what injustice he had done him, and begged them, if they had told it to any other persons, to contradict it. Several other persons whom he had wronged in his dealings with them he also visited; and fully redressed all these wrongs against his neighbors. He also confessed them to the Lord, and asked him to forgive him. Peccator was then restored to the Church; and, better still, he enjoyed a peace of mind, and confidence in God, which was a continual feast. His example, moreover, did more to enlarge the congregation at the Cross roads than did the preaching of Panlinus in a whole year. This was unequivocally, sincere repentance."

Dr. Adam Clark, in his commentary on Genesis, says: "No man should expect mercy at the hand of God, who, having wronged his neighbor, refuses, when he has it in his power, to make restitution. Were he to weep tears of blood, both the justice and mercy of God would shut out his prayer, if he make not his neighbor amend for the injury he has done him."

On this subject, it may be well to introduce a quotation from the Jewish law found in Num. vi 6-8. "When a man or a woman shall commit any sin that men commit, or do a trespass against the Lord, and that person be guilty; then they shall confess their sin which they have done: and he shall recompense his trespass with the principal thereof, and add unto it the fifth part thereof, and give it unto him against whom he hath trespassed. But if the man have no kinsman to recompense the trespass unto, let the trespass be recompensed unto the Lord, even to the priest." Now it will be seen that during the existence of this law a trespass against a man was regarded as a trespass against God who gave the Law, forbidding the trespass, And it was not only necessary to recompense to the party aggrieved, but he was required to add a fifth to it and if he could not find the party to whom recompense was due, he should make it to his kindred if he had any; and, if there were none, then it was required to be made to the Lord through the priest. There was no escape from making restitution. Indeed, it is difficult to conceive it possible for the heart of a man to be subjugated, wholly, to the Will of the Lord; and he not feel a desire to restore anything unjustly taken from any one. If his pretensions be real he will make restitution if in his power to do so. Tell me not to the contrary. We do not say that all this must be consummated before remission of sins and adoption into the family of God can take place; but we do insist that the disposition or purpose of heart must be present before the party is in a fit frame of mind to farther obey God in anything. And if the purpose thus formed is abandoned and not carried out, "It had been better for them not to have known the way of righteousness, than after they have known it to turn from the holy commandment delivered unto them." II Pet. i: 21. Zacchaeus said: "I have taken anything from any man-by false accusation, I restore him four-fold. And Jesus said, this day is salvation come to this house." Luke xix : 8, 9. Thus the principle of restitution met the approval of Jesus himself even to the extent of four-fold. Once more: Jesus once said to a distinguished lawyer "Thou shalt love thy neighbor as thyself." Matt. xxi: 39. If we do this will we not do by our neighbor as we do by ourselves? As in the golden precept that crowned the rich casket of jewels contained in the sermon on the mount it is said: "whatsoever ye would that men should do to you,

171

do ye; even so to them." Mat. vii: 12. Do we desire that others withhold from us that which they have wrongfully taken from us? Or do we not rather desire them to restore to us that which is our own? If so, are we not bound to make that restitution to others, which, under like circumstances, we would have them make to us. True, this is a straight and narrow path and few there are who walk therein; but it is nevertheless "The law and the prophet." ibid. See also Levit.vi: 1-7.

A few thoughts as to the order or place of repentance, and we lay down our pen for the present. From the fact that repentance is mentioned before faith in a few passages of Scripture, many have concluded that men must repent before they have or exercise faith. We will very briefly examine those Scriptures that we may see whether or not they certainly teach the doctrine in question.

"Now after that John was put in prison, Jesus came into Galilee preaching the Gospel of the Kingdom of God, and saying, the time is fulfilled, and the Kingdom of God is at hand: repent ye, and believe the Gospel." Mark: 14, 15. These persons were not required to believe the same Gospel that was to be preached to every creature, but simply the glad tidings that, the Kingdom of God was at hand. This was the Gospel Jesus preached to them. They had previous faith in God and toward him their repentance was directed. Paul preached to the Ephesians "Repentance toward God and faith in the Lord Jesus Christ." Acts xx: 21. Their repentance was toward God in whom they believed before the Messiahship of Jesus Christ was proclaimed to them. There is still another passage worthy of notice in this connection: "John came to you in the way of righteousness and you believed him not; but the publicans and harlots believed him; and you, when you had seen it; repented not afterwards that you might believe him." Mat. xxii: 32. Here repentance not only preceded faith but was in order to faith; but is from the original word *melomelomai*, indicating regret and not reformation. It was the pride of the self-righteous Pharisees that kept them from believing the proofs and accepting the ministry of John. When they saw the publicans and harlots acting more consistently in submitting to his teaching, as they believed in God by whom John was sent, they should have regretted that these outcasts outstepped them in obedience to the servant of the God in whom they believed; and had they been filled with such regret it would have prepared them for faith in the glad tidings proclaimed by John.

Having seen that the strongest proof relied on does not support the theory, may it not be well to see whether the interpretation given to these Scriptures by the advocates of the theory, be not contradicted by other Scriptures, the import of which we cannot mistake, Paul says: "Whatsoever is not of faith is sin." If repentance precedes faith it cannot be of faith and therefore is sin. See Rom. xiv: 23; "Without faith it is impossible to please Him for he that cometh to God must believe that he is and that he is a rewarder of them that diligently seek him." Heb. xi: 6. If repentance precedes faith it is without faith; and cannot be pleasing to God. Surely, there must be error in the theory. Finally: The advocates of this doctrine associate repentance with prayer, generally, at the mourner's bench. Now if these prayers, connected with repentance, are before faith, they are therefore, not in faith. James says: "Let him ask in faith nothing wavering, for he that wavereth is like a wave or the sea driven with the wind and tossed; let not that man think that he shall receive anything of the Lord." Jas. 1: 6, 7. Will God hear and answer these prayers made in connection with repentance before faith?

Perhaps it would be well to examine the history of a few actual cases of repentance, and see whether it preceded or succeeded faith. We have seen that Jesus, himself, said that the Ninevites repented at the preaching of Jonah; let us see whether or not faith in Jonah's preaching preceded their repentance. We will begin with Jonah. And Jonah began to enter into the city a day's journey, and he cried, and said, "yet forty days, and Nineveh shall be overthrown." Here is the preaching, what was the first effect of it "So the people believed God." Now bore their faith the first thing. What next? They "Proclaimed a fast and put on sack cloth from the greatest of them even to the least of them, for word came unto the King of Nineveh, and he arose from his throne, and he laid his robe from him, and covered him with; sack cloth, and put on ashes. And he caused it to be proclaimed and published through Nineveh by the decree of the King and his nobles let neither man nor beast, herd nor flock taste anything; let them not feed, nor drink water; but let man and beast be covered with sack-cloth and cry mightily unto God; yea, let them turn every one from his evil way and from the violence that is in their hands. Who can tell if God will turn and repent, and turn away from his fierce anger that we perish not. And, God saw their works that they turned from their evil ways. Here is their repentance. Who cannot see the order of events? First, Jonah preached the message God gave him to say to them; second, "The people believed God." Third, "They turned from their evil way." On the day of Pentecost the order was similar. Peter preached, they heard, believed, were cut to the heart, asked what to do, were commanded to repent and be baptized. In the narrative already twice quoted from Paul, II Cor. vii: 8-10, Paul wrote them a letter, they believed it, were made sorry by it. They sorrowed in a Godly manner and their Godly sorrow, worked repentance.

It will be admitted that repentance is produced in some way by something— that it is the effect of some cause. If it precedes faith, faith cannot be the cause of it; then we would like to know what does produce it. Do you admit that a belief with all the heart in God, Heaven, Hell, Jesus, Apostles, Prophets, and all things written and spoken by inspiration, precedes and causes repentance? Then will you please give as a minute description of the faith that follows repentance; what it is, and how it comes? We acknowledge the want of light along-here. We are not very well prepared to understand how we are to repent for transgressing the laws of a King in whom we have no faith. The doctrine seems not only contrary to the order of the Bible; but at war with every principle of reason and common sense.

In our next we will examine the "Confession."

8 GA vol10, #3, 1-16-68, page 63

THE CONFESSION

As myself and brethren are the only people with whom we are acquainted, who teach that God requires an acknowledged alien to confess his faith in the Divine character and mission of His Son, it may be well for us, at this stage of our investigation, to examine the Divine Volume, and see whether or not as have Divine authority for requiring it of him. Paul says, "All Scripture is given by inspiration of God, and is profitable for doctrine, for reproof, for correction, for instruction in righteousness, that the man of God may be perfect, thoroughly furnished unto all good works." 2 Tim. iii: 16,17. If the confession is to be required of the alien by the Son of God, It is certainly a good work, and if a good work, the man of God is, by the Scriptures, thoroughly furnished unto it—if he is not, therein, thoroughly furnished to it, it follows that it is not a good work, and should be abandoned.

In the 37th verse of the 8th chapter of Acts we have the following words: "And Philip said, if thou believest with all thy heart thou mayest and he answered and said, "I believe that Jesus Christ is the Son of God." While this verse is regarded as genuine, the question of authority for the confession is not debatable at all. Here is a plain, unmistakable precedent that we dare not ignore. Our practice must conform to it, or we must remove it from the Divine Volume. The limits of this article will not allow us to enter upon an extensive examination of the claims of this verse, nor have the means afforded us been such as to enable us to decide the matter, even to our own satisfaction. While they have been such as to cast suspicion upon the verse, we are not quite sure that there is, at this day, a possibility of knowing, with certainty, whether it be genuine or spurious. This narrative, (the Acts) like all the other books the New Testament, was, at first, a separate manuscript, and circulated by being copied by uninspired men. These copies were again copied, and copies of copies were copied, how far from the original we have not the means of knowing. The first copy taken was, in all probability, imperfect, as it is very difficult to copy any thing without imperfections. And these imperfections must have increased as the copies were more remote from the original, because each copy must contain the errors of the one from which it was taken, with the chance of incorporating others. As the only sure method of correcting these errors was to compare copies with the original, when it wore out, we see not how further corrections could have been made without risk. That the original, and all copies taken directly from it, have long since been worn out is next to certain; how then are the claims of the verse in question to be settled were it wanting in all the manuscript copies of the first thousand years, and only found in such as are of modern date, this would be a circumstance well calculated to cast suspicion upon it; but Dr. Becket tells us that this interpolation was known to Irenaeus as early as the year 170. Then it was bound to have been in copies taken at or before that period. It is fair to presume that the original, and all the first copies were circulated among, and read, and handled by thousands of persons, and were, most likely, worn out before that time, so that we are not sure that, even, Irenaeus had the privilege of comparing such copies as he saw with the original, so as to be assured that it was spurious.

Tregellus tells as that this verse "Was inserted by Erasmus, as being supposed to have been incorrectly omitted. From his edition this and similar passages have been perpetuated, just as if they were undoubtedly genuine." Are we to understand by this that the interpolation began with Erasmus.

If so, how could Irenaeus have known of it so early as A. D. 170? twelve hundred years before the time Erasmus lived?

The circumstance that casts the darkest shade upon the purity of the verse is the fact that the most profound critics, whose opportunities have been best for examining the subject, and whose peculiar labors called them directly into its examination, have decided against it. Tregellus tells us that "No part of this verse is recognized in critical texts." While the copy of the New Testament, put forth by the American Bible Union, relates the verse, the translators have appended a foot note, saying "It is wanting in the best authorities." As it was their object to give the English reader a pure version of the mind of the Spirit, we see not why they retained the verse at all, if satisfied that it was spurious. Anderson has excluded the verse from his translation, and many other men of great research have pronounced it an interpolation. But we think attacks upon a verse that has had a place in the Bible, according to the testimony of its opposers, since the year 170, nearly seventeen hundred years, should be very cautiously made, lest, unfortunately, we shake the confidence of the uninformed in the whole Bible. Now, we wish to call attention to what we think is plain to the most ordinary mind, that there is evidently a blank in the narrative without the 37th verse. We will quote from Anderson's Translation of the New Testament in which the verse is omitted.

"And as they went along the road they came to some water, and the Eunuch said, See here is water; what hinders me from being immersed ? And he commanded the chariot to stand still, and they both went down into the water both Philip and the Eunuch, and he immersed him." Now, please observe that when they came to water the Eunuch asked a question saying, "See, here is water; what hinders me from being immersed?" and to this important question his inspired instructor makes no answer whatever! None!! He knew that Jesus, in the very commission that authorized the act about to be performed, said, "He that believeth and is baptized shall be saved." Mark xvi: 16, and when asked what kindred baptism, he made no answer at all; but, acting upon the presumption that the Eunuch believed, proceeded to baptize him without asking whether he did believe or not! Why did the Eunuch command the chariot to stand still, until he knew whether or not Philip would baptize him? Are we to believe that Philip said nothing in answer to the question, and yet the Eunuch commanded the chariot to be still—that they both got out of it, and went down into the water his silence? Is there not a perceivable blank which the sense requires to be filled with just such language as we find in the 37th verse and are we prepared to believe that Luke, as a faithful historian, omitted so important a part of the conversation? We cannot pursue the subject further. We dismiss it with the remark that whether the verse be real or spurious, it is fairly deducible from the connection, and the confession can be just supplied by other Scriptures, the Divine authenticity of which will not be called in question.

Upon the banks of Jordan, in the presence of the multitude that waited on the ministry of John, God bore witness to the Divine character and mission of his Son, saying, "This is my beloved Son, in whom I am well pleased." Matt iii: 17. Upon the truth of the grand proposition that Jesus is the Christ, the Son of God, rests the salvation of the world, and in it is centered all the hopes which mortals can have that reach beyond the grave. It underlies the whole scheme of man's redemption; for if he be not the Son of God he was an imposter, the Bible is a fable, and no man was, or is under any obligations to believe in or obey him. On the contrary, if this is true, his pretensions are real, his claims are just, and every man who professes to believe it, puts himself under obligations to accept the terms he imposes. Hence, Jesus said, "Whosoever, therefore, shall confess me before men, him will I confess also before my Father which is in Heaven; but whosoever shall deny me before men, him will I also deny before my Father which is in Heaven." Here he gives us plainly to know the importance of confessing him before men; but how did they confess him? When the parents of the blind man, whose eyes were opened by Jesus, were questioned, they feared the people, for "The Jews had agreed already that if any man did confess that he was the Christ he should be put out of the synagogue." John ix: 22. Then to confess him was to confess that he was the Christ, and to deny him was to deny that he was the Christ. Of course, some were making this confession, and others denying it, or the Jews would not have made such an agreement concerning those who did make it These sayings among the people may have given rise to the question Jesus asked his Disciples, saying, "Whom do men say that I, the Son of man, am?" Matt, xvi: 13. In answer to this question, the Disciples gave some of the opinions which the people expressed concerning him, when he put the question directly to them, saying, "Whom say ye that I am?" And Simon Peter answered and said, "Thou art the Christ, the Son of the living God." Matt, xvi: 15, 16. Here the same grand truth is confessed by Peter, and Jesus assures him that on it his Church is to be built as much as to say, "All my claims upon the world rest upon this truth which you have now confessed, not because you have confessed it, but because it is true. You could not have known

179

it, but my Father, at my baptism, and also through the mighty works I have done in His name, in your presence, has revealed it to you. All who confess it put themselves under obligations, thereby, to accept the terms and oblige as I impose as much as if God, who sent me, did himself impose them; hence I will make this truth the foundation of my Church." By making this confession, the party puts himself under obligations to observe all the ordinances emanating from Jesus as head of the Church built upon the truth confessed. Hence, says John, "Whosoever shall confess that Jesus is the Son of God, God dwelleth in him and he in God." 1 John iv: 15, And again, "Who is he that overcometh the world, but he that believeth that Jesus is the Son of God." 1 John v: 5. Having seen that this fact, which was attested by God and confessed by Peter, is the truth to be believed in order to overcome the world, and confessed that God may dwell in the party submitting it, it may be well to see how it is confessed. First, we quote from Paul where he informs us that "At the name of Jesus every knee should bow of things in Heaven, and things in earth, and things under the earth, and that every tongue should confess that Jesus Christ is Lord to the glory of God the Father." Phil, ii: 10, 11. Also "As I live, saith the Lord, every knee shall bow to me and every tongue shall confess to God." Rom. xiv: 11. In these quotations two important facts are made apparent. First, that the confession is to be made with the tongue, and, secondly, that God has determined that it shall be made, and, therefore, cannot be displeased with. But from the pen of the same Apostle we have another lesson on this subject. He says, "That thou shalt confess with thy mouth the Lord Jesus, and shalt believe in thy heart that God hath raised Him from the dead, thou shalt be saved, for with the heart man believeth onto righteousness, and with the mouth confession is made unto salvation." Rom. x:9,10. We here learn that the confession is not only to be made with the mouth, but that it is a condition to, and therefore precedes remission of sins. Paul does not say "With a nod of the head confession is made unto salvation," nor does he say that by visiting the sick or other acts of obedience through life, confession is made, but it is made with the mouth unto salvation. And while Paul is thus specific, we dare not accept it made in any other way; provided the subject has the use of the tongue with which to make it.

Having learned that the confession with the mouth is a condition to, and unto salvation, and, therefore, before it, and as Jesus says that "he that believeth and is baptized shall be saved." Mark xvi: 16, It follows that confession precedes baptism. As the baptized believer is saved, there Is no period between his baptism and his salvation in which to make the confession, and hence if it is made before salvation, it is certainly made before baptism.

As it is with the heart man believeth that Jesus is the Christ, the Son of God, and with the mouth he confesses what the heart believes, it follows that the confession with the mouth is subsequent to faith or belief. Hence, clearly, the confession is located after faith, and he before baptism. Indeed, were a man to make the confession with the mouth before he believed with the heart, It would be a down right falsehood, for he would thereby say he believed what he did not believe.

Now, if the reader will review the ground over which we have traveled, he will find that God has determined that he shall confess, with the mouth, his faith in Jesus Christ, as being the Son of God, before he is baptized, and by so doing, he puts himself under obligation to observe all the law emanating from him as head of the Church built upon the truth he thus confesses. Paul's account of Timothy's confession is in perfect harmony with this view of the whole subject. We quote from Anderson's Translation as follows: "Fight the good fight of faith; lay hold on eternal life, to which you have been called, and for which you confessed the good confession before many witnesses." 1 Tim. vi: 12.

181

Jesus proposed to confess them which as confessed Him before men—Timothy made the good confession before many witnesses. Paul tells the Romans that confession is made unto salvation; and when we supply the antecedent to which the relative "which" refers in his account of Timothy's confession, we find it reading thus, "For which, eternal life, you confessed the good confession." Then Timothy made the confession unto salvation, or for eternal life "whereunto he was called" by the Gospel, when Paul preached it to him.

That the "good confession," made by Timothy, consisted in confessing that Jesus was the Christ, the Son of God, is further shown by the foot that in the next verse Paul applies the very same words, the good confession, to the confession made by Jesus before Pontius Pilate. And though in the account given by Matthew of what he said in answer to Pilate, the words "I am the Son of God," are not given; yet we are assured by the testimony of his enemies, that this was embraced in his confession. In derision, they said "If thou be the Son of God come down from the cross." And again, "He trusted in God, let him deliver him now. If he will have him for he said I am the Son of God." Matt, xxvii: 40, 43. If this, then, was what Paul called the good confession when made by the Savior, it is also what be called the good life, where unto he was called by the Gospel.

But it is sometimes insisted that there was not time enough on the day of Pentecost, after Peter quit preaching, for three thousand to have made this confession before the baptism. Will the objector tell us how long it would have taken, on that occasion, for this same three thousand to have each told such an "experience" as he requires previous to baptism? While it would have been possible for one speaker (and there were twelve present) to have propounded the question, "Does each one of you believe with all the heart that Jesus is the Christ, the Son of God ?" and the response, "I do," to have come simultaneously from three thousand tongues, in as little time as it could have been asked of and answered by a single person, it could not have been possible for such "experiences" as are now told, to have been told in that way. They may all differ in the details, and must, therefore, be told, listened to, and decided upon separately. Say, then, how long would it take to hear three-thousands of them in that way? Were it profitable, we might entertain the reader with a feast of fat things, sometimes narrated in these so-called experiences, but we forbear. A few plain questions for the reflection of our readers, and we are done.

If the belief of the fact that Jesus is the Son of God is the faith that overcomes the world, will believing that He is the very and eternal God do the same thing? If this is what is to be confessed with the mouth, unto salvation, after faith and before baptism, and it is not made, will we get the salvation unto which it should have been made? If Timothy made this good confession for eternal life, may we displease with it, and still get the eternal life for which he made it? If God has determined that every tongue shall confess that Jesus is Lord to the glory of God the Father, and we fail to make it unto our salvation, will we not have to make it in the final day to our condemnation? If Jesus has promised to confess, before His Father, such as confess Him before men, will He confess us if we fail to confess Him? If God dwells in those who confess that Jesus is the Son of God, will He also dwell in those who do not confess this fact? If this is what has to be confessed, will it be safe to substitute a narrative of our dreams, feelings and imaginations in the shape of an experience instead of this confession? And If these dreams, feelings and imaginations constitute all the confession made prior to baptism, when do the parties confess that Jesus is Lord to the glory of God the Father, to their own salvation, and for eternal life, and which secures the dwelling

183

of God in those who make it? In our next we will begin the subject of baptism.

GA vol.10, #4 1-23-68, page 89

WHAT IS BAPTISM?

The Bible. If we speak not as the oracles of God speak, then prove all things and hold fast that which is good. First, then, we inquire WHAT IS BAPTISM?

Worcester, in his unabridged dictionary-Baptism. The subject of baptism has engaged the attention of many of the wisest heads, and employed the tongues and first defines the Greek word *bappeas* of many of the ablest speakers *tismos* a dipping, and then proceeds and writers that have adorned the earth to define the same word as an English since the days of the Apostles. In the word, (less two letters) and says: An examination of a subject, upon which of baptizing, a Christian rite or sacrament there is much spoken and written, symbolical of initiation into the will not be expected that we will be able, Church, and of consecration to a pure to present a single thought that has not life, performed by immersion, ablution been presented, in some shape, by some or sprinkling, and accompanied with a one who has preceded us. If there is a form of words. Now, how are we to a subject connected with man's salvation, reconcile his definition of *baptismos* "that has been exhausted, surely this one dipping," with his definition of baptism has. Indeed, the great mind of Alexander "performed by immersion, ablution, or Campbell seems to have grasped sprinkling?" The former is the subject in all its aptitude, and there use of the Greek, when Jesus used can be but little profitably said about it to indicate his will in commanding that may not be found in his writings of baptism; while the latter is the modern somewhere. And were every one in abuse of the term, defined in accommo-possession of every thing he has written, we would deem it wholly unnecessary to write a sentence about it. In the nature of things, however, we know this cannot be so. The class of persons for whom we write are not presumed to have read everything that he and others have written. Not only do every few years change the readers of a paper, but each of the various papers, published at the same time has, In the mind, its own readers, most of whom read no other. We have read every thing that has come in our way on the subject; had ever been written about it before. All our Father blesses us with health sufficient, and other labors more important do not encroach upon our time, it is our purpose to present, in our own way, everything we may deem important to modern theology. How can the same word mean a dipping in Greek, and when adopted into English, mean immersion, ablution, or sprinkling? Surely, it was transplanted into good soil, for its meanings have rapidly increased since its adoption. Children resemble their parents not more than modern dictionaries and lexicons resemble the religious persuasion of their authors. If we would comprehend the subject we must not stop with definitions given by authors whose works are made to reflect the faith of the party to which but we will write just as though nothing they belong; but we must get at the import of the words used by the Savior at the time he employed them.

It is scarcely necessary to say to our readers that the words baptist, baptism, baptize, baptized and baptizing are all Greek words, anglicized in termination to a thorough examination of the subject to satisfy the demands of English without regard to the source from aphony and adopted into our language which we learned it; whether from the by order of King James. Among the Bible or the writings of men, tried by roles he gave to the forty-seven men he employed in translating the Bible, are the following:

" Rule I. The Bishop's Bible the basis of the version.

185

Rule II. The names of the prophets and the Holy writers, with the other names in the text, to be kept as near as may be, according as they are vulgarly used.

Rule III. The old ecclesiastic words to be kept."

Had not the translators been trammeled by these rules, they had ran, slated these words, their labor would have done much toward preventing the unfortunate controversy on the action of baptism. The word *baptisma*, rendered baptism, occurs in the New Testament twenty-two times. *Baptismos* occurs four times, three times rendered washing, and once baptism. *Baptistes* occurs fourteen times connected with John, and is rendered baptist. *Baptiso* occurs eighty times, seventy-eight of which it is rendered *baptise* and one time each wash and washing. The family of words is derived from the primitive word *Bapto*, and each partakes of the import of this word. It occurs six times with its compound *embapto*. Mat. xxvi: 23, Mark xiv : 20, Luke xvi: 24, John xiii: 26, twice; and Rev. xix: 13. This word not being used to indicate baptism, its translation was not prohibited by the king's rules, and therefore you will find it translated dip, dippeth, dipped. And even *baptiso*, the very word rendered baptise in the New Testament, is rendered dipped in II Kings v: 14. "Then went he down and dipped himself seven times in Jordan." Now can any one doubt what would have been the rendering of this word had the translators been permitted to faithfully translate it. Language, no law that is better established than that derivative words inherit the radical form and primary meaning of the radical words from which they are derived.

This being so, and the primary meaning of the root *bapto* being dip, does it not follow that Its derivative *baptiso* must be rendered dip, immerse or some word equivalent thereto. If baptism may be performed by sprinkling or pouring, is it not strange that we never have the word *bapto*, or any word derived, from it rendered sprinkle or pour? They often occur, but never from the word *baptiso*. Sprinkle is always from *ratasiend* pour is from *cheo*, each indicating a specific action differing widely from the other. While the primary meaning of *bapto*, and per consequence of its derivative *baptiso* is dip, immerse, overwhelm; the meaning of sprinkle is to scatter in drops; and pour to turn, out in a stream. As well might we expect purely English parentage to produce a progeny of baboons and monkeys as for *baptiso*, or any other word derived from *bapto*, to mean sprinkle or pour. We have only one Greek lexicon, and it is by Pickering. He defines *baptiso* as follows: To dip, immerse, submerge, plunge, sint, overwhelm ; to steep, to soak, to wet, to wash or bathe." Now If sprinkle or pour, either or both, are meanings of the word, why are they not given as such? We have, collated by others, the definitions given by Scapula, Henrecus, Stephanus, Robertson, Thesaurus, Sohrevelliua, Schleaaner. Tasor, Porkhurat, Donnegan, Jones, Greenfield, Rost, Bretachneider, Bass, Sloklus, Seudas, Gitovea, Ewing, Schellgenius, Alstedlua, Wilton, Bailey, Young and Richardson; and with great unanimity they give the meaning, dip, immerse and words of similar Import, also such figurative meaning is may be the result of dipping, Immersion, etc.

Ours is a living, growing, and, therefore, a changing language, and the import of adopted words is as liable to be changed by usage as native English words. It would have astonished the Greek writers of eighteen hundred years ago to have found a definition to baptism in such a dictionary as Worcester's, saying "It may be performed by immersion, ablution, or sprinkling." Yet, how many speakers and writers so use the term. Josephus the justly celebrated Jewish historian, lived cotemporaneous with the Apostles, and wrote in the Greek language, immediately after the days of the Savior. It is fair to presume that he understood the language in which he wrote as well as the Grecians themselves. In speaking of the murder of Aristabulus he said, "Whereupon the child was sent, by night, to Jericho, and was there dipped (baptized) by the Gauls, at Herod's command, in a pond till he was drowned." Wars of the Jews, Book I, chapter xxii. We have by us, at this writing, near one hundred extracts from the Greek writers, in which the word occurs; which we might transcribe to show the real import of this word in those days; but they would not be perused with interest by many readers. The above from Josephus we have taken from Whiston's edition of his work, and it may serve as a sample of them all. In every instance it is rendered dip, or some equivalent word, such as immerse, submerge, overwhelm, etc. Many of these extracts are in debates when they were presented in the presence of able opponents whose duty it was to expose any false position taken. Now can we suppose that Jesus used a word in which to express a command, to those by whom he expected be understood and obeyed; a command, too, of so much importance as to have for its object the introduction of the obedient subject into his Kingdom, and yet he used the term selected, to indicate his will, In a sense entirely different from its ordinary acceptation at the time he employed it. Well may those, who so teach, regard the words of Jesus as a mystery. If we are to understand the words employed by him in some other than their ordinary acceptation at the time he used them, how are we to tell when we have the sense intended? "When they accord with our creed they are to be understood in their ordinary acceptation, if not, they must mean something else," is the Pandora's box from which have sprung the evils that have ruined the world.

Professor Stuart, of the Andover Theological School, in the Biblical Repository for 1833,. page 298, says: *Bapto* and *Baptizo* mean to dip, plunge or immerse into any liquid. All LEXICOGRAPHERS AND CRITICS OF ANY NOTE ARE agreed in this." There is no higher scholastic authority in all the ranks of orthodoxy than this. That dip, immerse or some equivalent word is necessary to express the primary meaning of baptizo, is admitted by all; but it is insisted that wash, wet, stain, dye, etc., are figurative meanings; and as washing, wetting, staining and dying may be done by pouring or sprinkling, therefore, baptism may be performed by sprinkling or pouring. These meanings are bound to be purely metonymical—that is, they are effects of the true or real meaning of the word. No two meanings can be given to the same word which are antagonistic to each other. Stains are removed by washing, and therefore, the same word cannot literally mean both wash and stain. Washing may be the effect of immersion in clean water, while staining and dying may be done by immersion in impure or coloring fluids. Hence, these opposite meanings cannot be otherwise than metonymical, and then it follows that they are effects produced by the real meaning, dipping or immersion, otherwise they would not be metonymical at all. All these figurative meanings, so-called, may be the effect of Immersion, but they cannot all be the effect of pouring or sprinkling. Washing and dying are not done in either of these ways. Sprinkling a few drops of water on a filthy garment would not be likely to wash it well; nor would pouring a little dribble on one end of a garment be very apt to wash or cleanse the balance of it. And if it were coloring-fluid, it would not be a good process by which to dye a whole web, to sprinkle or pour a little of the fluid on one end of it. By the way, we have never been able to see any more authority for putting water on the head and calling it baptism, than for making the application to the hands, feet or any other part of the body. We speak most reverently when we say that if baptism is rightly performed by sprinkling or pouring a few drops of water only; and it has come in the room of circumcision, as the advocates of this theory are wont to maintain, then most certainly do they make the application at the wrong place. As immersion is admitted by all to be the primary meaning of the word representing baptism, we wish to know why it is to give place to figurative or metonymical meanings such as wash, wet, stain, dye, etc.? All philological laws require preference to be given to the primary meaning unless good reason be shown for its removal. In seeking the specific action required by the command "Be baptized," if we are to take the word in its common acceptation and give preference to the primary meaning, there can be no mistake that immersion is the act required. Prof. Charles Anthon, of Columbia College, New York, one of the most profound scholars in America, says: "The primary meaning of the word [baptizo] is to dip or immerse; and its secondary meanings, if it have any, all refer to the same leading idea. Sprinkling, etc., are entirely out of the question." Letter to Dr. Family, of March 27th 1843.

A good rule by which to try the meaning of a word in any given sentence, is to substitute the meaning of the word for the word Itself, and if it be a correct interpretation it will make as good sense as the word for which it is a substitute. By this rule we will try the meaning of the word baptize in a few passages, and see whether or not it may mean sprinkle or pour. Before applying the test, we may remark that the verb sprinkle means to scatter in drops, and is always followed by the material to be sprinkled, either expressed or understood. We may sprinkle blood, water, sand, of ashes on a man, but we cannot sprinkle a man on anything. We sometimes speak of sprinkling a man with water, when we mean to sprinkle water upon him; but the language is an outrage upon all grammatical accuracy. If we say "we sprinkle a man with water," the language must mean one of two things; first, that we sprinkle (that is scatter in drops) both the man and the water together, as we eat butter with our bread; or that water is the instrument with which we sprinkle, or scatter the man; as, we sprinkle water with a broom. In the first construction, the nouns man and water are the object of the action expressed by the verb sprinkle; and in the second construction the noun man is alone the object, and water the instrument either of which involves a physical impossibility.

We have not forgotten that Paul says, "When Moses had spoken every precept to all the people according to the law, he took the blood of calves and of goats with water, and scarlet wool and hyssop and sprinkled both the book and the people." Heb. ix: 19. This sentence is evidently elliptical, and when the ellipsis is filled, it will read thus: "He took the blood of calves and of goats with water, scarlet wool and hyssop and sprinkled them upon both the book and all the people." Hence this passage does not efface the position we have taken. The verb pour means to turn out in a stream, and is also followed by the thing poured which must be something fluid or composed of small particles. It is as much impossible to pour a man as to sprinkle him. We are now prepared to read the passages and submit these definitions to the rule stated.

"Then went out to him Jerusalem and all Judea, and all the region round about Jordan and were sprinkled (scattered in drops) of him In Jordan confessing their sins. But when he saw many of the Pharisees and Saducees come to his sprinkling (scattering In drops) he said unto them, etc." Mat. ill: 5-7. Were the people scattered in drops by John in Jordan? "He that believeth and is sprinkled (scattered in drops) shall be saved." Mark xvi:16. "Repent and be sprinkled (scattered in drops) every one of you." Acts ii: 38. "When they believed Philip preaching the things concerning the Kingdom of God and the name of Jesus Christ, they were sprinkled (scattered in drops) both men and women." Acts viii: 12. These Scriptures need only to be read—no comment is necessary to show that sprinkle will not bear the test. Will pour do any better? We will try it. "Then went out to him Jerusalem and all Judea, and all the region round about Jordan and were poured (turned out in a stream) of him in Jordan." He that believeth and is poured (turned out in a stream) shall be saved." "Repent and be poured (turned out in a stream) every one of you." "When they believed Philip preaching the things concerning the Kingdom of God and the name of Jesus Christ, they were poured (turned out in a stream) both men and women." Thus we see -that the sense is as completely destroyed by substituting pour as sprinkle. Now let us subject immersion to the same ordeal; If it will do no better, away with it. "Then went out to him Jerusalem and all Judea, and all the region round about Jordan and were immersed of him in Jordan confessing their sins. But when he saw many of the Pharisees and Sadducees come to his immersion he said unto them, etc." "He that believeth and is immersed shall be saved." "Repent and be immersed every one of you." "When they believed Philip preaching the things concerning the Kingdom of God and the name of Jesus Christ they were immersed, both men and women." Thus, we might try every place in the New Testament where the word occurs and the result would be the same. A man may be immersed in water, blood, oil, grief, suffering, debt, etc.; but sprinkled or injured he cannot be and live.

As the Holy Spirit was shed forth on the day of Pentecost when the Apostles were baptized with it, it is sometimes insisted that this is the meaning of baptize. Then let us try It. "Go teach all nations shedding them forth in the name, etc." Mat xxvi: 19. "And they went down into the water, both Philip and the Eunuch, and he shed him forth: Acts viii: 38. Will this do? Once more: At the house of Cornelius "The Holy Ghost fell on all them which heard the word." Acts x : 44. It Is therefore insisted that fell on is the meaning of the word baptize, and indicates the manner in which it should be performed. Then we will try this also. " Go teach all nations falling on them In the name of the Father, etc." "And they went down into the water, both Philip and the Eunuch, and he fell on him. We will not offer a word of comment to make these definitions more ridiculously absurd than they are in their own native deformity.

This article is long enough; some will think it too long. We will lay down our pen for the present.

GA Vol 10, #5, Jan. 30,1868 Page 114

THE HOLY SPIRIT

It is not our purpose to write a dissertation upon the nature, origin of relationship of the Holy Spirit. Paul said, "Foolish and unlearned questions, avoid, knowing that they do gender strife." 2 Thes. ii: 23. We are persuaded that there can be but little known of these subjects because there is but little revealed concerning them. "Secret things belong unto the Lord our God: but those things which are revealed belong unto us and to our children forever." Deut, xxix: 29. Why then should we worry ourselves over questions which our Father never revealed to us and therefore never intended us to know? We have read most of what has been written on these subjects and we do not remember a book or essay of any considerable length that does not speak of the Holy Spirit as a person. The denominational writings abound with the phrase, "The third person of the Trinity." While our brethren, with great unanimity, have pruned off the words third and trinity, they have generally retained the word person. Why is this? Is the notion of personality essential to the reception of any truth on the subject, or the enjoyment of the Spirit in any way? We think not. Indeed, we are inclined to think that it has prevented good men from receiving the truth with regard to the presence of the Spirit in Christians. As they could not see how one person could literally dwell in another person, they have been inclined to reject the thought entirely. We feel sure that if the term person is applicable to the Holy Spirit at all, it must be in, a highly accommodated sense; for the Scriptures nowhere teach that it is really a person in the current acceptation of that term. True, they teach that the Spirit speaks, reproves, comforts, bears witness, etc.; and it is hence insisted that it must be a person, as it performs the work of a person. But this proof is not quite conclusive. The fact that two things perform similar labor and fill similar functions cannot prove their identity. But we are told that the Holy Spirit is represented in the Scriptures by personal pronouns of the masculine gender. Yes, and we apply the same pronouns to the sun and other things which have no real claims to personality. The English noun Spirit, and Pneuma its Greek representative are both of the neater gender, and cannot be represented by pronouns of the masculine gender; and had the translators been free from trinitarian bias it is quite lively that no such pronouns would have been introduced by them. We are aware of the fact that some forms of the word Pneuma rendered Spirit, and also of the word *Paraclete* rendered comforter, are of the masculine gender; but it is termination and not signification that makes them so. Our idea of sex is not in them at all. What would be thought of a translator who would represent the nouns tree, river, mountain, etc., by pronouns of the masculine gender in English because their terminations make them masculine in Greek? We do not believe that the Holy Spirit can be correctly represented by pronouns of the masculine gender, either grammatically or theologically, the translators to the contrary notwithstanding. We, therefore, most respectfully decline to use them, only as we quote them. If any one still insists that the Holy Spirit is really a person we will make no quarrel with him about it; but would like to know the family relationship of the person he calls the Holy Spirit. Is God his Father? If so, Jesus is not the only Son of the Father. (See John i: 14,18 ; iii: 16, 18. 1 John iv:9.

God said, "I will pour out of my Spirit upon all flesh." Peter said, "He hath shed forth this which you; now see and hear. Are these passages compatible with our ideas of personality? Can a person be poured out or shed forth? But there is yet another feature of the phrase "Pour out of my

Spirit," which is fatal to the notion of personality. The preposition of in the phrase implies division, hence the obvious meaning is that God would pour out a portion or measure of his Spirit, May we divide and pour out a person by measure? Or was Heaven exhausted of the Holy Spirit when the person called the Holy Spirit was sent from there to Jerusalem on the day of Pentecost? Of Jesus it is said, "God giveth not the Spirit by measure unto him." John iii: 34. This language clearly implies that God gives the Spirit by measure to others. With what propriety can we speak of measuring out a person to other persons?

But there are more practical questions connected with the Holy Spirit of "which we may know something, because God has spoken, to us more definitely concerning them, and it is of them we propose to write. We are aware, too, that even these are not to be comprehended without effort; nor are we vain enough to suppose that we are able to write an unexceptionable essay concerning them. Strong minds and devoted hearts have prayerfully perused the sacred pages of Holy Writ until their eyes have grown dim in age; and after all their toil, have closed their labors confessedly ignorant of the modus operandi of the Holy Spirit. Indeed, the incomprehensibility of the subject is the theory advocated by many very able pleas. By such, those who claim to understand the subject are at once suspected of denying the influence of the Spirit in conversion entirely. If you deny an incomprehensible influence of the Spirit, they know of no other, and hence conclude that you deny all spiritual influence. They are ever ready to quote John iii:8. "The wind bloweth where it listeth, and thou hearest the sound thereof, but canst not tell whence it cometh, and whither it goeth: so is every one that is born of the Spirit." In vain may you call their attention to the fact that the passage does not say "so is the Spirit," or "so is the operation of the Spirit." They have learned to so interpret it, and this is quite sufficient to end the investigation of the subject.

They will regard it presumptuous in us to even attempt an examination of it. They will quote the old adage, "Fools rush on where angels fear to tread." But we beg them to remember that if we are ignorant of the subject, we will not be more likely to remain so, than those who do not examine it at all. If they and we, close our Bibles and cease to investigate, we will all remain ignorant together. The divine volume contains many lessons on the subject, and surely our Father would not have said so much to us on a subject of which he intended us to remain entirely ignorant. We are therefore encouraged to pursue our study of the sacred pages, with all the assistance we can get, in the hope that we may, at least, acquire a sufficient knowledge of what is taught concerning the Holy Spirit to enable us to enjoy its comforting influences in God's appointed way.

Our Bible teaches us that there is not only one God and Father, and one Lord Jesus Christ the Son of this Father; but also that there is one Holy Spirit which proceeded from God, divine as is God from whom it proceeded. As the sun is the great center of the solar system from which emanates light and heat to the natural world; so God is not only Spirit, but the great center of the Spiritual world from whom emanated the Holy Spirit: giving light and comfort to the denizens of earth through the inspired word and the institutions and service appointed therein.

John the Baptist said to those who came to be baptized of him in the Jordan, "I indeed baptize you with water unto repentance; but he that cometh after me is mightier than I, whose shoes I am not worthy to bear; he shall baptize you with the Holy Ghost and with fire." Mat. iii: 11.

Paul says, "Now concerning spiritual gifts, brethren, I would not have you ignorant." And again: "Now there are diversities of gifts but the same Spirit." 1 Cor. xii: 1, 4.

After Jesus had told his Disciples that it was needful for them that he should go away in order that the Holy Spirit might come to and remain with them as an abiding comforter, he said to them, "When he is come he will reprove the world of sin, and of righteousness, and of judgment." John xvi: 18.

Paul in his epistle to his brethren at Rome said, "Ye have received the Spirit of adoption, whereby we cry, Abba, Father." Rom. viii: 15.

Thus, we find the Scripture speaking of the baptism of the Holy Spirit; secondly of the gifts of the Spirit; thirdly the operation or work of the Spirit in reproving the world of sin, righteousness and judgment and the reception of the Spirit by the children of the Father. Paul charged Timothy, saying, "Study to show thyself approved unto God, a workman that needeth not to be ashamed, rightly dividing the word of truth." 2 Tim. ii: 15. We know of no subject to the study of which this admonition is of more importance than that of the Holy Spirit. If we can rightly divide and apply the word of truth to the subject in hand, we will be aided much in attaining to a knowledge of it. If we fail to do this we may correctly learn something concerning it, but understand the subject as a system we never will.

We have seen four separate departments of our subject spoken of in the passages quoted. Let us draw the line deep and wide between them, that we may keep them well apart until we examine them in the light of the Scriptures. Should we indiscriminately apply what was Written with reference to any one of them, to any or all the others, we would certainly do violence to the teaching of the Spirit, and make an incomprehensible: logomachy of the whole subject. Let us rightly divide our subject and apply the Scriptures accordingly. First in order we will examine.

THE BAPTISM OF THE HOLY SPIRIT.

That God promised the baptism of the Holy Spirit to certain persons, through John the Baptist and also through Jesus His Son, is not disputed by any one, and that this promise was verified on the day of Pentecost and at the house of Cornelius is believed by all. The matter in controversy is as to whether or not the baptism thus promised was to be special or general, temporary or perpetual. In other words, was it confined to the days of miracles? or was designed for, and promised to the Christians of our day, yea of all time?

First, then, we will examine the Scriptures relied on to prove that persons are now baptized with the Holy Spirit. The first passage we will examine may be found in the prophecy of Joel ii: 28-30. "And it shall come to pass afterward that I will pour out my Spirit upon all flesh; and your sons and your daughters shall prophecy, your old men shall dream dreams, your young men shall see visions; and also upon the servants and upon the handmaids in those days will I pour out my Spirit; and I will shew wonders in the Heavens and in the earth, blood and fire, and pillars of smoke." That this prophecy had reference to the baptism of the Holy Spirit to take place on the day of Pentecost is certain from the fact that Peter quotes it as fulfilled in the events of that day. Acts ii: 16-19. As it is here said that the Spirit was to be poured out upon all flesh, it is insisted that those living now are a part of all flesh as well as those who lived then, and hence it must require all time to fulfill the prophecy, because if its fulfillment was restricted to the events of that day it was not poured out upon all flesh. But if there are to be no restrictions placed upon the phrase "all flesh" then the passage will prove entirely too much. Paul tells us that "All flesh is not the same flesh; but there is one kind of flesh of men, another flesh of beasts, another of fishes, and another of birds." 1 Cor. xv: 39. Therefore if the phrase "all flesh" is not to be limited. Not only have all been baptized with the Spirit, but also all beasts, birds and fish. Well, but it means all human firth. This proves too much yet; for this would include the most wicked man of earth as well as the host Christian. But it means all Christians. Stop, you set out with the position that there are no restrictions to be put on the phrase all flesh; now you cut off not only all beasts, birds, and fish but also the larger portion of human flesh, for few go the narrow path while the many go the broad road; and these you will not-allow to be baptized with the Spirit at all. This is doing pretty well. These restrictions are right, may there not be others? The sons and daughters who were the subjects of this baptism were to prophecy, the old men were to dream dreams, and the young men were to see visions. Are these phenomena exhibited by all Christians now? If not, the phrase all flesh must be pruned down until it embraces such, and only such, as can do the things spoken of. When Peter said, "This is that which was spoken by the prophet Joel," (Acts ii: 16) the Disciples were prophesying, speaking with tongues, and doing the things spoken of by Joel, hence we feel authorized to restrict the phrase "All flesh" to such as exhibited the signs predicted in the prophecy. Again: We have the fulfillment of this prophecy to take place at a specified time. "It shall come to pass in the last days, saith God that I will pour out of my Spirit upon all flesh." Acts ii: 17. Certainly the last days here spoken of cannot be the last days of time, for more than eighteen hundred years have gone by since Peter said, "This is that which was spoken by the prophet Joel." And it would require great boldness to affirm that the phrase last day was intended to include all the days from the day of Pentecost to the end of time; yet such must be the interpretation given to it to make the fulfillment of Joel's prophecy include the Christians of all time, and therefore those of this day. The last days here spoken of by Joel must have been the last days of the Jewish dispensation, for it was in them that Peter tells us, "This is that which was spoken." The argument drawn from this prophecy to support the notion that persons are now baptized with the Holy Spirit is, therefore, evidently defective.

The language of John the Baptist next claims our attention, he said to those demanding baptism of him in the Jordan "I indeed baptize you with water unto repentance; but he that cometh after me is mightier than I, whose shoes I am not worthy to bear: he shall baptize you with the Holy Ghost and with fire: whose fan is in his hand and he will thoroughly purge his floor, and gather his wheat into the garner; but he will burn up the chaff with unquenchable fire." Mat. iii:11,12. This address is recorded by Luke (iii: 16, 17,) in very nearly the same words. Mark records an abridgment of it, thus: "There cometh one mightier than I ; after me, the latchet of whose shoes; I am not worthy to stoop down and unloose. I indeed have baptized you with water; but he shall baptize you with the Holy Ghost." Mark i: 7, 8. It is not important to our investigation that we stop to enquire who were to be the subjects of the baptism of fire spoken of in the records by Mathew and Luke, as it is the baptism of the Holy Spirit which concerns us at present; nor will we stop to enquire whether this was to be a figurative or a literal baptism in the Holy Spirit. That it was literal is all that can be claimed; and this we are not only willing to grant but firmly believe. But do these quotations prove that persons are now baptized with the Holy Spirit? If they prove it at all, they must do it in one of two ways. First, the language employed must be sufficiently comprehensive to include us; or the principle taught must be applicable to as. First, then, who were the persons represented by the pronoun you in the sentence "He shall baptize you with the Holy Ghost" That this word could not have included even all John's audience is clear from the fact that some of them were wicked, comparable to chaff and to be burned with unquenchable fire. But even had it embraced every one to whom he spake, both wicked and good, it would still require very elastic rules of interpretation to make it embrace the Christians of all time. "I indeed baptize you with water * * * he shall baptize you with the Holy Ghost and with fire. Can any fair rules of interpretation make the last you include more than the first you? Surely not. Then it follows that those who were here promised the baptism of the Holy Ghost were among those baptized by John in water.

Again: We have a rule of grammar saying "Pronouns must agree with the noun for which they stand in gender, number and person." If we respect this rule at all, how can we make these pronouns include more, or other persons than their antecedents in the preceding part of the chapter?

Once-more: In oral discourse, the persons indicated by pronouns of the second person are always present with the speaker. This rule knows no exception. In written communications, persons represented by pronouns of the second person may be absent from the writer; but to a speaker they must be present. Let us apply this rule to the speech made by John the Baptist to the multitude on the banks of the Jordon, "I indeed baptize you with water * * * he shall baptize you with the Holy Ghost" How can these pronouns of the second person, embrace any persons not present before John when he used them? If we apply this promise to other persons we must derive authority for doing so from other sources than the language employed, for evidently it is not there. Then is there a principle taught, applicable to us? If so we can not see it. The passage was a prophetic promise made to certain persons, to be fulfilled to them; and when so fulfilled, there was no general principle remaining applicable to any persons only such as are shown to be subjects of the baptism in question. That Christians are now such subjects is the matter to be proved—to assume it is to assume the whole controversy. We have seen that the language of John is incapable of providing it, either expressly or by implication. We would not be understood, however, to deny that any were baptized with the Holy Ghost who were not of those baptized by John the Baptist in water. We know that others were so baptized, but this is not quite efficient to prove that the language employed by John included them. We have been seeking to test the power of this passage to prove the doctrine in question. We know that it is confidently relied on to sustain the theory; hence we have thought for the extent of its application, and the time of its fulfillment. When Jesus was assembled with the Apostles on one occasion, he "commanded them not to depart from Jerusalem, but wait for the promise of the Father which, saith he, ye have heard of me; for John truly baptized with water, but ye shall be baptized With the Holy Ghost not many days hence." Acts i: 4, 6. As Jesus here associated this promise of the Father with John's baptism, it is next to certain that he here refers to the same promise which the Father made by John. This being so, we can scarcely fail to recognize its fulfillment on the day of Pentecost at Jerusalem where they were commanded to wait for it. And though, in the three recorded accounts of John's discourse, we have no specific allusion to the time of its fulfillment, yet when Jesus quotes it, he says it shall be not many days hence, and commanded them not to depart from Jerusalem until it was fulfilled. When, therefore, we connect these passages together we see not how it is possible to look beyond the day of Pentecost for the complete fulfillment of the promise of the Father made through John concerning the baptism of the Holy Spirit.

But we may be told that Peter quoted this language at the house of Cornelius as applicable to the Gentiles saying, "As I began to speak the Holy Ghost fell on them as on us at the beginning. Then remembered I the word of the Lord, how that he said, John indeed baptized with water, but ye shall be baptized with the Holy Ghost." Acts xi: 15,16. This is sufficiently near the language quoted from Acts i: 4, 5, to make it probable that both passages refer to the same conversation. As God baptized the Disciples with the Holy Spirit when the Gospel was first proclaimed to the Jews, it was proper, for reasons which we will see in due time, that He should attend its introduction to the Gentiles by the like gift. But if the baptism of the Holy Spirit was then bestowed upon all converts, as we are told, it now is why did Peter associate it with the beginning. Why not have said, "As I began to speak the Holy Spirit fell on them as on all others converted?" Surely some such style would have been appropriate. Many thousands had been converted from the day of Pentecost to that time, yet the language employed is calculated to make the impression that such an event had not come under their notice from the beginning until that time.

We will notice one more passage only. "For by one Spirit are we all baptized into one body, whether we be Jews or Gentiles, whether we be bond or free; and have been all made to drink into one Spirit." 1 Cor xii: 13. Although this passage was written in close proximity to Paul's explanation of the miraculous gifts of the Spirit, yet we are willing to admit the principle taught in it, to be applicable to Christians generally; but it falls very far short of proving that they, or any of them, are baptized with the Holy Spirit. So far from it that it says not one word about it. By one Spirit are we all baptized into one body. There is one body. (Ep. iv : 4) This is the Church, (Col. i: 18 and 24.) There is one baptism, (Eph. iv : 5) by which we enter this one body. Are we now prepared to see the import of the passage? By (the teaching of) one Spirit (the Holy Spirit) we are all baptized (in water) into one body (the Church.) This seems to be the obvious import of the passage; and it is in harmony with the whole tenor of the Spirit's teaching on the subject. But if we insist that it means "In one Spirit are we all baptized into one body," then we make Paul contradict himself saying there is "one baptism." When he says, "There is one Lord, one Faith, one Baptism, one God and Father of all, he as clearly teaches that there is but one baptism, as he does that there is but one Lord or but one God and Father of all. The denominations themselves agree that by water Baptism we enter the Church if therefore they make this passage mean Holy Spirit baptism they not only contradict Paul but they contradict themselves. Surely, they will not do this.

It is admitted by all that God's works, everywhere, are a most wonderful exhibition of harmony and order. He has a place for everything, and everything in its place an office for everything to fill, and everything filling its own office. It is altogether probable, then, that the baptism of the Holy Spirit was designed for some appropriate work, and not given to accomplish anything, everything, or nothing as might chance to happen. It is, then, of the first importance that we seek for the office assigned it in the Gospel plan of salvation. What say you gentle reader on this subject? What do you think with it? What do you expect it to do for you? The first work usually assigned it in the theories of modern times, is the removal of the depravity, or corruption of nature supposed to have been inherited from our illustrious progenitors as a result of their sin, or rather, our sin in them. It is assumed that man comes into the world totally depraved, wholly defiled in all the faculties and parts of soul and body, opposed to all good and wholly inclined to all evil, in consequence of which he cannot will or desire anything good accompanying salvation until this depravity is removed, or mortified by the baptism of the Holy Spirit. For an examination of this assumption the reader is referred to the chapter on Hereditary Total Depravity.

Suppose, however, that this is really a true picture of man's nature, and he can do nothing until God enables him to do it by baptizing him with the Holy Spirit. What then? If God has to administer it, and man can do nothing until it is done, and it is never done at all, who is to blame for it? Will God sentence the sinner to hell and there punish him forever for not obeying the Gospel when it was no fault of his that he did not do it? The baptism of the Holy Spirit was emphatically a miracle, performed by Jesus himself. If, therefore, all converts of our day are baptized with it, it follows that there is a miracle performed every time a conversion takes place, and miracles will continue as long as there is a subject converted to God; and the conversion of every man is suspended upon the performance of a miracle of which he has not the slightest control, for until it is performed he cannot even desire it, or will anything good ac-companying it. But was the removal of depravity the object to be accomplished by the baptism of the Spirit anciently? The first case, of which we have a record, took place on the day of Pentecost and the Disciples were the subjects of it on that occasion. Had the Apostles been more than three years with the Lord, and been sent by him to preach the ap-proach of the Kingdom "to the lost sheep of the house of Israel," Matt, x: 5-7, with power to perform miracles in his name; and finally to preach the Gospel to every creature, with power to bind and loose on earth, with the assurance that their acts should be ratified in Heaven, and yet their hearts totally depraved, wholly disposed to evil and op-posed to all good until they were baptized with the Holy Spirit on the day of Pentecost? Are we prepared for this? But we are told that the three thousand converts of that day were also baptized with it is there any proof of this? The record says, "Peter stood up in the midst of the Disciples, the number of names together were about a hundred and twenty." Acts i: 5. "And when the day of Pentecost was fully come, they were all with one accord in one place * * * and they were filled with the Holy Ghost, and began to speak with other tongues as the Spirit gave them utterance." Who were with one accord in one place? The Disciples. Who were all filled with the Holy Ghost? The Disciples. Who began to speak with other tongues as moved by the Holy Ghost? The Disciples. Not a word about any one else being with them. But "when this was noised abroad the multitude came together." ver. 6. Then it was not until after the baptism of the Disciples with the Holy Spirit that the multitude came together from among whom the three thou-sand were converted. Not a word in the narrative about their having been baptized with the Holy Ghost. They were promised the gift of the Holy Spirit if they would "repent and be baptized in the name of Jesus Christ for the remis-sion of sins," but even this was not until they had heard and believed Peter's preaching and were cut to the heart by it, which modern teachers insist they could not have been until they were baptized with it.

We will next examine the case of Cornelius. Please notice his character before he was baptized with the Holy Spirit. He was "a devout man and one that feared God with all his house, which gave much alms to the people, and prayed to God always." Acts x: 2. And was his heart totally depraved, wholly corrupt, the opposite of all good? Really it seems he had good thoughts and did good deeds before he was baptized, either with Spirit or water. Then it follows that the baptism of the Holy Spirit was not intended to remove his depravity and make him devoted, charitable or prayerful for he was all these before. We insist, that if you purify the heart by the baptism of the Holy Spirit you thereby annul the office of faith. With reference to the Gentiles, Peter said, "God, which knoweth the hearts, bare them witness, giving them the Holy Ghost even as he did unto us; and put no difference between us and them, purifying their hearts by faith." Acts xv: 8, 9. Here we find that in cases where the Gentiles received the Holy Spirit, it was not to purify the heart for this was done by faith. Suppose you have a clock, the machinery of which is propelled by weights. You remove the weights from their place and propel the machinery of the clock by springs, what further use have you for the weights? So, if you purify the heart by the baptism of the Holy Spirit what further use have you for faith? But we are sometimes told that the baptism of the Holy Spirit is to produce Faith. Then when Paul said, "So then faith cometh by hearing, and hearing by the word of God." Rom. x: 17, he should have said "So then faith cometh by the baptism of the Holy Spirit."

Again: It is insisted that the baptism of the Holy Spirit is for or in order to the remission of sins, and that this is its office in the Gospel plan of salvation. Then it follows that the Apostles were three years the chosen companions of

Jesus, sent by him to preach to the lost sheep of the house of Israel with power to perform miracles in his name, and still unpardoned until baptized on the day of Pentecost. "John did baptize in the wilderness and preach the baptism of repentance for the remission of sins. And there went out unto him all the land of Judea and they of Jerusalem and were all baptized of him in the river of Jordan, confessing their sins." Mar. i: 4, 5. Thus John made "Ready a people prepared for the Lord." Jesus selected his Apostles from the material thus prepared for him. Does any one believe that when they were baptized by John for the remission of sins that they were still unpardoned until baptized with the Holy Spirit on the day of Pentecost? If not then the baptism of the Holy Spirit was not for the remission of their sins. Paul informs us that there is "one Lord, one Faith and one Baptism." Eph. iv: 5. That this one baptism is for the remission of sins, we believe, is admitted by all. All agree that the one Body, Spirit, Hope, Lord, Faith, Baptism, God and Father of all, spoken of in this connection, by the Apostle to his Ephesian brethren, are essential to the remission of sins, spiritual growth and final happiness of intelligent men and women in a land of Bibles. But those who would disparage the worth of baptism in water, always insist that this one Baptism is "Holy Ghost baptism." If we can dispel this delusion we will have done much to settle the unfortunate controversy with regard to the design of baptism in water. First, then, we would enquire of those who advocate this theory; and believe themselves to have received this one baptism in the Holy Spirit, why they still submit to baptism with water in any form? Surely, if they have been baptized with the Holy Ghost, that is one baptism; yes verily, if their theory be true it is the one baptism; hence, if they subsequently add to this, another in water, they have not one, but two baptisms, and Paul should have said, "There is one Lord, one faith, and two Baptisms." But we may be told that "Cornelius was baptized with the Holy Spirit and was

207

subsequently baptized with water, in obedience to the command of God through Peter, which proves that we may have two baptisms." If this proof is conclusive, will the objector be so good as to assist Paul in extricating himself from the difficulty in which he is placed by saying "There is one baptism." If he will say, with us, that the baptism of the Gentiles at the house of Cornelius, with the Holy Spirit, was a miracle, such as has not occurred from that time to the present (of which we have a record) and allow that when Paul said "There is one baptism," he alluded to the baptism to which the taught of all nations are to submit; Mat. xxviii: 19; and that was enjoined upon "every creature" who would believe the Gospel and be saved, Mark xvi: 10, which was connected with repentance for the remission of sins, Acts ii: 38, that now saves the people who rightly submit to it, 1 Peter iii: 21, and to which all must submit or fail to enter the Kingdom of God, John iii: 5, then we can see perfect harmony in the Scriptures, and a fitness in Paul's language saying "there is one baptism."

Again: When persons were baptized with the Holy Spirit on the day of Pentecost "They were all filled with the Holy Ghost and began to speak with other tongues as the Spirit gave them utterance." Acts ii: 4. There was an absolute impact of the Holy Spirit with the human Spirit and hence, being filled with the Holy Spirit, their spirits were energized—inspired by the Holy Spirit which took possession of them and through them spake forth the wonderful and mighty works of God in languages hitherto unknown to them. The same cause produces the same effect on all occasions if surrounded by the same circumstances. Baptism with the Holy Spirit, on the day of Pentecost, enabled those who received it to speak with tongues, hence if we can find another case on record we may expect the same results, for of this law in nature, God is as much the author as he is the author of the Bible. Accordingly, when Cornelius and his house were baptized with it, "They heard them speak with tongues and magnify God." Acts x: 46. Now as this law obtained in the cases recorded, we must insist that those who claim to have been baptized with the Holy Spirit, must under its influence speak in languages before unknown to them, or give us some good reason why their cases are exceptions to the rule. And were they even to speak with other tongues, this would not be conclusive for although this always followed the baptism of the Holy Spirit and its absence would bar the claim to such baptism, yet there were persons enabled to speak with tongues, and prophecy who had not been baptized with the Spirit. This we will see more clearly when we come to examine the subject of spiritual gifts. As Paul tells us that there is "one baptism" we have only to show that baptism in water is enjoined upon all nations, and every creature who believes the Gospel and would be saved in order to show that there is now no such a thing as Holy Spirit baptism, and hence that there is not a man, woman or child alive to-day who has been the subject of it. In the commission Jesus says, "Go ye, therefore, and teach all nations, baptizing them into the name of the Father, and of the Son, and of the Holy Ghost." Matt, xxviii: 19. Now here is a baptism to which he taught of all nations are to submit, for it would have been anomalous had Jesus commanded the Apostles to baptize them without, at least, an implied obligation on their part to submit to it. Hence if there be one baptism, and only one, this is the baptism, besides which there is not another. There is no escape from this position. Then the only remaining question to be settled, is, did the Savior here allude to water baptism? Does any one doubt it? If so, from whence comes their authority to baptize with or in water, in the names here set forth; that is, in the names of Father, Son and Holy Ghost? And as Jesus was to baptize with the Holy Ghost, and no human being ever had power to administer this baptism; and as the Apostles were commanded to administer one, it is certain that it was not Holy Ghost baptism. Once more: This was to be administered in the name of the Holy Ghost, and as it is not probable that the baptism of the Holy Ghost would have been administered in its own name, it is not probable that this was that kind of baptism.

We have seen that there was an; implied command in the commission to the taught of all nations to submit to this baptism, and in keeping there with we find the Apostles commanding persons to be baptized. "Repent; and be baptized every one of you." Acts ii: 38. "And he commanded them to be baptized in the name of the Lord." Acts x: 48. The baptism of the Holy Spirit was not a command but a promise. "And being assembled together with them, commanded them that they should not depart from Jerusalem, but wait for the promise of the Father, which saith he, ye have heard of me." What promise? "For John truly baptized with water, but ye shall be baptized with the Holy Ghost not many days hence." Acts i: 4, 5. As baptism in water is a command, and the baptism of the Holy Spirit is a promise and not a command, it follows that when the Apostles commanded baptism they meant water baptism. Paul speaks of himself and Roman brethren as having been buried with Christ by baptism, and finally tells them, "ye have obeyed from the heart the form of doctrine which was delivered you; being then made free from sin." Rom. vi: 17, 18. When were they made free from sin? When they obeyed the form of doctrine. What form of doctrine? He was speaking of a baptism in submission to which they obeyed, and were then made free from sin. Was this Holy Ghost baptism? No there was no, obedience in that—it was a promise not a command. Promises may be enjoyed but cannot be obeyed. Commands are to be obeyed in order that the promises connected therewith, if any, may be enjoyed. Water is the only element in which the Romans were commanded to be baptized, and hence baptism in it, was the only baptism they could have obeyed in order that they might be made free from sin. This form of doctrine we will examine hereafter.

But it is insisted that we must have the baptism of the Holy Spirit as evidence of pardon and acceptance with God. Then we ask, had the apostles, who received it on the day of Pentecost, no evidence of their acceptance during their personal intercourse with the Savior prior to that day? And did it give evidence to Cornelius of his acceptance before he obeyed the Gospel? Now we propose to show that persons, were pardoned under the Gospel dispensation, and had reliable evidence of the fact, who had not been baptized with the Holy Spirit. Let us see. "Then Philip went down to the city of Samaria and preached Christ unto them." Acts viii; 5. "When they believed Philip preaching the things concerning the Kingdom of God and the name of Jesus Christ, they were baptized both men and women." Ver. 12. Now are they, saved? Does any one doubt it? So, the advocates of modern Holy Ghost baptism command men and women to be baptized, whom they regard as unsaved when they have been baptized? Nay, verily! So far from it that they believe them pardoned before baptism. Then according to their own theory these persons were saved. If men are saved by faith only, before baptism they believed and were therefore saved; and if it required faith and baptism, they had believed and been baptized and were still saved. So, they were saved in any aspect of the case. But they had still further evidence of pardon. Jesus had said "He that believeth and is baptized shall be saved." Mark xvi: 16. This language is not ambiguous, we can not fail to understand it. Luke says they did believe and were baptized hence if Jesus spake truly when he issued the proclamation and Luke correctly recorded what they did, it follows unmistakably that they were pardoned and had the word of the Lord as evidence of the fact. Were they yet baptized with the Holy Ghost? "Now when the apostles which were at Jerusalem heard that Samaria had received the word of

211

God, they sent unto them Peter and John, who when they were come down, prayed for them that they might receive the Holy Ghost, for at yet he was fallen upon none of them, only they were baptized in the name of the Lord Jesus" Acts viii: 14,16. While it is true that the baptism of the Holy Spirit was not the measure of it which Peter and John designed to confer upon the disciples at Samaria yet the context clearly shows that it had not fallen upon any of them in any form, they having only received what ordinarily followed adoption into the family of God; still they were pardoned—saved beyond a peradventure. Then if the Samaritans could and did believe the Gospel and be baptized in the name of the Lord Jesus, and have his word as evidence that they were saved without the baptism of the Holy Spirit why may we not do the same thing? If any one supposes himself to have been baptized with the Holy Spirit in order to his conversion, then we would like to know whether or not he supposes himself to have been converted as were the Samaritans? Should he claim to have been pardoned in a different way, then we would inquire, how many ways of pardon are there for the same class of persons.

But we have not yet found the purposes for which the baptism of the Holy Spirit was administered in the cases of which we have a record. Soon after his baptism, Jesus selected twelve men to whom it was his purpose to commit the first proclamation of the Gospel which was to be the power of God for the salvation of men. These he required to forsake parents, friends, occupations, every thing, and follow him that their minds might be free to receive the instruction necessary to a thorough preparation for the work assigned them. For three and a half years he ceased not to instruct them in the things pertaining to his Kingdom; and though they had left all to follow one so poor that he had not where to lay his weary head, he comforted them saying "I appoint unto you a Kingdom, as my Father hath appointed unto me; that ye may eat and drink at my table in my

Kingdom, and sit on thrones judging the twelve tribes of Israel." Luke xxii: 29, 30. Knowing the events that were soon to occur in their presence, that he should be put to death, and go to his Father, leaving them to plead his cause in the midst of persecution and death, he faithfully told them of all that should befall them; but that he would remember them in prayer to his Father; "I will pray the Father, and he shall give you another comforter, that he may abide with you forever; even the Spirit of truth whom the world can not receive, because it seeth him not neither knoweth him; but ye know him; for he dwelleth with you and shall be in you." John xiv: 16, 17. This comforter was not, like him, to be taken from them but to remain with them forever. But said he "Because I have said these things unto you sorrow hath filled your hearts; nevertheless, I tell you the truth, it is expedient for you that I go away, for if I go not away the Comforter will not come unto you; but if I depart I will send him unto you." John xvi: 6, 7. Why was it expedient for them that he should go away? "When the Comforter is come, whom I will send unto you from the Father even the Spirit of truth, which proceedeth from the Father, he shall testify of me." John xv: 26. They trusted that it had been he which should have redeemed Israel." Luke xxiv: 41. But when he was crucified their hopes died with him; and in despair they went, each one, to his former occupation. When he gave them proof that he had risen from the dead they took courage and determined to await the promised power from on high. But when the Holy Spirit came from Heaven bearing to them the glorious tidings of his coronation as King of kings and Lord of lords it filled their hearts with joy and gladness; yea they rejoiced to know that he was at his Father's right hand as their adorable High Priest and Mediator, and would there remain to make intercession for his children until his foes should become his footstool. Truly did the Comforter on that day bear witness, of him, for then were they bold to declare that he was "By the right hand of God exalted, and having received of the Father the promise of the Holy Ghost he hath shed forth this which ye now see and hear." Acts ii: 33.

Again: Notwithstanding he had been with them, and had faithfully instructed them in the great scheme of man's salvation, still they were human, and liable to forget the important lessons he had given them; hence he told them that "The Comforter which is the Holy Ghost, whom the Father will send in my name, he shall teach you all things, and bring all thing to your remembrance whatsoever I have said unto you." John xiv: 26. Though he had many things to say to them, which, in their weakness, they were not able to bear; and which, for their good he graciously declined there to reveal, he assured them that "When he, the Spirit of truth is come he will guide you into all truth," (John xvi: 13) and thus he prepared them to eventually receive what he could not then tell them.

Once more: their commission required them to "Preach the Gospel to every creature," to "Teach all nations." How could these ignorant Galileans preach the Gospel among "all nations" to every creature in the numerous languages then spoken?

"There were dwelling at Jerusalem Jews devout men out of every nation under Heaven." Acts ii. Truly here was a difficulty. But they were to "Tarry at Jerusalem until endued with power from on high." This power they were to receive after that the Holy Ghost came upon them? This completed the preparations. How could they then err? They could not despair, for the Spirit gave them comfort from Heaven. They could not forget anything for the Spirit was to strengthen their memory. What Jesus lacked of perfecting their instructions, the Spirit supplied by guiding them into all truth. Were there many nations and divers' languages? The baptism of the Holy Spirit enabled them to speak to every man in his own tongue wherein he was born; and thus they were enabled to preach to every creature, among all nations; and the Comforter through them re-proved the world of sin, of righteousness and of judgment. Only one thing more and the scheme is complete. "Other sheep have I which are not of this fold, them also I must bring, and they shall hear my voice, and there shall be one fold and one shepherd." John x: 16. But how shall this be done? The Jews then, like the Calvinist now, regarded themselves as the favored few for whom Jesus died, and thought it not meet to take the children's bread and give it to dogs. Hence it took a miracle to convince Peter that it was his duty to preach the Gospel to the Gentiles. Six of his Jewish brethren accompanied him to the house of Cornelius where God poured out the Holy Ghost on the Gentiles as on the Disciples at Jerusalem on Pentecost. And they of the circumcision which believed were astonished, as many as came with Peter, because that on the Gentiles also was poured out the gift of the Holy Ghost for they heard them speak with tongues and magnify God." Acts x: 45,46. This satisfied those of the Jews who were with Peter and wit-nessed it and when he rehearsed the whole matter from the beginning, to the Apostles and brethren who were at Jerusa-lem "They held their peace and glorified God, saying, then hath God also to the Gentiles granted repentance unto life." Acts xi: 18. Thus, we see a necessity for God to baptize the Gentiles at the house of Cornelius with the Holy Spirit, not to convert those who received it, or in anyway benefit them; but that the Jews might "perceive that God is no re-specter of persons; but in every nation, he that feareth him and worketh righteousness is accepted with him." Acts x: 34,35.

We wish, in conclusion, to call attention to the striking difference in the forms of speech used with reference to water baptism and Holy Spirit baptism. "Go teach all na-tions baptizing them." "Preach the Gospel to every crea-ture, he that believeth and is baptized shall be saved." Eve-ry creature, among all nations, who is capable of hearing and believing the Gospel may be baptized with the baptism connected with faith as a condition of salvation. How very different the style when speaking of Holy Spirit baptism. "He shall baptize you with the Holy Ghost and with fire." "Ye shall be baptized with the Holy Ghost not many days hence." When speaking of that coming down to us and designed to be perpetual, the style is all nations, every creature; but when speaking of Holy Spirit baptism it is you, ye, and this is the extent of it. Kind reader is not this significant?

12 GA vol.12, #9, 3-10-70, page 217

THE GIFTS OF THE HOLY SPIRIT.

Speaking of the Son of God, John the Baptist said, "God giveth not the Spirit by measure unto him." John iii: 34. This language clearly implies, as stated elsewhere, that God gave the Spirit by measure to others. Indeed, it may be safely said that Jesus was the only person who ever possessed the Spirit without measure- who was always speaking and doing the things suggested by it. The prophets and apostles spake and acted under its influence occasionally, he always. But we have seen that there was a baptism with the Spirit which was a measure of it sufficient to temporarily possess and inspire those who received it. This measure of the Spirit was the promise of the Father, and was given by him through his Son to the disciples on the day of Pentecost, and to the Gentiles at the house of Cornelius. (See Acts xi: 17.) But we must be careful that we do not confuse the Spirit with the gifts of the Spirit. The inspiration and energizing influences of the Spirit are not the Spirit. But there was another measure of the Spirit which was capable of imparting extraordinary gifts to the disciples which we propose to examine for a time. That this measure of the

Spirit was different from the baptism of the Holy Spirit is evident from the fact that the latter always required a divine administrator, while the measure under consideration was imparted by the laying on of apostolic hands. That this measure of the Spirit was different from the ordinary measure received by all Christians is clear from several considerations. First: It was imparted by the apostles through the imposition of their hands, as before stated, while the ordinary measure was received by the hearing of faith. See Gal. iii: 2. Second: Miraculous power was always imparted by it, and manifested by those who received it, while no such manifestations attend the ordinary measure. Third: At Samaria and other places, persons believed the Gospel and were baptized; and therefore enjoyed the ordinary measure of the Spirit for some time before this measure was imparted to them by the apostles. The power to impart this measure of the Spirit' was what Simon sought to purchase with money and was called by Peter "The gift of God," (Acts viii: 20) because God gave it to the apostles who alone possessed it. Though this power of imparting the Spirit by the imposition of apostolic hands was the gift of God, it was neither the Spirit nor the gift of the Spirit. And the Spirit itself though given in different measures, at different times, to different persons, in different ways, for different purposes, was always the gift of God and the same Spirit. There is one Spirit, and only one; hence Paul says, "There are diversities of gifts but the same Spirit." 1 Cor. xii: 4. We have seen that baptism with the Holy Spirit required a divine administrator, hence on the day of Pentecost and at the house of Cornelius it came from Heaven in its amplitude. "The self-same Spirit dividing to every man severally as he would," the measures and manifestations appropriate to each.

The phrase "The gift of the Holy Ghost" occurs Acts ii: 38, and x: 45; and in both places must be understood as equivalent to "The Holy Spirit as a gift." Yet we are persuaded that the same measure of the Spirit is not alluded to in both places.

"While Peter yet spake these words, the Holy Ghost fell on all them which heard the word. And they of the circumcision which believed were astonished, as many as came with Peter, because that on the Gentiles also was poured out the gift of the Holy Ghost; for they heard them speak with tongues and magnify God." Acts x:44-46. That this was that measure called the baptism of the Holy Spirit is plain from the fact that when Peter rehearsed the matter before his brethren he said "As I began to speak the Holy Ghost fell on them as on us at the beginning. Then remembered I the word of the Lord, how that he said, John indeed baptized with water but ye shall be baptized with the Holy Ghost;" (Acts xi: 15, 16) thus quoting the language of the Lord concerning baptism with the Holy Ghost as applicable to this event. But it was not until after the Holy Spirit had been poured out on the disciples "at the beginning," on the day of Pentecost that the multitude came together, to whom Peter promised the Holy Ghost as a gift; hence, it could not have been the baptism of it to which he referred when he said "Ye shall receive the gift of the Holy Ghost." Acts ii: 38. But did Peter here mean the Holy Spirit itself in some measure of it; or did he mean that they should receive something imparted to them by the Spirit? Paul says "There are diversities of gifts but the same Spirit." Peter, did not say "Ye shall receive the gifts, a gift, some gift, or any gift of the Spirit; but the gift of the Holy Spirit. He uses the singular number and definite article, hence we conclude he must be understood to mean some measure of the Holy Spirit itself. But to what measure of the Spirit did the Apostle allude? We have seen that he did not allude to the baptism of it; then it only remains for us to enquire whether he alluded to the ordinary measure which always follows as a necessary result of adoption into God's family? Or did he mean to promise them an extraordinary endowment of it

218

peculiar to the apostolic times We cannot regard it very important to settle this matter in favor of one question or the other. All agree that there were extraordinary endowments of the Spirit conferred upon those, or at least many of them, who believed and obeyed the Gospel in the apostolic times; and all agree that all Christians, from then until now, receive the Spirit of adoption—that all Christians may unite in saying "The love of God is shed abroad in our hearts by the Holy Ghost which is given unto us." Rom. v:5. While good and true men differ as to how the Spirit is received, all agree that it is received, and in some case dwells in every Christian. It is not important, therefore, whether Peter referred to this or that measure of the Spirit. Yet it may not be amiss to state, that as the apostles had power to communicate the Spirit in an extraordinary measure to such as believed and obeyed the Gospel under their ministry; and as they deemed it so important that the primitive Christians should thus extraordinarily receive it, that they sent Peter and John from Jerusalem to Samaria to confer it upon the disciples first made there; we are inclined to think that Peter intended to promise something more than the ordinary measure of the Spirit to those he addressed at the beginning. Surely it was as important that the first disciples made at Jerusalem should receive the extraordinary endowment as it was that those of Samaria, Ephesus and other places should receive it. Nay more; There were dwelling at Jerusalem Jews, devout men, from every nation under Heaven and it is fair to suppose that some of every nation were converted on that occasion. And it is more than probable that it was through these men that the commission was carried out. The apostles preached to all nations on that day; and when the persons there converted returned to their homes bearing the Gospel to every creature, the commission was carried out, "Their sound went into all the earth and their words unto the ends of the world." Rom. x:18. Surely, if these gifts of the Spirit were for the confirmation of the word in Jerusalem, Samaria and Ephesus at its first proclamation, it was not less important that these converts, who were to go into all the world with the Gospel, should be able to confirm its truth when they first preached it in their respective countries. Hence, we conclude that Peter promised the Spirit to such as would believe and obey the Gospel there in as ample measure as he had power to impart it to them. Why should he not thus amply bestow it upon them having the power to do so? And why should he not thus amply promise it to them? Did he wish to bestow it upon them without apprising them of it, that he might afford them an agreeable surprise? But as a settlement of this matter could have no practical bearing upon our investigation, the subject is not worth debating, and we will not consume further space with it. Our purpose is, more particularly, to show that there were extraordinary manifestations of the Spirit in the apostolic times, what they were, and how they were conferred; that they were to cease, have ceased, how and when they ceased and consequently need not be expected now.

Jesus said in the final commission "Go ye into all the world, and preach the Gospel to every creature. He that believeth and is baptized shall be saved; but he that believeth not shall be damned. And these signs shall follow them that believe. In my name shall they cast out devils; they shall speak with new tongues; they shall take up serpents; and if they drink any deadly thing, it shall not hurt them; they shall lay hands on the sick and they shall recover." Mark xvi: 15-18. By this we see that signs were not confined to the apostles alone, but were to follow them that believe. This has been a sweet morsel to infidels from the time miracles ceased until now. The Mormon claims to exhibit these signs now, and he sneeringly tells you that you do not believe your own book. It says, "He that believeth and is baptized shall be saved, but he that believeth not shall be damned." You believe that, O yes, but when it says, these

signs shall follow them that believe you don't believe that."
Yes, we believe it all, but we will not allow an infidel to
divide and interpret it for us. We were once asked by an
infidel why these signs do not follow them that believe?
Jesus said they should follow them that believe. Persons
profess to believe and still we do not see the signs following. What is the reason? Until such persons learn to discriminate between things ordinary and extraordinary—until
they can "Rightly divide the word of truth" it will ever be
unintelligible to them. They never will understand it and
therefore never will have any well-grounded faith in it. Nor
do we think it at all strange that persons should fail to understand the subject of the Spirit's influence, and therefore
teach that it is enveloped in mystery; entirely incomprehensible to finite minds, who mix up the baptism, gifts, reception, and operation of the Holy Spirit. Nor is it strange that
they fail to understand us and continue to misrepresent our
teaching; for when we deny them the baptism of the Holy
Spirit which they have failed to distinguish from the operation of the Spirit, and therefore regard them as one and the
same thing, it is natural that they should understand us to
deny the operation of the Spirit in denying the baptism of it.
But Jesus said these signs should follow them that believe.
Did they follow? At Samaria "The people with one accord
gave heed unto those things which Philip spake hearing and
seeing the miracles which he did. For unclean Spirits crying
with loud voice, came out of many that were possessed
with them and many taken with palsies, and that were lame,
were healed. And there was great joy in that city." Acts
viii: 6-8. Here we find that the very things which Jesus said
should follow, really did follow. We next propose to show
that these signs which Jesus said should follow them that
believe, and which we have seen did follow, were among
the gifts of the Spirit." What were the gifts? "To one is giv-
en by the Spirit the word of wisdom; to another the word of
knowledge by the same Spirit; to another faith by the same

Spirit; to another the gifts of healing by the same Spirit; to another the working of miracles; to another prophecy; to another discerning of Spirits; to another divers kind of tongues; to another the interpretation of tongues; but all these worketh that one and the self-same Spirit dividing to every man severally as he will. 1 Cor. xii: 4-11. Thus, we see that these gifts of the Spirit were the same things which Jesus said should follow them that believe, and which we have found at Samaria and other places did follow. Before leaving this quotation, it may be well to remark that no one man possessed all the gifts, but they were given, one to this, and another to that man, "The self-same Spirit dividing to every man severally," the gifts appropriate to each.

Now, then, was the Spirit imparted by which these gifts were conferred? As the baptism of the Holy Spirit enabled those who received it to speak with tongues, and speaking with tongues is here said to be one of the gifts of the Spirit, is it true that all these miraculously endowed persons were baptized with the Spirit? We think not. The baptism of the Spirit was the gift of the Father (Acts ii: 4) sent from Heaven by the Son. No human being was ever entrusted with the administration of it; but when these spiritual gifts were to be manifested "Then laid they their hands on them and they received the Holy Ghost." And when Simon saw that through laying on of the apostle's hands the Holy Ghost was given he offered them money, saying give me this power that on whomsoever I lay hands, he may receive the Holy Ghost." Acts viii: 17-19. Then it was through the laying on of the Apostle's hands that God gave the Holy Ghost to believers, by which these extraordinary gifts of the Spirit were conferred. And it is expressly said that Simon "had neither part nor lot in this matter." Acts viii:21. And we suppose he had as much part and lot in it as had any one else save the apostles.

That these spiritual gifts were uniformly imparted by the laying on of apostolic hands is made probable by the fact that the presence of an apostle was indispensable to the reception of them. Had it been possible for the apostles to have imparted these gifts by prayer, it occurs to us that a useless trip from Jerusalem to Samaria was imposed upon Peter and John. Certainly, their prayer would have been as efficacious in that city as in this. They would have been addressed to God who could hear in one place and answer in another, and did so in numerous instances (See Mat. viii: 5-13.) He was God afar off as well as near by. Paul said to his brethren at Rome, "I long to see you that I may impart unto you some spiritual gift." Rom. i: 11. This shows most clearly, that however much Paul desired to impart spiritual gifts, he had not the power until he could visit those to whom he would impart them. When he passed through the upper coasts of Asia and came to Ephesus he found certain disciples of whom he enquired, "Have ye received the Holy Ghost since ye believed?" By this it seems to have been customary for the apostles to impart this endowment of the Spirit to the disciples wherever they met them, unless they had previously received it. Hence finding that these disciples were entirely ignorant of it; and that they had been baptized with John's baptism after its validity had ceased, he instructed them in the way of the Lord more perfectly, after which "They were baptized in the name of the Lord Jesus. And when Paul had laid his hands on them, the Holy Ghost came on them; and they spake with tongues and prophesied." Acts xix: 2-6. Then whether this endowment was ever imparted otherwise than by the laying on of apostolic hands, or not; it is certain that they did impart it in this way, and we have no account of its ever being imparted in any other way, and they could not impart it without being present, where their hands at least could have been laid on.

From this standpoint it is easy to see when and how these signs, or spiritual gifts ceased. As none but the apostles, as instruments in the hands of God, had power to impart this endowment of the Spirit to those who believed and obeyed the Gospel, it is obvious that when they died, the power to work miracles necessarily ceased to be conferred upon any person; and when all died who had received the power at the hands of the apostles, they, of course, ceased to be performed. That none but the apostles had power to impart that measure of the Holy Ghost, by which these gifts were conferred is plain, from the fact, that "When the apostles, which were at Jerusalem, heard that Samaria had received the word of God, they sent unto them Peter and John, who, when they were come down, prayed for them that they might receive the Holy Ghost." Acts viii: 14,15. Philip, it seems had the power to exercise the gifts of the Spirit; but, not being an apostle, he could not transfer this power to any one else; hence the necessity of sending Peter and John to them for that purpose, the apostles alone possessing such power.

As we have said that this Philip, who preached the Gospel to the Samaritans, was not an apostle, and as one of the apostles was named Philip it may be well for us to turn aside long enough to examine this matter a little. Some years ago, we made a similar statement, and a good brother thought it a mistake of sufficient importance to induce him to write to the editors of the paper in which our article was published to know if we were not mistaken; and it became necessary to write and publish an essay by way of explanation. The New Testament clearly speaks of three persons named Philip.

First: Philip, the brother of Herod, whose wife was Herodias, at the request of whom, Herod had John the Baptist's head taken off. This Philip was "Tetrarch of Ituria and of the region of Trachonitis." Luke iii: 1.

Second: The Apostle Philip, of whom we have an account of one of the twelve, Mat. x: 3, Mark iii: 18, Luke vi: 14. And as one of the eleven, after the fall of Judas, and before the election of Matthias, Acta i: 13. This Philip "was of Bethsaida of Galilee." John xii: 21.

Third: Philip, the evangelist, who lived in Caesarea, into whose house Paul and company entered ; and who " had four daughters, virgins, which did prophecy." Acts xxi: 8, 9. He "was one of the seven." Acts xxi: 8. What seven? "Then the twelve called the multitude of the disciples unto them and said, it is not reason that we should leave the word of God and serve tables. Wherefore, brethren, look ye out among you seven men of honest report, full of the Holy Ghost and wisdom, whom we may appoint over this business. But we will give ourselves continually to prayer and the ministry of the word. And the saying pleased the whole multitude; and they chose Stephen, a man full of faith and of the Holy Ghost, and Philip, and Prochorus, and Nicanor, and Timon, and Parmenas, and Nicolas a proselyte of Antioch, whom they set before the apostles. Acts vi : 2-6.

Could anything be more plain? The Apostle Philip was one of the twelve who declined to leave the ministry of the word, and commanded the selection of seven others from among the disciples, one of whom was Philip; hence the language, "We entered into the house of Philip, the Evangelist, which was one of the seven; and abode with him." Acts xxi: 8. Following up the history of these seven from their appointment in the 6th chapter of Acts, we find in the seventh chapter an account of the death of Stephen. The second verse of the eighth chapter speaks of his burial; then, in close connection, the fifth verse declares that "Philip went down to the city of Samaria and preached Christ unto them." Then can we be mistaken in saying that this was Philip the evangelist but not the Apostle Philip? "Now when the apostles which were at Jerusalem heard that Samaria had received the word of God, they sent unto them Peter and John, who, when they had come down, prayed for them that they might receive the Holy Ghost: (for as yet he was fallen upon none of them; only they were baptized in the name of the Lord Jesus.) Then laid they their hands on them and they received the Holy Ghost." Acts viii: 14-17.

Had this Philip, who was already at Samaria, been an apostle why the necessity of sending Peter and John from Jerusalem to Samaria that they might impart the Holy Spirit to the Samaritan disciples? Surely, one apostle could have done this as well as others. Are our readers sufficiently acquainted with the Samaritan preacher? we will return to the examination of spiritual gifts.

These gifts were not given as toys to be sported with by those to whom they were given as they might think proper. Even the apostles, themselves, possessed them only to a limited extent. When Paul was shipwrecked on the island called Melita, he gathered a bundle of Sticks, and laid them on the fire, and there came a viper out of the heat, and fastened on his hand, yet he shook off the beast into the fire and felt no harm. Acts xxviii: 3, 5. Did Jesus say "They shall take up serpents; and if they drink any deadly thing, it shall not hurt them?" Surely, the ever faithful Son of God remembered this promise to his humble persecuted disciple just then. But this was not all Jesus further said "They shall lay hands on the sick and they shall recover." Hence, he not only protected Paul's person from harm; but "It came to pass that the father of Publius lay sick of a fever, and of a bloody flux: to whom Paul entered in, and prayed, and laid his hands on him, and healed him. So, when this was done, others also, which had diseases in the island, came and were healed." Acts, xxviii: 8, 9. By this we learn that Paul possessed in an eminent degree, the power to heal the sick, which is enumerated among the spiritual gifts; nevertheless, he informs us that he left Trophimus at Miletus sick. 2 Tim. iv: 20. Why would Paul leave his friend and traveling companion sick, having the power to heal him? Surely, if he could have done so, he would have cured him. The reason why he did not, can only be found in the fact that he only possessed such power when the glory of God would be exhibited by its exercise.

But for what were these spiritual gifts bestowed upon the primitive disciples? After Jesus had given to the apostles their commission to preach the Gospel to every creature, promising salvation to those who would believe and obey it; and assuring them that these signs (gifts of the Spirit) should follow them that believe, we learn that they went forth and preached everywhere, the Lord working with them and confirming the word with signs following." Mark xvi : 20. Then these signs were for the confirmation of the word at its first proclamation. Hence Paul said to the Romans; I long to see you, that I may impart unto you some spiritual gift, to the end ye may he established; that is, that I may be comforted together with you by the mutual faith both of you and me." Rom. i: 11, 12. In the infantile state of the Church, when it was dependent upon oral instructions for all things pertaining to life and godliness, the Lord graciously attended, and confirmed the word preached, by these extraordinary demonstrations of the Spirit. Hence, says Paul to the Corinthians, "And I, brethren, when I came to you, came not with excellency of speech or of wisdom, declaring unto you the testimony of God; for I determined not to know anything among you, save Jesus Christ, and him crucified. And I was with you in weakness, and in fear and in much trembling. And my speech and my preaching was not with enticing words of man's wisdom, but in demonstration of the Spirit and of power; that your faith should not stand in the wisdom of men. but in the power of God." 1 Cor. ii: 1-5. Persons sometimes say of a preacher "He is so smart that he can make error appear as truth—he would make you believe a crow is white as a swan were he to make the effort." Though this is not very complimentary to the intelligence of the people; the devil sometimes seeks thus to catch away the seed sown, by making the people believe that it is the shrewdness of the preacher and not the truth which makes his positions look plausible. The apostle made no effort to fascinate and charm the Corinthians by his eloquence, excellency of speech; nor by his learning, enticing words of man's wisdom. As to these, he was with them in weakness. But that they might be established and their faith unshaken his preaching was confirmed by signs following, here called demonstration of the Spirit and of power that their faith should not stand in the wisdom of men, but in the power of God. When Jesus ascended up on high, he led captivity captive and gave gifts unto men. How did he give these gifts, and what were they? By the Spirit he prepared some men to be Apostles; and some, prophets; and some, evangelists; and some, pastors and teachers." And what were these for? "For the perfecting of the saints, for the work of the ministry, for the edifying of the body of Christ." And how long were these gifts to remain? "Till we all come in the unity of the faith and of the knowledge of the Son of God, unto a perfect man, [perfect Church] unto the measure of the stature of the fulness of Christ; that we henceforth be no more children, tossed to and fro, and carried about with every wind of doctrine." Eph. iv: 11-14. Paul tells us "Whether there be prophecies they shall fail whether there be tongues they shall cease whether by knowledge it shall vanish away." 1 Cor. xiii: 8. These were among the spiritual gifts, and it is here expressly stated that they should have an end; and we have clearly seen just how and when they did end. Having a perfect record of these signs given by inspiration of the Holy Spirit there is no necessity for them to be repeated now; and to wish to see them, but to confess our want of confidence in the Bible— virtually saying "I know God therein says they occurred, but I am not sure the record is true, I would prefer to see them myself." "If the word spoken by angels was steadfast, and every transgression and disobedience received a just recompense of reward, how shall we escape, if we neglect so great salvation, which at the first began to be spoken by the Lord, and was confirmed unto us by them that heard him; God, also, bearing them witness, both with signs and wonders, and divers miracles and gifts of the Holy Ghost according to His own will?" Heb. ii: 2-4. Kind reader, let us ponder well this soul stirring question. This great salvation, first spoken by the Lord, was confirmed by them that heard him, God, also, bearing them witness with signs and wonders, and divers miracles and gifts of the Holy Spirit according to his will, and they are written, as were the signs of Jesus, that ye might believe that Jesus is the Christ the Son of God and that believing you might have life through his name. How then, how shall we escape if we neglect it? As surely as every transgression and disobedience, under the law, received a just recompense of reward so surely will we be rewarded according to our works.

13 GA vol. 12, #11, 3-17-70 page 241

THE OPERATION OF THE HOLY SPIRIT IN CONVERSION,

That it is necessary that man be converted in order to the enjoyment of the favor of God is not a matter of controversy with any save Universalists and we are not quite sure we could do any good by stopping to debate the question with them just now. They say they believe the Bible to be a revelation from God and therefore true. It says, "These shall go away into everlasting punishment; but the righteous into life eternal." Mat. xxv; 46. "The hour is coming, in the which all that are in the graves shall hear his voice, and shall come forth; they that have done good, unto the resurrection of life, and they that have done evil unto the resurrection of damnation." John v: 28, 29. "The rich man also died, and was buried; and in hell he lifted up his eyes, being in torments." Luke xvii: 22-3. And what more? The fearful, and unbelieving, and the abominable, and murderers, and whoremongers, and sorcerers, and idolaters, and all liars, shall have their part in the lake which burneth with fire and brimstone." Rev. xxi: 8. These are enough for us; and if they will not suffice for those who profess to believe the Bible, then they would not be persuaded though one should arise from the dead. That all intelligent men and women in a land of Bibles must be converted or lost we will assume as a settled fact.

That the Spirit does operate in conversion is admitted by all who are expected to be benefitted by our labors; hence we offer no argument to prove that which no one denies. Though we have sometimes, nay often, heard of a people who deny the operation of the Holy Spirit in conversion, we have never met a single man who so taught nor have we ever read any thing from the pen of any man who had so written. Lest, therefore, we waste our ammunition in " shelling the woods we will wait for the appearance of the enemy before we make war upon him. Nor do we propose any examination of what the Spirit can or cannot do. The questions which concern us are, What does it do and how does it do it. We have seen, in another department of our work, that on the day of Pentecost God established upon the earth a system of government, variously styled, the Kingdom of God—the Kingdom of Heaven—the Kingdom of God's dear Son—the Church of God—the Temple of God—the House of God—the Household of Faith— the Body of Christ, etc. Concerning this organization we are now prepared to see

First: That those who established it were directly instructed by the Holy Spirit.

Second: That from the time of its organization it became the dwelling place of the Holy Spirit through all succeeding time; and,

Third: That it is the medium through which the Holy Spirit puts forth its power for the conversion and salvation of man.

To an examination of these propositions, in their order, we solicit the attention of the reader for a time.

First, then, that those who established it were directly instructed by the Holy Spirit. This has been so thoroughly examined already that it need not detain us long. Still it is important to remember that "They were all filled with the Holy Ghost, and began to speak with other tongues, as the Spirit gave them utterance." Acts ii: 4. Then their teaching was but the teaching of the Holy Spirit through them. Every announcement made, every condition imposed, every blessing promised, and every punishment threatened was spoken by the Holy Spirit through men selected for the work and was made binding on men here and ratified in Heaven.

Second, that it became the dwelling place of the Holy Spirit through all succeeding time is apparent from several considerations:

1. "The body without the Spirit is dead." Jas. ii: 26. The body is the Church. Col. i: 18 and 24. Then if there was ever a time when the Spirit was not in the body of Christ or Church it was surely a dead body.

2. When Paul said, "There is one body and one Spirit," it is next to certain that he meant to teach that there is one body and one Spirit in this body.

3. In speaking of it as a Temple or building and the disciples as living stones in it, the Apostle says, "Know ye not that ye are the temple of God, and that the Spirit of God dwelleth in you." 1 Cor. iii: 16.

4. Jesus said to the disciples before his death, "I will pray the Father, and he shall give you another Comforter, that he may abide with you forever." John xiv: 16. "The Comforter is the Holy Ghost." ver. 26. From these Scriptures, it is apparent that when the Holy Spirit came, and the Church or body was organized by its directions, it took up its abode in it; not for a season only, but as an abiding guest and Comforter forever; and thus it is that the disciples are

"Builded together, for an habitation of God through the Spirit." Eph. ii: 22.

Third: We come now to an examination of our third proposition; namely, that the Church thus Organized by the Spirit, is not only its dwelling place, but is the medium through which it puts forth its power for the conversion and salvation of man.

The Kingdom or Church of God, and the Kingdom of Satan are the great antagonistic governments or powers of earth. They are engaged in a perpetual war against each other; and each is seeking to capture the subjects of the other. They do not discharge their prisoners on parole; but each one taken, is forthwith made a recruit in the ranks of the captors. Paul minutely describes the armor furnished the soldiers of the cross in this great struggle. After describing the character of the enemy he says, "Wherefore take unto you the whole armor of God, that ye may be able to withstand in the evil day, and having done all to stand. Stand therefore, having your loins girt about with truth, and having on the breastplate of righteousness; and your feet shod with the preparation of the gospel of peace; above all taking the shield of faith wherewith ye shall be able to quench all the fiery darts of the wicked. And take the helmet of salvation, and the sword of the Spirit, which is the word of God." Eph. vi: 13-17. There are many valuable thoughts suggested by the different parts of this armor which we have not time to notice. We wish to call attention to the fact that the disciples are to don this armor and use it, not lay it on the center-table as a keepsake, but use it. That this spiritual war is both offensive and defensive is suggested by the fact that there is both a sword and shield belonging to the armor. This is for protection against the darts of the enemy—that is for making wounds upon him. He that enters the army taking only the shield, that he may protect himself, while others fight the enemy makes rather a worthless soldier. Soldiers of the cross are required to take the whole armor of God that they may "fight a good fight," for their own salvation and the salvation of others.

The word of God is the sword of the Spirit, and the disciples are to use it in order to rescue their fellow-man from the enemy and enlist him as a soldier against him—that he may be delivered from the power of darkness and translated into the Kingdom of God's dear Son. Are we letting the sword of the Spirit rust in its scabbard? "Ye are the salt of the earth; if the salt have lost his savor, wherewith shall it be salted? It is thenceforth good for nothing, but to be cast out, and to be trodden under foot of men." Mat. v : 13.

The Holy Spirit dwelling in the body, operates through its members by its teaching upon such material as comes within the range of its influence. The teaching of the Spirit put forth through the members of the body is both theoretic and practical. The Gospel is the power of God unto salvation to every one that believeth; and he has ordained that it shall be preached to all nations— every creature, that he may learn the theory by which God proposes to save him. But this is not all of it. There must be a practical exhibition of the Christian religion in the life of the disciples, hence Jesus said to them, "Let your light so shine before men, that they may see your good works, and glorify your Father which is in Heaven." Mat. v: 16. That this be spiritual light, the good works must be those "Which God hath before ordained that we should walk in them." Eph. ii: 10. Every thing necessary to a thorough exhibition of the Christian religion, both theoretically and practically, is comprehended in the Scriptures "Given by inspiration of God," for they are profitable for doctrine, for reproof, for instruction in righteousness; that the man of God may be perfect, thoroughly furnished unto all good works." 2 Tim. iii: 16,17. The man of God is designed to be perfect and the Scriptures given by inspiration were designed to make him so. They not only furnish him, but thoroughly furnish him, not only to some good works but to all good works. Does it not follow, then, that there is nothing left discretionary with man? Nay, if there be any work to which the man of God is not thoroughly furnished by the Scriptures does it not follow that it is not a 'good' work? "As his divine power hath given unto us all things that pertain unto life and godliness, through the knowledge of him that hath called us to glory and virtue." 2 Peter i: 3.

But we have seen that the promised Comforter was to reprove the world of sin, righteousness and judgment, That this Comforter was the Holy Spirit, and that it did come to the disciples and was received by them we have already seen. That it did reprove, and is reproving, the world of sin, righteousness and judgment is a fact so generally admitted that we need not stop to offer proof of it. The controverted question is, how did it do it? To this question we will; give our attention for a time. Did the Spirit come from Heaven to the world? What do we understand the Savior to mean by the term world in the passage under consideration? Certainly it will be conceded that he did not mean the material universe, but that he meant the wicked people who committed sin of which to be reproved, in contrast with the disciples.

Then was the Holy Spirit given directly to the wicked, that it might enter their hearts and reprove them? No, it was promised to the disciples. Jesus said to them "I will pray the Father, and he shall give you another Comforter, that he may abide with you forever; even the Spirit of truth whom the world cannot receive, because it seeth him not, neither knoweth him; but ye know him for he dwelleth with you and shall be in you." John xiv: 16,17. Then the Spirit was not only promised to the disciples to dwell with, and be in them but it is said, in great plainness, that the world, which was to be reproved by it, could not receive it. On the day of Pentecost, the promised Spirit came, and through Peter used words calculated to convey to those who heard, just such ideas as were necessary to be communicated to them

234

to make them sensible of the sin of which they were to be reproved. Believing Jesus to be an imposter they had crucified and slain him, but Peter used such arguments as convinced them that in this they were mistaken. At the close of his speech he said "Therefore let all the house of Israel know assuredly, that God hath made that same Jesus, whom ye have crucified, both Lord and Christ. Now when they heard this they were pricked in their heart" Acts ii: 36, 37. This is all plain. The Spirit reproved them through Peter's words which they understood and believed, and thus operated sensibly upon them, cut them to the heart. When God created man, he gave him an organization capable of receiving just such impressions as he designed should be made upon him. He placed within him a mind capable of appreciating communications from his Creator and his fellow man; and he gave him certain senses through which to receive such impressions as are necessary to the accomplishment of his mission on the earth. Hence, we conclude that in order for man to receive instructions from, any source they must be embodied in words adapted to his comprehension and directed to the mind through the avenues which God has opened to it. In keeping with this arrangement, we find that in every period of man's existence, when God wished to communicate an idea to him he embodied it in words adapted to his capacity and gave it to him either in person or through some agent selected for that purpose. Even so, when the Spirit reproved man of sin it is said "ye men of Israel, hear these words; Jesus, of Nazareth, a man approved of God among you by miracles and wonders, and signs which God did by him in the midst of you, as ye yourselves also know: him, being delivered by the determinate counsel and fore-knowledge of God, ye have taken, and by wicked hands have crucified and slain." Acts ii: 22-3. When the angel of the Lord told John in the Isle of Patmos what to write to each of the seven Asiatic churches, each message closed by saying "He that hath an ear to hear let him hear what the Spirit saith unto the Churches." Hence the words which John wrote by inspiration of the Spirit were the words of the Spirit, and by hearing them we hear, what the Spirit said to the Churches. Then it follows that when we hear the words of an inspired man we hear the words of the Spirit, and when we have the thoughts legitimately belonging to such words, we have the thoughts communicated by the Spirit. In this way even "Now the Spirit speaketh expressly that in the latter times some shall depart from the faith, giving heed to seducing spirits and doctrines of devils." 1 Tim. iv:1. The Spirit then does not speak in mysterious and incomprehensible ways but it speaks expressly, in words easy to be understood. "Holy men of God spake as they were moved by the Holy Ghost." 2 Peter i: 21. We have a faithful record of what they said, hence "They being dead yet speaketh." Heb. xi: 4 Paul said "Eye hath not seen, nor ear heard, neither have entered into the heart of man, the things which God hath prepared for them that love him; but God hath revealed them unto us by his Spirit; for the Spirit searcheth all things, yea, the deep things of God. Which things also we speak, not in the words which man's wisdom teacheth, but which the Holy Ghost teacheth; comparing spiritual things with spiritual." 1 Cor. ii: 9-13.

And again: " For this cause I, Paul, the prisoner of Jesus Christ for you Gentiles, if ye have heard of the dispensation of the grace of God which is given me to you-ward; how that by revelation he made known unto me the mystery as I wrote afore in few words; whereby, when ye read, ye may understand my knowledge in the mystery of Christ, which in other ages was not made known unto the sons of men, as it is now revealed unto his Holy Apostles and Prophets by the Spirit." Ep. iii: 1-6. Here we learn that things which in other ages had been a mystery to other people were by the Spirit revealed and made known to Paul and other Apostles and prophets, and that Paul had written them to his brethren so that when they read they could understand his knowledge of what had previously been a profound mystery. "And what shall I say more for the time would fail me," to quote all the Scriptures which prove that the lessons taught by the prophets and apostles were nothing less than the teaching of the Holy Spirit. David said "To-day if ye will hear his voice, harden not your heart, as in the provocation, and as in the day of temptation in the wilderness, when your fathers tempted me, proved me, and saw my work. Forty, years long was I grieved with this generation, and said, It is a people that do err in their heart, and they have not known my ways." Ps. ix: 7-10. Paul quotes this language, saying, "wherefore as the Holy Ghost saith, To-day if ye will hear his voice," etc. Heb. iii: 7-10. Why did the apostle thus quote the language of David as the language of the Holy Ghost? Because "David, the son of Jesse said, and the man who was raised up on high, the anointed of the God of Jacob and the sweet psalmist of Israel said, the Spirit of the Lord spake by me, and his word was in my tongue." 2 Sami xxiii: 1, 2. Hence it was, too, that Peter quotes David saying "The Holy Ghost by the mouth of David spake," etc. Acts i: 16. Thus we see why Paul and Peter quote the words of David as the words of the Holy Spirit spoken by him. And therefore, any effect produced upon the heart as properly growing out of such language can be nothing less than an effect produced by the Holy Spirit.

Having found that the Holy Spirit has clothed its ideas in words adapted to the comprehension of man we can see a beauty and fitness in the parable of the sower and the explanation of it by the Savior: He says, "The seed is the word of God. Those by the way-side, are they that hear; then cometh the devil, and taketh away the word out of their hearts, lest they should believe and he saved." The devil knows well that if he can keep the people away from the word of God, or get it away from them after they have heard it, all are his. Hence, he makes every effort he can, to keep it from them. He will bolt church doors against it—call it all the ugly names he can think of to keep people from hearing it—if, in spite of him they hear it, he offers every gratification that the flesh can desire, to choke it out. "They on the rock, are they, which, when they hear, receive the word with joy, and these have no root, which for a while believe, and in time of temptation fell away. And that which fell among thorns, are they which, when they have heard, go forth and are choked with cares, and riches, and pleasures of this life, and bring no fruit to perfection. But that on the good ground, are they, which in an honest and good heart, having heard the word, keep it and bring forth fruit with patience." Luke viii: 11-15. As the farmer cannot reap a crop without seed has been sown, neither can there be a spiritual crop without spiritual seed. And as the word of God is the spiritual seed, it follows that where the word of God is not preached, or the seed in some way sown, there can be no spiritual crop. This is so very evident that we need not offer arguments to support it. "Faith cometh by hearing and hearing by the word of God." Rom. x: 17. Where the word of God is not, it cannot be heard and hence there can be no faith and "he that believeth not shall be damned." Mark xvi: 16. Hence no word of God, no faith; and no faith, no salvation for intelligent men and women in a land of Bibles. Before there was a written word, "It pleased God, by the foolishness of preaching, to save them that believe." 1 Cor. i: 21. The press is now a very extensive sower of the word of God; but then, men went everywhere preaching the word. Hence Paul asks "How shall they believe in him of whom they have not heard? and how shall they hear without a preacher? and how shall they preach except they be sent?" Rom. x: 14, 15. Before the Gospel was written so as to afford preachers an opportunity of learning it by study, God miraculously called, qualified and sent men to preach; but now, if they would know anything they had better observe Paul's charge to Timothy "Give attendance to reading."

That we may, if possible, more clearly see the medium through which the Spirit operates we will notice another Scripture or two. "The Lord said, my Spirit shall not always strive with man." Gen. vi: 3. How did the Spirit of the Lord anciently strive with the people? "Yet many years didst thou forbear them, and testifieth against them by thy Spirit in thy prophets: yet would they not give ear." Neh. ix : 30. Thus we see that the Spirit strove with, bore with and testified against the people, but was located in, and did its work through the prophet, and by resisting their words the people resisted the teaching of the Holy Spirit. The devoted Stephen said to his persecutors, " Ye Stiff-necked and uncircumcised in heart and ears, ye do always resist the Holy Ghost: as your fathers did so do ye." How did their fathers resist the Holy Ghost? "Which of the prophets have not your fathers persecuted?" Then by persecuting the prophets they resisted the Holy Ghost. "When they heard these things they were cut to the heart"—reproved of sin— operated on by the Holy Spirit; but did they receive the Spirit? Surely not. "They gnashed on him with their teeth; but he being full of the Holy Ghost looked up steadfastly into Heaven and saw the glory of God, and Jesus standing on the right hand of God, and said, behold I see the Heavens opened, and the Son of man standing on the right hand of God. Then they cried out with a loud voice, and stopped their ears, and ran upon him with one accord and cast him out of the city, and stoned him." Acts vii: 61-58. By this narrative we see clearly that the Spirit was located in Stephen, and through his words operated on the people; yet they did not receive the Spirit, but resisted it. The Holy Spirit was in Stephen but the spirit of the wicked one was in the people. It is one thing therefore to be operated on by the Spirit, and quite another thing to receive the Spirit. On the day of Pentecost, the Spirit operated in the same way, but the result was very different. It was in Peter and through his words cut the people to the heart, "Then they that gladly received his word, were baptized: and the same day there were added unto them about three thousand souls." Acts ii: 41. In place of gladly receiving Stephen's words they resisted the Holy Spirit and put Stephen to death. Persons operated on by the Spirit may receive or reject its teaching as they may elect.

All bodies, or organizations have Spirits within them, and cannot exist without them. Not only so, but every organization or body has its own peculiar spirit. The Free Mason, Odd Fellow, Sons of Temperance and Good Templar organizations, each has its own peculiar spirit. And they are working, operative spirits too, operating through the members by their teaching on such material as comes within the range of their influence. And when they make any thing, they make material for their own respective bodies, and nothing else. That is, the Spirit of Masonry, if it makes anything, makes Masons, and never makes an Odd Fellow or Son of Temperance. The spirit of Odd Fellowship makes Odd Fellows, but never makes Masons or anything else. Mormons, Baptists, Presbyterians, Methodists and Christians all have spirits peculiar to their own respective organizations or bodies. These spirits too, are working Spirits, operating through their members by their teaching on the people. When the spirit of Catholicism operates it always makes a Catholic, and never makes a Mormon, Baptist, Presbyterian, Methodist or a Christian. When the Mormon spirit operates, it always makes if anything at all, a Mormon, and never makes a Catholic, Baptist, Presbyterian, Methodist or Christian. To this all but Catholics and Mormons will agree. Shall we take another step? When the Holy Spirit operates by its teaching it always makes Christians, and never makes a Catholic, a Mormon or anything else. Will all agree to this? "No," says an objector, "I see what you are at, and you are mistaken. I will give you an instance where the Spirit made Methodists, Baptists, and Presbyterians. There was a protracted union meeting in our town (or neighborhood as the case may be) in which these several denominations were engaged. The Spirit was profusely poured out, and the meeting was abundantly blessed to the conversion of scores of persons, some of whom joined each of the denominations mentioned. Very well. It yet remains to be shown that this was the work of the Holy Spirit. Let us see. Perhaps this meeting was gotten up by these parties, not to oppose the powers of darkness, or put to flight the armies of Satan; but to put down what the preachers were pleased to call Campbellism. They told the people not to hear such stuff. They had bolted their doors against all who dared to say as Jesus did, "He that believeth and is baptized shall be saved," or as did the Spirit by Peter, "Repent and be baptized every one of you in the name of Jesus Christ for the remission of sins." But still the people would go to hear, and this union meeting was gotten up as an effort to create, if possible a deeper prejudice in the minds of the people to keep them from hearing. "It is but the teaching of the Bible, and as sure as the people continue to hear it they will believe it. Our peculiarities are all in danger, and we must unite to put them out of the way. This done, we can then fight and devour each other as we did thirty years ago." Now as the spirit of this meeting was hatred and malice towards those who taught and acted according to the Spirit's directions, and as Paul tells us "The fruit of the Spirit is love, joy, peace, long-suffering, gentleness, faith, meekness, temperance," etc., Gal. 6: 22-3, fruit so very unlike the fruit of this meeting, it is clear that the very main spring of the whole affair was not the Spirit of Christ, but the spirit of anti- Christ.

But let us examine the teaching at this meeting, and see whether or not it resembles the teaching of the Spirit. The preachers say to sinners "Ye wicked and uncircumcised in heart, the Lord's arms of mercy are open wide to receive and bless you, but you will not come to him that he may bless you. The horrors of Hell and the joys of Heaven are painted in glowing colors before the audience, until some conclude they will secure these, and avoid those; and they at once put themselves under the instructions of the preachers with hearts subdued to the will of God as far as they know it. And how do they direct them? Do they say to them as the Spirit by Peter said to those wishing to know; how to be saved on the day of Pentecost, "Repent and be baptized every one of you, in the name of Jesus Christ for the remission of sins?" Nay, verily! Such a declaration would put out all the excitement as effectually as water puts out fire. What then? Come into the altar or to the mourner's bench." Did the Spirit so teach the Pentecostian enquirers? Nay, did the Spirit ever teach a son of Adam thus from the beginning of time until now? Not a word like it. But the sinners willing to do anything to obtain the blessing, come to the altar as directed by the preacher (not the Holy Spirit.) Then what follows? The congregation must all engage in prayer to God for them; and among the first petitions made in their behalf is something like the following: "O God, come now, we beseech thee, to pardon and bless these mourners." First, they told the people God was willing, but they were not willing: Now they are willing, but God is not. Hence, they pray, beg and beseech God to do that which they had previously declared him always ready and willing to do. Is this the teaching of the Holy Spirit? It cannot be. Surely God trifles not with his creatures in this way. But the preacher prays very earnestly to God to baptize them (us, says he,) "With the Holy Ghost and with fire, right now." And perhaps he has prayed for the same thing at every meeting he has attended, perhaps a dozen times at some of them. Did God anciently baptize the same persons with the Holy Ghost and fire, day after day repeatedly? When we hear such a petition we involuntarily think, if we do not say, Lord forbid! But the excitement in some is now sufficiently high, and they rise, shouting, jumping, falling over benches, or on the floor, until it has become necessary for the friends to interpose, and restrain them by force to prevent them from being injured or killed. What is the matter now? Will the Holy Spirit kill the people in converting them? Not so. If we believed in the operation of the Holy Spirit, we would say, hands off gentlemen, it is God's work. Fear not, he will do right. If he kills them, they ought to die. Others, who are not blessed with a temperament so highly exciteable, are not so easily moved by excitement, (which, by the way, is the very pabulum upon which the whole meeting subsists) hence the preacher says to them, "you have got it. Get up and shout, and tell the people what the Lord has done for you." And it takes all the assurance the preachers and Spirit can all give to get them through. Others, who have a little higher intellectual development, have to get up and go home without "getting through" at all. Pray what is the reason? Did any of the Pentecostian applicants fail? The preachers told them God was willing, and would bless them if they could come. They have come and they have honestly and faithfully done as they were directed, and yet they have been disappointed. What is the matter? Were they not as honest and as humble as they ever could be? Had they not full confidence in the efficacy of the blood of Jesus? If they had not they would not have gone into the altar. Did they not from the great deep of their hearts desire pardon? Were they any worse than those who get through, that it should cost them a harder struggle? Then we again ask why were they disappointed? Not to be tedious, we must leave these unfortunate subjects to brood over and account for their disappointment, upon the ground that they are not of the elect, or by supposing that there is no reality in religion, and thus merge into the stygian pool of infidelity, while we attend to those who were fortunate enough to "get through."

They must each tell an " Experience of grace," for which there is not a word of authority in the Bible. Persons under the instruction of the Spirit anciently were required to confess their faith in the Son of God, but these tell the workings of their own imaginations. And not to be tedious in our examination of the many absurdities detailed, they usually contain the following four main points:

1st. They felt like, and therefore believed themselves the worst sinners living.

2nd. They felt like, and therefore; believed that their day of grace had forever passed.

3d. They felt like, and therefore believed that God could not be just and pardon persons so wicked as themselves.

4th. They felt like, and therefore; believed that God for Christ's sake had pardoned them.

As these four points enter into almost every experience we have listened to, we will examine them briefly.

1st. They never had killed any person or stolen anything; others having done both, were worse than they, therefore when they believed themselves worse than all others they believed a falsehood.

2nd. They were then telling an "Experience of grace," claiming to have found a day of grace, hence when they believed their day of grace forever passed, they believed a falsehood.

3rd. They all believed God to be infinitely just, and were then saying that they believed he had pardoned them; so, if in this they were not mistaken, when they believed God would not be just and pardon them, they believed a falsehood.

Now as their feelings had led them to believe three admitted falsehoods, out of but four propositions, may we not at least suspect the truth of the fourth? Paul told his brethren that they were chosen to salvation "Through sanctification of the Spirit and belief of the truth." 2 Thess. ii: 13. Then if these persons were not mistaken in thinking themselves pardoned, Paul's rule was reversed as to them, for they were not chosen in the belief of the truth but in the belief of three falsehoods as they themselves admit. And as the fourth proposition consists in believing that God had pardoned them without a compliance, upon their part, with the conditions upon which he had suspended their pardon, we must be permitted to think that there is as much probability in the truth of either of the other proposition as in this one. The vote is taken, however, and they are received. But we are rather ahead of the proceedings; we must go back a little, Each one asks, "What Church shall I join?" The preachers are all present. No one will say join my Church; that would be too selfish. But they say "Go to the grove and secretly pray to God to direct you by the Spirit, then come back and join the Church to which the Spirit, through your feelings, may incline you." Very well. All go and pray to the same God, and are guided by the same Spirit, yet when they return, one will join the Presbyterians and he will have water sprinkled on him as baptism. Another guided by the same Spirit will join the Methodists, and have water poured on him as baptism. Another, under the guidance of the same Spirit will join the Baptists, and nothing will do him for baptism but immersion. And though when he "got religion" twelve months before, he may, under the direction of the Spirit, have been immersed by one of the Methodist preachers in the present meeting, he must now have it administered by a Baptist minister. The Methodist preacher who immersed him a year before, though now fully competent to preach, pray, exhort, sing and assist in his present conversion, is nevertheless incompetent to administer baptism though it be "a mere nonessential" and his former baptism is therefore invalid, though it may have been immersion. Paul says "By one Spirit are we all baptized into one body." 1 Cor. xii: 13. Now as these were not all baptized into one body, but into several bodies, it is quite clear that they were not guided by the Spirit of which he spake. Now kind reader is this picture overdrawn? Have you not seen all this and much more? We most solemnly aver that we have seen all this and many other things at such meetings too absurd to be spoken of in an essay like this without a compromise of our self-respect. Then in the fear of God allow me to ask, did the Holy Spirit originate, preside over, or conduct the meeting?

There are a few thoughts connected with these revival meetings to which we respectfully invite the attention of those who believe that the Spirit operates, directly, abstractly or immediately on persons to effect their conversion. First: Why is it necessary that there be a meeting? Is it because the Spirit cannot or will not operate on the people at their respective homes as well as when they are congregated? Or is it not true that they are called together that the preacher may have an opportunity of calling their attention to their spiritual interests? If so, it must follow that the Spirit is expected to operate through the preacher by such preaching, praying, singing and exhortation as he may be able to bring to bear upon them. Again: Why is it important that the best revivalists be secured to conduct the more successful meetings? If the Spirit operates immediately on the people we cannot see any use for a preacher at all. Or if one must be had, it would not matter whether he have ten talents or one. An immediate operation of the Spirit cannot be a mediate operation, and hence the preacher could have nothing to do with it and one preacher would do as well as another. From our standpoint, we can easily see why one preacher may be more successful in conducting a meeting than another; but we can not reconcile it with the doctrine of immediate Spiritual influences. The Spirit is in the Church and operates through its members by its teaching upon such material as comes within the range of its influence; and it is to bring the people where they may hear its teaching that the meeting is called in the first place. Then the Spirit operates, not immediately but mediately, the stronger the medium the more potent the influence. The word of God is the sword of the Spirit; and as earthly governments wield their swords through their soldiery, so God wields the sword of the Spirit through his soldiery. And as an adroit fencer will use the instrument of death more successfully in carnal warfare, even so will skillful workmen more successfully wield the sword of the Spirit in fighting the battles of the Lord. God gives us bread by giving us soil, rain and other means of producing grain of which to make it; but the richer the soil and better the season the more abundant will be the crop. So, of everything we enjoy through means; the more potent the means the richer the blessing.

But we are told that the devil operates on the people immediately. It is assumed that he has no written law or revealed will, nor does he make any verbal communications in man, hence he must either operate without words, arguments or other visible means, or not operate at all. And if the Holy Spirit only operates on man mediately, and the devil immediately, then it follows that the latter has more power than the former. We would respectfully suggest that the modus operandi of the Holy Spirit is not a question of power. We care not to examine whether the Spirit can or cannot operate in this or that way. It is sufficient that we know how it does operate. Nor are we prepared to admit that the devil, even now, makes no verbal communications to men; on the contrary he makes very many both oral and written. It is true that there are no books bearing his name as author; nor did he write immediately any book known to us. But the same may be said of Jesus and the Holy Spirit. Neither of them wrote any part of the New Testament immediately, yet we accept it as the last will and testament of the one, and inspired by the other. We most firmly believe that four-fifths of the books extant are doing efficient service in behalf of the devil. Does any one doubt it? Then let him look at the Mohammedan and Mormon Bibles leading

247

multiplied thousands away from Christ after Mohammed and Joe Smith. Look, too, at the writings of infidels of every grade and hue; whose avowed purpose is to make the people believe that the word, of God is a fable, and his Son an impostor. The time would fail us to mention even the general, to say nothing of the species, of the devil's literature; and yet we are told that the devil makes no verbal communications to man at all!! Surely even this is an example of such communications from his satanic majesty. We have seen that God has his government, and operates through his subjects, by his teaching upon such material as comes within the range of its influence; even so, the devil has his government, and operates through his subjects, by his teaching, upon such material as comes within the range of its influence. Jesus said "He that is not with me is against me; and he that gathereth not with me, scattereth abroad." Mat. xii: 30. Luke xi:3. Therefore, all responsible persons who are not the disciples of the Lord are the children of the devil, and engaged in his service. "Ye are of your father the devil, and the lusts of your father ye will do." John viii: 44. When he wished to operate on our progenitors in the garden of Eden he talked to them; and as there was no human being through whom he might address Adam and Eve, he made a medium of the serpent, the shrewdest of all beasts; for which there would have been no necessity had wicked men and women been numerous then as now. When he wished to torture Job, he talked to God about him. When he tempted Christ he talked to him, and offered him inducements to serve him; some of which are not unlike the inducements presented by him now. It is said in the explanation to the parable of the sower that the devil catches away the word sown in the heart. Do we not see this verified almost every day? Through his subjects he calls it "Campbellism," and one of his subjects had recently written a book in which he calls it "Bold-faced infidelity," "Water salvation," and many other ugly names for no other purpose than to make it odious to the people lest they believe it. Should they believe and obey the Gospel then he appeals to their ambition by offering them places of honor in his government; or to their avarice by offering them wealth; or to their appetites, passions or fleshly lasts by offering them any and every gratification which their carnal natures can desire. Surely his resources are ample without resort to immediate communications upon any person, or class of persons. The word and service of God are our only sure means of defence against him and his subjects. "Know ye not, that to whom ye yield yourselves servants to obey, his servants ye are to whom ye obey" Rom. Vi. "If God has given us a full and perfect revelation of his mind and will concerning the redemption, conversion, salvation, government, spiritual growth, and final happiness of man in his word; what need have we for influences of, or communications from the Spirit without the word? We cannot conceive of an impression necessary to be made upon the heart of man which the word of the Lord is not capable of making. If we wish to be enlightened; "The commandment of the Lord is pure, enlightening the eyes." Psalm xix: 8. If we wish to be made wise unto salvation, "The testimony of the Lord is sure, making wise the simple." Ps. xix: 7. Paul told Timothy that "From a child thou hast known the Holy Scriptures, which are able to make thee wise unto salvation through faith which is in Christ Jesus." 2 Tim. iii: 15. If we wish our souls converted to God, "The law of the Lord is perfect, converting the soul." Ps. xix: 7. He that is dead in trespasses and in sins may be quickened by the Gospel: "Thy word has quickened me," Ps. cxix: 50. " I will never forget thy precepts; for with them thou hast quickened me." Ibid 93. If any one wishes to be spiritually begotten, Paul says "In Christ Jesus I have begotten you through the Gospel." 1 Cor. iv: 15. Indeed, the Corinthians were saved by the Gospel if they were saved at all. Paul says "Moreover brethren I declare unto you the Gospel which I preached unto you, which also ye have received, and wherein ye stand; by which also ye are saved." 1 Cor, xv: 1, 2. "0 the depth of the riches both of the wisdom and knowledge of God" What can we desire to perfect the scheme of salvation to which we are not thoroughly furnished in the Gospel? We can see no use of sending the Gospel to the heathen if the doctrine of abstract spiritual influences be true. If God converts sinners here where Bibles are plenty, without the word, he will certainly be as kind to the heathen and convert them without the word where they have no chance to hear it. If we believed this doctrine we would not contribute one dollar to send Bibles, or missionaries to them, for God will as surely convert them without the word as he will any one here. If you tell us you do not want influences of the Spirit without the word; but an accompanying influence with the word, then is this not an attack upon the sufficiency and truth of the word? It seems to virtually say, "I will not believe and obey the Lord in full assurance of faith in his word until there is accompanying influence of the Spirit through my own feelings confirming its truth." If the Spirit makes impressions through our feelings not conveyed by words, we would like to have the rule of interpretation. How shall we decide whether it confirms & contradicts the word? If the message be that God has pardoned our sins, how shall we determine that it is not a message of condemnation? We cannot see how communications from a dumb spirit can be reliable. It occurs to us that we would about as soon undertake to translate the tappings of table-legs into good English as any other kind of communications not made through words. Again: Paul said "Faith comes by hearing, and hearing by the word of God." Rom. x:17 Then faith that comes by an abstract operation of the Spirit cannot be the kind of faith of which Paul wrote. If he had been taught in the theological schools of modern times he would have said " Faith cometh by feelings, and feelings by the Holy Spirit. If God gives man faith and converts him to

Christianity by an abstract operation of the Spirit we cannot see why he will not give him all information necessary for his present and eternal happiness in the same way. Certainly, we can as readily conceive of sanctification by the Spirit without the word as of justification by the Spirit without the word. Hence the Bible is a dead book if not "a dead letter." A judge of the circuit court whose name is quite familiar in this country, was celebrated for his ignorance of everything but the law. On one occasion the connection of Scripture containing the "Lord's prayer" was read in his hearing, whereupon "his honor" remarked in all sober earnestness "There is some right good reading in that book." So, we suppose the Bible may be respected for its antiquity and the "Good reading" it contains but as a way-bill from earth to Heaven it is worth nothing if the feelings and speculations of men are allowed to supersede it. It was a useless application of the blood of Jesus when the New Covenant was dedicated with it. If there are new revelations being constantly made by the Spirit, they become the last will of the Savior; and as the last will abrogates all former wills these abstract revelations must supersede the one dedicated by the blood of Jesus. And if these impressions are not new revelations but simply the same that are in the word, made known without the word, then they are worthless, nay mischievous; for it were much better to have them in the word where they may be understood.

Finally: This doctrine opens the door to every species of imposition as wide as the speculations of men may desire it. We cannot conceive of a doctrine so odious that it may not be confirmed by the same kind of testimony. The feelings of the Roman Catholic tell him that the Priest can pardon his sins for money, and sell him indulgences to commit others. Surely, he believes it real pardon, or he would not give his money for it. The feelings of the Moslem tell him that Mohammed was a prophet equal to Jesus of Nazareth; and that he conversed with God and received the Koran from him in person as Moses did the law at Sinai. The feelings of Brigham Young tell him that Joe Smith was the prophet of God and that the Book of Mormon, and not the word of the Lord is the rule of faith and practice. And can we object to what the Spirit tells him through his feelings, and at the same time offer him the same kind of testimony as evidence of our acceptance with God? We know not how any man, who admits the doctrine of abstract spiritual influences can object to the faith of the Moslem, the Mormon, the Catholic, the Spirit Rapper or any one else who believes that the Holy Spirit; or any other spirit communicated to him that upon which his faith is predicated, unless they can discredit the spirit which is said to have made the communication to him. Whenever they claim, as generally they do, that the Holy Spirit was the source of the communication, further objection cannot be made by those who are committed to that kind of testimony.

Before dismissing the subject, it may be well to call the attention of the reader to a few things which have been improperly blended with the ordinary influence of the Spirit in conversion, at least by some. The cases of conversion recorded in the Acts all occurred in the days of miracles, and there were miracles connected with most of them. We have taken some pains to disconnect ordinary from extraordinary manifestations of the Spirit; we need only here remind the reader that, however prominent a miracle may appear in the record of any case of conversion; as we do not live in the days of miracles he must not expect the miracle to be reproduced in him.

Again, the influence of circumstances, whether accidental or providential are not the work of the Spirit in conversion. A merely accidental circumstance may take a man within range of the Spirit's teaching; e. g. a young man goes to meeting to see a young lady—to see some friend — simply to be in company or transact some business, the Gospel is preached, he becomes interested, and is finally converted. The accidental circumstance, whatever it may have been, which induced him to go to preaching was not the influence of the Spirit; for this began when he came in contact with the teaching of the Spirit through the preaching and other service at the meeting. The Scriptures furnish numerous examples illustrative of this fact. Lydia's occupation as a vender of purple took her from Thyatira to Philippi, where Paul preached the Gospel to her, by which God opened her heart— enlightened her mind, and she was converted; but the influence of the Spirit upon her heart began not until Paul's preaching saluted her ears.

Again: The Jailor's occupation as keeper of the prison in the city of Philippi caused him to hear the word of the Lord preached by Paul and Silas, by which he was converted. But he had not a spiritual idea until they spake to him. Even after the miracles had ceased he would have committed suicide had they not prevented him. Had some one else been keeper of the prison, such one, and not he might have been the beneficiary of the preaching.

A providential circumstance may prepare a man to favorably receive the Spirit's teaching; e. g. the death of a friend, or near relative, or physical suffering. When death fastens upon the vitals of a lovely child, brother, sister or parent, with whom our affections are borne away to the realm of Spirits; or when our physical powers are exhausted by the blighting influence of disease and trouble, then it is that we realize the insufficiency of human aid, and the instability of all earthly things. Our dependence upon God is brought home to us, and thus the heart is prepared for a favorable consideration of Spiritual instruction; but not a ray of Spiritual light can we derive from such afflictions. We are simply prepared to consider what light we previously had, and to receive additional instruction if it is presented to us. We are not prepared to regard the mellowing influence of such afflictions as the work of the Holy Spirit in conversion; nor are they even within the line of special providences for they are the common lot of all men—the result of general providence or natural law. Nor would we be understood to deny the doctrine of special providence. Nay we not only admit, but believe it; but it is for God's children and not to convert sinners. Paul says, "We trust in the living God, who is the Savior of all men, but specially of those that believe." 1 Tim iv: 10 God has a general providence of which all are the recipients, but he specially provides for them that put their trust in him according to his word. Hence "We know that all things work together for good to them that love God, to them who are the called according to his purpose." Rom. viii: 28. "The eyes of the Lord are over the righteous, and his ears are open unto their prayers; but the face of the Lord is against them that do evil." 1 Pet. iii; 12. But, we have no disposition to enter upon a discussion of this subject here. It is important to a proper understanding of the Holy Spirit's work in conversion that we keep it disentangled from every thing foreign to it. If we can do this; and then quit hunting for difficulties and mysteries; we will not find many. The truths of God often sparkle as gems upon the surface of his word, and are unobserved by those who are always digging tunnels, but never examine the virgin soil in its native simplicity.

THE RECEPTION OF THE HOLY SPIRIT.

Having seen that the Spirit dwells in the body or Church—that the disciples are builded together for a habitation of God through the Spirit, and that the Church is the medium through which the Spirit's power is exerted for the conversion and salvation of man we come now to consider the relationship it sustains to each member of the body. Before leaving the disciples, Jesus said to them, "I will pray the Father and he shall give you another Comforter that he may abide with you forever, even the Spirit of truth whom the world cannot receive because it seeth him not, neither knoweth him, but ye know him, for he dwelleth with you and shall be in you." John xiv: 16, 17. There are several very important matters in this quotation for which we will have use as we proceed; but at present we are here to see that the Holy Spirit was promised as an abiding with and comforter to the disciples and as such it was to dwell with and be in them forever. That this was not a figurative, but a literal indwelling of the Holy Spirit in the disciples is plain from the fact that when the Spirit came as promised "They were all filled with the Holy Spirit and began to speak with other tongues as the Spirit gave them utterance." Acts ii: 4 It will scarcely be said that the disciples were only figuratively filled with the Holy Spirit on the day, of Pentecost. Nay, it was literally in them as the Savior promised them it should be. Then are we to believe that it was literally in them as an inspiring monitor, but as a comforter only figuratively? If not, and it was literally in the apostles to inspire them, we can see no reason why it should not be as literally in them as a comforter. And if it dwelt literally in them as a comforter and as such was to abide with them forever, we conclude that it must dwell in the disciples now as literally as it was in them. And here we must not forget that the Spirit was given to man by measure; and we have seen some of these measures fill their mission and pass away. It was to guide the apostles into all truth, and bring to their remembrance everything said to them by the Savior. It has done this and as we have a perfect record of what they said and did when inspired by it, we have no use for it now as an inspiring monitor; but as a comforter it abideth ever. But we may be told that this promise was made to the apostles only, and was to them fulfilled. And as they were inspired by its presence, the absence of such inspiration proves the absence of the Spirit in all who are not so in-

255

spired. A careful examination of the Scriptures will show that, while there was no promise that the inspiration should remain, as a comforter it was to abide with the disciples forever. As such it was to dwell with and be in them. As an inspiring monitor, it did not abide forever. Nay even the apostles, during their lives, were not always under its inspiration. Paul sometimes spake as a man, at other times he thought he had the Spirit of God, (See 1 Cor vii: 40.) How could he so speak if he knew himself to be at all times under the influence of inspiration. When it was necessary for something to be revealed or confirmed by the Spirit, it took possession of some spiritual man or men through whom the work was accomplished. Had Peter been all the time under the influence of inspiration it would not have taken a special miracle to teach him that he might go to the house of Cornelius with the Gospel to the Gentiles. This case clearly shows that the Gospel was progressively developed to the apostles and that they did not know all its provisions when first baptized with the Holy Spirit on the day of Pentecost. "While Peter thought on the vision the Spirit said unto him, Behold, three men seek thee, arise therefore, and get thee down, and go with them, doubting nothing; for I have sent them." Acts x: 19, 20. Then he knew something he never knew before. And when the messengers told him for what they had come he knew something more. And when Cornelius rehearsed the things seen and heard by him "Then Peter opened his mouth, and said, of a truth I perceive that God is no respecter of persons; but in every nation he that feareth God and worketh righteousness is accepted with him." Acts x: 34,35. These important lessons, the other apostles, though inspired, did not know yet. But Peter rehearsed the whole matter to them from the beginning, and "when they heard these things, they held their peace, and glorified God, saying Then hath God also to the Gentiles granted repentance unto life." Acts xi: 18. Here for the first time these inspired men knew that the Gentiles were fellow heirs with the Jews in the privileges of the Gospel. But as a comforter, was it designed for the apostles alone. If so, why did Jesus promise that it should abide with them forever. They could not live here forever; nor can we conclude that Jesus intended to promise them the Holy Spirit as a comforter forever, meaning that it should go with them into the future state; for he assures them that there they should again be with him. "I go said he to prepare a place for you and if I go and prepare a place for you, I will come again and receive you unto myself; that where I am there ye may be also." John xiv: 2,3. While clothed with humanity, Jesus was not omnipresent, and hence could only be with and comfort his disciples in a single place at one time. As to the apostles alone, this would not have made another comforter necessary for he could have kept them with him; but when the time came for them to go into all the world and pro-claim the Gospel to every creature, he could not, as son of man, be in Jerusalem, Rome, Corinth, Philippi, Samaria and other places at the same time; hence it was expedient, in this respect as well as others, that he should go away and send another comforter, even the Holy Spirit, who could dwell with and be in every disciple, any and every where until he should come again. There is a remarkable similari-ty in the style of the Savior when he promised the comfort-er to the disciples, and that of Paul in his letter to his breth-ren at Rome. He says "But ye are not in the flesh, but in the Spirit, if so be that the Spirit of God dwell in you. Now if any man have not the Spirit of Christ, he is none of his. And if Christ be in you, the body is dead because of sin; but the Spirit is life because of righteousness. But if the Spirit of him that raised up Jesus from the dead dwell in you, he that raised up Christ from the dead shall also quicken your mortal bodies by his Spirit that dwelleth in you." Rom. viii: 9-11. That this passage is applicable to Christians now is admitted by all; how strikingly similar the phraseology to that used by the Savior. He says "He dwelleth with you and

257

shall be in you." Paul says, "If so be that the Spirit of God dwell in you" "If the Spirit of him that raised up Jesus from the dead dwell in you." "Shall also quicken your mortal bodies by his Spirit that dwelleth in you." What can this language mean? We cannot say that God will quicken our mortal bodies by his Spirit that dwelleth figuratively in us; and to say that he will quicken our mortal bodies by his Spirit that dwelleth metonymically in us would be no better. Nor will it do to say that God will quicken our mortal bodies by his disposition that dwelleth in us. To our mind the passage admits of one interpretation, and only one; namely that the Spirit of God—the Holy Spirit, dwells literally and really in every Christian, and by it God will reanimate his body in the great day. With this agrees the teaching of Paul when he wrote to the disciples at Corinth. He says "What know ye not that your body is the temple of the Holy Ghost which is in you." 1 Cor vi: 19. He here manifests astonishment that they should not ever keep this thought before them. And again: "Know ye not that ye are the temple of God, and that the Spirit of God dwelleth in you?" 1 Cor. iii:16. Had Paul been "Seeking to impress the disciples at Rome and Corinth with the fact that the Spirit did really dwell in each of them, we know not how he could have selected a set of words better calculated to convey the thought than those he employed in the passages quoted.

Thus far we have not approached our position by any process of reasoning, but by positive declarations of holy writ. "The Spirit dwelleth in you," has met us every where. Upon such Scriptures there is not much room to reason; and here we could well afford to rest this position. But we think we can arrive at the same thought by a process of reasoning altogether satisfactory, even in the absence of direct testimony. Paul, more than once likens the Church to the human body; an example of which may be found, 1 Cor. xii: 12-27, to which the reader is referred; we can only transcribe a sentence or two. Addressing the disciples he says "Now ye are the body of Christ, and members in particular." The blood freighted with the pabulum of life must freely circulate in all the members of the body great and small. And should such circulation cease in any member, death and disintegration of such member must inevitably follow; and unless it is separated from the body all must perish. Even so "The body without the Spirit is dead." Jas. ii: 26. If the Spirit ceases to dwell in and vitalize every member of the Church or Spiritual body, Spiritual death to such a member is inevitable. And if the circulation cannot be restored, painful as the operation may be, the amputating knife must be used; for "When one member suffers all the members suffer with it." As it is better for one member to perish than for the whole body to be cast into hell" (Mat. v:29, 30) sacred as the relationship may have been, a separation must take place. Are we not here taught that the presence of the Spirit in the Christian is indispensable to the maintenance of Spiritual life?

Again: Jesus illustrated the relationship his disciples sustained to him by a vine and its branches. See John xv: 1-7. Said he "I am the vine, ye are the branches. he that abideth in me, and I in him, the same bringeth forth much fruit." As every branch must maintain its connection with the vine so that the sap may circulate from vine to branch, and keep it alive; even so must every member of the Church or body of Christ maintain his connection with the body so that the Spirit circulate in and keep him alive, lest "he be cast forth as a branch and is withered, and men gather such, and cast them into the fire and they are burned." So the Lord taught, and so we believe.

But we are sometimes told that the Spirit dwells in us simply by its teaching received through the inspired word; hence all that is meant by it is that we are well instructed by the Spirit. When Paul told the Romans that God would quicken their mortal bodies by his Spirit that dwelt in them, did he only mean to teach that God would reanimate their sleeping dust by the instructions they had received from the Spirit? If this be all then we see not why the world cannot receive it. An infidel may be as wise in the Scriptures as the most devoted disciple. It took a man mighty in the Scriptures to meet Mr. Owen in debate upon the authenticity of the Bible, and yet it will scarcely be contended that the Holy Spirit dwelt in his infidel heart. Every man who is adopted into the family of God must be taught by the Spirit before he is adopted; but the Spirit is given to him because he is a son and not to prepare him for adoption or make him a son. If the reception of the word of truth be all that is meant by the reception of the Spirit, then Paul's rule is reversed, and every man receives the Spirit, not because he is a son but that he may become one. Yea, Jesus was mistaken when he said, "world cannot receive it," because they must receive its instruction, while of the world and before entering the Church, Kingdom, or body as certainly as hearing precedes faith and faith precedes obedience. Paul said to the Ephesians that they were sealed, with the Holy Spirit after they heard and believed the Gospel and trusted in Christ. "In whom ye also trusted after that ye heard the word of truth," the Gospel of your salvation: in whom also, after that ye believed ye were sealed with the Holy Spirit of promise, which is the earnest of our inheritance until the redemption of the purchased possession." Eph. i: 13, 14. Then it follows, most certainly, that if we are now sealed with the Holy Spirit as these Ephesians were, it takes place after, and is something more than hearing, believing, and receiving the word. Their sealing was to them an earnest of the inheritance that is a pledge of God's faithfulness in giving them the promised inheritance, hence he admonishes them to faithfulness on their part, that they "Grieve not the Holy Spirit of God, whereby ye are sealed unto the day of: redemption." Eph. iv: 30. The same Apostle writes to the Corinthians thus, " For all the promises of God in him are

260

yea, and nay him Amen, unto the glory of God by us. Now he which establisheth us with you in Christ and hath anointed us, is God; who hath also sealed us, and given the earnest of the Spirit in our hearts." 2 Cor. i: 20-22. God established them in Christ by giving them the Holy Spirit as an earnest or pledge of the fact that his promises were yea and amen in Christ, hence they were sealed with the Spirit.

"Now he that hath wrought us for the self-same thing is God, who also hath given unto us the earnest of the Spirit." 2 Cor. v:5. That God gave these Corinthians the Holy Spirit as an earnest of the promised inheritance is clear; and when we associate these quotations with the language quoted from Eph. i: 13 is clearly shown that it was given after they were instructed in and believed the Gospel; and hence was something more than the information thus received by them. From this conclusion we can conceive of but one possible way of escape; namely, that the measure of the Spirit by which, the Ephesians and Corinthians were sealed was the extraordinary measure by which spiritual gifts were imparted; and not the ordinary measure following adoption into God's family. But it is the business of him who so affirms to furnish the proof of such affirmation and he would do well, in the mean-time, to see that he does not explain away all the Bible in special applications of it; leaving nothing applicable to us at all.

It may not be amiss to remark here that the words in which a truth or thought is expressed are not the thought itself; nor is the thought or truth suggested by a person or thing the person or thing which suggested it. Hence, the words in which a spiritual idea is suggested are not the idea; nor is the idea suggested by the Spirit the Spirit itself. A school boy may have the words of an author committed to memory most perfectly and yet not have the thought which the author designed to convey by the words, nevertheless the thought was in the words. Even so he may get the thoughts of an author without drinking in or imbibing

261

the Spirit of the author who suggested the thought, nevertheless the Spirit was in the thought. Hence it is possible for us to comprehend a thought or truth suggested by the Holy Spirit, and yet fail to receive the Spirit which inspired the thought. You will say these are nice distinctions: we admit it but they are distinctions nevertheless, and he who fails to make them may never fully understand the subject of the Holy Spirit. If he would profit by an examination of it he must keep wide awake all the time devoted to the study of it.

BUT HOW DO PERSONS RECEIVE THE HOLY SPIRIT?

Suppose we acknowledge ourselves incapable of answering the question at all; what then? Does it follow that we must repudiate a plainly taught fact because we cannot comprehend and explain the philosophy of it? For just such a crime Zacharias was made dumb and not able to speak until the fulfillment of the words which he refused to believe because he could not see how he and Elizabeth were to be blessed with a child when both were well stricken in years. When God speaks the man of faith believes, whether he can or cannot explain the philosophy of what he says. Hence, we are prepared to believe that the Holy Spirit dwells in God's people whether we can or cannot explain the manner of its reception because he says he will quicken our mortal bodies by his Spirit which dwelleth in us. But we would not have the reader suppose the Bible a blank, even on this subject. Paul says, "The love of God is shed abroad in our hearts by the Holy Ghost which is given unto us." Rom. v:5. By this we learn that the Holy Spirit is given to the disciples. But how is it given? This is the troublesome question. Well it is either given mediately, or immediately—through means, or, without means. Jesus once said "If ye then, being evil, know how to give good gifts unto your children; how much more shall your heavenly Father give the Holy Spirit to them that ask him." Luke xi: 14.

262

Here we are taught that the Father gives the Spirit to such of his children as ask him for it, but we are not told how he gives it to them. He gives us bread, and taught his disciples to pray for it, yet he gives it through means and not otherwise; hence we may find that the Father has provided a system of means by which to convey the Holy Spirit to his children. "This only would I learn of you, received ye the Spirit by the works of the law, or by the hearing of faith." Gal. iii; 2. Two thoughts are here implied:

First, that the Galatians did not receive the Spirit by the works of the law.

Second, that they did receive it by the hearing of faith.

This question, then, is pertinent to our inquiry. We wish to know how the Spirit is received, and it is here assumed to have been received by the hearing of faith, But, this is a queer sentence; what can it mean. Does hearing belong to faith? No, faith comes by hearing, hence hearing must precede faith; indeed, hearing may be where there is no faith. Then the Apostles could not have meant by faith that confidence only, with which we receive testimony. He must mean something more than that. In this chapter, as in many other places, he is evidently contrasting the Mosaic Law and its service, with the Gospel and its service; and the word faith in the verse quoted, is the synonym of Gospel, and comprehends the whole plan of salvation presented in the Gospel. If we comprehend the passage we must notice the word hearing for it must mean something more than the reception of sound. In the New Testament compiled by A. Campbell from the works of Doctors George Campbell, MacKnight and Doddridge, the passage is rendered "The obedience of faith." We might quote many passages from the common version where the word hear implies obedience but a single example must suffice. "And it shall come to pass that every soul which will not hear that Prophet shall be destroyed from among the people." Acts iii: 24. Certainly the word fear must be understood to mean obedience to the commands of Jesus. In collating these items the account stands thus; The Galatians received the Spirit by obedience to the Gospel; and hence obedience to the Gospel is the Father's appointed means of imparting the Holy Spirit to his children. Thus, we see why it is that the world cannot receive the Spirit; they do not obey the Gospel that they may receive it. We have seen that it is given by the Father to his children; hence Paul said to them, "Because ye are sons, God hath sent forth the Spirit of his Son into your hearts crying Abba Father." The children obey the Father, hence as the Gospel is the law by which he governs his children and as obedience to it is the medium through which he gives them the Spirit, by obeying the Gospel the children receive the Spirit.

We have seen that there are two great opposing kingdoms; namely, "The Kingdom of God " and the "Kingdom of darkness." The subjects of that are called the children or "Sons of God." 1 John iii: 1. The subjects of this are called, "The world," and Jesus says they cannot receive the Spirit. Nor is it at all strange that they cannot receive the Holy Spirit while citizens of the Kingdom of darkness laboring for and serving their father, the devil. If we would receive the Spirit of God we must become citizens of his government—members of his family. Then, and not until then may we receive the Spirit of the family which entitles us to the privilege of calling God our Father. The linen of the world have not the Spirit of God and have not the right to call him their Father. Jesus said to such, "Ye are of your father the devil, and the lusts of your father ye will do." John viii: 44. The Church is God's spiritual family into which we enter as "Babes in Christ." 1 Cor. iii: 1. And we are admonished. "As new-born babes to desire the sincere milk of the word that we may grow thereby."- 1 Pet. ii: 2. Reading and feeding upon this spiritual food the children of God are "Filled with the Spirit;" not because the word is the Spirit, for it is not; but because the Spirit is ever present in the inspired word; and the service appointed therein is God's ordained means of giving them the Spirit. Hence says Paul "Let the word of Christ dwell in you richly, in all wisdom." Col. iii: 16. By so living-we may grow up to the stature of men and women, full grown in Christ Jesus, the Lord, " Till we all come in the unity of the faith and of the knowledge of the Son of God, unto a perfect man, unto the measure of the stature of the fullness of Christ." Eph. iv: 13. If we take a child of Indian parentage and adopt it into a family of civilization and refinement, it ceases to imbibe the Spirit of the family from which it is adopted. It henceforth manifests a different disposition, and speaks a different language. Its manners, habits, occupation, everything, save its personality undergoes a corresponding change. So when a person is taken from "The world," and adopted into the family of God, he or she ceases to imbibe the Spirit of the world, and hence to "conform to the world," and imbibes—" Drinks into," that measure of the Holy Spirit which the Father promised to his children by living in the Father's family, receiving his instruction, and being governed by his laws.

Every time the faithful child obeys a command of the Father, he drinks into, or imbibes a measure of the Spirit connected with that service. It matters not whether it were the service of the Lord's day, Worship in the family, visiting the sick, relief of the poor, or any other service required by the Father of his children, he has connected himself through the Spirit with his service; and he who faithfully serves him receives the Holy Spirit as an earnest of the promised inheritance. Hence "He that keepeth his commandments, dwelleth in him, and he in him. And hereby we know that he abideth in us, by the Spirit which he has given us." 1 John iii. 24. And again, "If we love one another, God dwelleth in us and his love is perfected in, us." "Hereby know we that we dwell in him, and he in us, because he hath given us of his Spirit." Ibid iv: 12, 13. The devoted disciple goes to the house of worship on the Lord's day and there is greeted heartily by his brethren and sisters in the Lord, and he feels the cords of love strengthen as he takes them by the hand. He joins with them in singing psalms, and hymns, and spiritual songs; and as he makes melody in his heart to the Lord, his thoughts soar away to a place where he hopes to join with the redeemed in singing the "New song before the throne" in sweeter strains than mortal tongues can make. A lesson of instruction is read from the word of the Lord "Whereby are given unto us exceeding great and precious promises; that by these we might be partakers of the divine nature." 2 Pet. i: 4. Are we made partakers of the divine nature by the precious promises of the Lord ? Then what has he promised? Nay what has he not promised us? Eye hath not seen nor ear heard, neither has it entered into the heart of man to conceive the things which God hath in reservation for them that love him. And though God has revealed them by his Spirit, language is beggared when called upon to furnish drapery in which to present them. He has promised that he will never leave nor forsake his children—that he will comfort and support them while crossing, the deep rolling river—that he will quicken their mortal bodies by his Spirit that dwelleth in them; and give them bodies fashioned like unto the glorious body of his Son— that, their homes shall be in the city of God where God and angels will be their associates—That they shall have right to the tree of life and drink of the pure river of life that flows from beneath the throne—that they shall bask in the sunny smiles of God's eternal love for ever and ever. O great, exceeding great and precious promises. Who can contemplate them without partaking of the divine nature? Nay, without drinking copious draughts of the Holy Spirit that is ever present in them?

While the disciple eats of the bread, and drinks of the wine which symbolize the broken body and shed blood of a crucified Savior, who died that he might live, his memory fastens by faith upon the scenes of Calvary and his heart swells with gratitude and is stirred with deepest emotion as he feels the love of God shed abroad in his heart by the Holy Spirit which is given to him through the appointments of the Lord. He prostrates himself at the golden alter and offers thereon the increase of a humble and devoted heart. Feeling his unworthiness, he pleads for mercy through Jesus Christ. Truly grateful for favors received, he humbly, yet in faith asks his Father for blessings and protection in time to come. "Likewise, the Spirit also helpeth our infirmities for we know not what we should pray for as we ought, but the Spirit itself maketh intercession for us with groanings which cannot be uttered." Rom. viii: 26. Thus God s children are "Strengthened with might by his Spirit in the inner man," (Eph. iii: 16) by the service of the Lord's day at the house of worship. Oh! precious season of refreshing from the presence of the Lord. Surely it is good for them to be there that they may sit together in heavenly places in Christ Jesus; and drink of that treasure of the Holy Spirit with which God designed to comfort and strengthen his children amid the persecutions and trials incident to their pilgrimage through life. But Jesus called the Holy Spirit a Comforter and truly it did comfort them. It not only dwelt in them, but it inspired men to write and speak words of cheer for them. It inspired Paul to write a graphic description of their victory over death and subsequent reign with the Lord. He says "'The Lord himself shall, descend from heaven with a shout, with the voice of the archangel, and with the trump of God: and the dead in Christ shall rise first: then we which are alive and remain shall be caught up together with them in the clouds, to meet the Lord in the air; and so shall we ever be with the Lord. Wherefore comfort one another with these words." 1 Thess, iv: 16-18.

"Hope of our heart, O Lord, appear,
Thou glorious star of light,
Shine forth, and chase the dreary night,

267

With all our tears, away.
Strangers on earth, we wait for thee;
O, leave the Father's throne;
Come with a shout of victory, Lord,
And claim us as thine own.
O, hid the bright archangel now,
The trump of God prepare,
To call thy saint—the quick, the dead
To meet thee in the air."

As Hannibal's soldiers, after triumphing over the frozen Alps, were vanquished by the luxuries of Capua, so has many a strong spirit after its victories over adverse fate, been conquered by the prosperity it wearied every energy to obtain,

Love is not a judge, but a benefactor.

GA vol.12, #13, 3-31-70, pg. 289

Bibliography

The Life of Dr. Brents by John Cowden

Marshall County, Tennessee Compilation

The Gospel Plan of Salvation by T.W. Brents

Gospel Sermons by T.W. Brents

Search For the Ancient Order 1 & 2 Earl West

The Gospel Advocate 1855-1905

Made in the USA
Columbia, SC
25 May 2024

36192965R00154